LLEWELYN POWYS:

A SELECTION

LLEWELYN POWYS

A selection from his writings

made by

KENNETH HOPKINS

MACDONALD : LONDON

THIS SELECTION FIRST PUBLISHED IN 1952 BY
MACDONALD & CO., (PUBLISHERS) LTD.
16 MADDOX STREET, W.1
MADE AND PRINTED IN GREAT BRITAIN BY
PURNELL AND SONS, LTD.
PAULTON (SOMERSET) AND LONDON

INTRODUCTION

I T IS seventeen years since, one wet November morning, I set out
from Bournemouth on my bicycle to visit Llewelyn Powys.
Of his work I then knew very little, and of himself nothing.
It was enough for me, a lad of twenty, that he was a famous
writer; for I hoped to become a famous writer, too.

Accordingly, with a sheaf of my poems in my pocket and with
my waterproof cape and leggings keeping out the worst of the
weather, I pedalled through Poole, Lychett, Wareham, and across
the rain-washed solitude of Thomas Hardy's Egdon Heath to the
remote Dorset village of East Chaldon. All this was familiar
ground, and Mrs. Legg at the Sailor's Return was an old friend;
but how was I to find the cottage in which Mr. Powys lived?
Over my bread-and-cheese lunch at the inn I made enquiries.

Mr. T. F. Powys lived just beyond the church—you could see
his little square house from the inn yard—but Mr. Llewelyn was
another matter. His house lay between the village and the cliffs,
a good half-hour's brisk walk over the bare downs. On my map
the house appeared as a tiny speck in the sea of green, close-
cropped grass. The rain fell steadily.

And so, past a row of thatched grey cottages and up the slope
I climbed until I reached the first smooth shoulder of the downs.
Below me the small village of Chaldon—thatch and slate shining
wet—appeared unpeopled under the racing clouds, except for
the chimneys smoking. Before me lay nothing but slippery grass
and a thin track worn into the chalk by centuries of rain and
generations of wayfarers. This disappeared abruptly over the
edge of the hill and reappeared across the valley on the side of an
even steeper hill. Down the track—which to-day I shared with
a small river—I made my way, and at last, under the curious
gaze of a group of cows, sheltering tail to wind in the lee of a
sturdy barn, I came to Chydyok.

This farmhouse in which Llewelyn Powys lived stands almost
at the summit of the second range of hills that divides East

v

Chaldon from the coast. Just above Chydyok the cliffs fall five hundred feet sheer into the sea. It is one of the grandest sights in England to stand at the top of White Nose and look along the curving coastline under a brilliant summer sun, or when the sea-mists are curling along the valleys, to the hills and tall headlands—Bats Head, Swyre Head, Hambury Tout, Bindon and the rest—solitary and bare as they were ten thousand years ago. It was here that the ashes of Llewelyn Powys were buried, and here is set above them the rugged block of Portland stone upon which his name is carved.

On the day of my first visit Llewelyn Powys, who had then been consumptive for twenty-five years, was recovering from a severe haemorrhage. I had promised to stay with him only five minutes.

He lay in a great bed almost filling the upper room to which his wife led me. A lattice window looked westward along the hillside, and he could see the sloping garden beside the house. But to-day the room was darkened by the low storm clouds.

The man I had come to visit was now fifty. To me he looked older, for his face was lined by illness and his eyes were deep set. He had a mass of curly, almost white hair, and a thick beard. The hand he held out to me was thin, with the blue veins clearly visible. His voice was not strong, but I thought its slow, rich tones the most remarkable I had ever heard. Every word he spoke he seemed to enjoy the sound and use of, as though there were pleasure in the simple exercise of speech and language.

In later years, as I came to know him better, I learned that he delighted in things many people think commonplace, or do not think of at all—a spider in its web against the sunlight, the sound of a creature moving in the hedgerow, the feel of cuckoo-spit on the fingers—like Hardy, 'he was a man who used to notice such things.' Surely no great writer has ever been more passionately aware of the delight of drawing breath.

Consider the glow, the glory of being alive, the incredible chance of it! How heart-piercing, how shocking, how supremely beautiful in this unexplained, wavering movement that troubles all that is, from the Milky Way to a common sting-nettle! It balances into restless vaults the blue troughs of the ocean, it stirs each thin leaf in the wild woods, and it shows to the lovers of every succeeding season, casting for each other with meshed nets, the infinite delight of an actual paradise. [1]

He lay propped against his pillows, yet, for all his illness, his eager interest in life was as strong as a young man's. I admired a red plaid shawl he was wearing, bright against the faded blue distemper of the wall. He told me the shawl had belonged to Edward FitzGerald, the translator of Omar Khayyam. He showed me an engraving of the cottage in which Rabelais was born; a handful of prehistoric worked flints collected in the ploughed fields near Chydyok; and an Egyptian scarab—which he gave to me—carved three or four thousand years ago from the rock of the Nile Valley.

After this meeting Llewelyn Powys wrote to me letters of advice and encouragement which would be of service to any young man who wanted to become a writer. These letters were published in 1949 with the title *Advice to a Young Poet*.

Of the three famous Powys brothers whose writings celebrate the West Country, only the youngest, Llewelyn, was born in Dorset. John Cowper Powys and T. F. Powys were born at Shirley, in Derbyshire, where their father was vicar. But the Rev. C. F. Powys returned to his native county and took a curacy in the ancient county town and there—at Rothesay House, Dorchester—Llewelyn was born in 1884.

As one of the youngest members of a large family—there were eleven children—Llewelyn Powys grew up almost in a private world. When he was eighteen months old his father moved again, this time to become vicar of the small village of Montacute, in Somerset, and in his books Llewelyn gives a remarkable picture of the life there sixty years ago—an account which is supplemented by those in John Cowper Powys's *Autobiography* and in Louis Marlow's book about the family, *Welsh Ambassadors*.

Llewelyn was sent to the famous West Country school at Sherborne and from there to Corpus Christi College, Cambridge. He had no settled plans for a career, and on leaving the University he became a schoolmaster for a short time, but found himself temperamentally unsuited to this profession. After this he gave a series of lectures in America, where his brother John was already

---

[1] *Now that the Gods are Dead.*

well established in the profession he followed for nearly forty years. But Llewelyn had none of John's wonderful gift for 'inspired rhetoric' from the platform and he returned home.

And then without warning he was struck down by tuberculosis. This was in November 1909, and in *Skin for Skin* he gives a vivid account of his reactions:

> The shock of finding myself to be really ill had the strangest effect on me. I became like one drunken with wine. A torrent of words issued from my mouth. I acted as if death were not the end of every child born into the world, but an event which in some mysterious way had been reserved for me alone. I felt nothing but pride in finding myself laid by the heels so neatly. I liked to get what sensation I could out of it; and yet, at the same time, deep in my heart, I refused to realize how grave my sickness was. I liked to talk about dying, but I had no mind to die. I liked to rail against God, but I had no mind that He should hear me. In every possible way I dramatised my situation. My head became completely turned, and I chittered at Death like a little grey squirrel who is up a fir tree out of harm's way.

When he was strong enough to travel he was sent to Switzerland, and at first under the treatment at Davos he appeared slowly to get well. It seemed that he might be cured, and he returned to England, but during another visit to Switzerland the following year he went for a long climb over the mountains and brought on a new haemorrhage of the lungs which almost proved fatal. At last, however, he was again able to return home.

He decided to join his youngest brother William, who was a stock-farmer in Africa. The war of 1914 had just commenced, and soon after Llewelyn's arrival at Gilgil, in British East Africa, William joined the local defence forces. Llewelyn, with little experience, was left to do his brother's work.

Llewelyn's letters and diaries of this period, and the sketches of African life in *Black Laughter* and *Ebony and Ivory*, show his intense interest in every manifestation of life. His years in Africa were not entirely happy—he had too many hardships and responsibilities—but he was much influenced by his experiences there, and, as always, he turned everything to account in his writings:

With the coming of the night the whole air became vibrant, quivering, palpitating. From innumerable minute scaly throats a song of praise rose to the creator of the world. In shrill and high tones that fantastical chorus throbbed and hummed against my ear drum. Now and again far above my head would sound the romantic alien call of some wild fowl winging its solitary way through the night. I waited and waited. A damp air, chilling and invisible, rose from the lake. It had about it the smell of thousands of unrecorded years that had passed in quiet procession over these remote waters, while century after century trees grew to their prime and rotted to water-logged decay, while century after century the bones of fabulous equatorial animals accumulated upon the slimy mud of the lake's bottom. It had about it the smell of water-pythons, of incredible crustacea, and of the fecund spawn of insects.

Then suddenly, loud and clear, breaking in upon the stillness of that wide moonlit stretch of water till every flag and every reed seemed to tremble, sounded the harsh note of a hungry leopard.[1]

The African life suited his health and during those war years he kept his illness in check, but he was glad to return to England in the autumn of 1919. Again he had to think of his future.

In 1916 passages from his diaries had been published in the United States, with some autobiographical reflections by his brother John, under the title *Confessions of Two Brothers*. Once more, Llewelyn decided to join John Cowper in America and late in 1920 he sailed for New York.

I set sail for America with the vaguest idea as to what I intended to do. I had lost every penny I possessed from investments in German marks. My plans for the future were most fanciful. Sometimes I imagined that I might become a salesman, sometimes I dreamed of success in business through the influence of some benevolent magnate. It seemed quite obvious that I could never hope to make a living out of writing. How could I expect to do so when all that I wrote remained unpublished?[2]

Nearly all writers of originality have experienced similar difficulties. Llewelyn's early months in New York brought him little material success, but he began to make friendships that were to last all his life. He travelled extensively in America,

---

[1] *Ebony and Ivory.*
[2] *The Verdict of Bridlegoose.*

accompanying his brother John on his lecture tours, and joining his American friends in expeditions. He spent the spring of 1924 in the Rocky Mountains, and soon after his return to New York he felt another attack of his illness upon him. He left at once for the country, where he lay for two months slowly regaining his strength. That winter he spent in the Catskill Mountains with his wife, Alyse Gregory. Miss Gregory, herself a writer, was managing editor of a distinguished literary magazine, *The Dial*, in which some of Llewelyn's first sketches had appeared.

For gradually his sketches and articles had begun to sell. One morning, in New York as he was returning to his room in the apartment house where he lived before his marriage, he entered into conversation with a stranger on the stairs. The stranger began to praise the writings of a man named Llewelyn Powys. On another occasion, as he signed his name in a hotel register, the clerk said: 'Are you the Llewelyn Powys who writes on Africa?'

In 1923 he had collected enough sketches to make a book and *Ebony and Ivory* was published, with a preface by Theodore Dreiser. Soon afterwards he was able to publish a second collection, *Thirteen Worthies*, essays in literary appreciation, and *Black Laughter*, another (and maturer) gathering of African impressions. He was now launched as a writer.

In 1925 he and his wife decided to leave America, and by August they were settled in Dorset. For the next ten years Llewelyn's reputation grew steadily, although more slowly here than in America. His illness was always with him, but by exercising care he was able to live a full life. He went abroad a good deal, spending eight months in Italy and visiting Greece, Cyprus, Capri and Palestine. He returned to the United States as visiting critic for the New York *Herald Tribune*, and visited the West Indies. In France he wrote *Apples be Ripe* which was the most popular of his books. In Capri he wrote *The Cradle of God*, an imaginative interpretation of the old testament in which he was able to use his first hand knowledge of the Palestinian background. But despite the range of his travels he remained a countryman of Dorset, and his settled home was among the hills and people he loved.

'I am like Ulysses, I have seen many cities,' he once said to me, and in all of them something had been added to his wisdom. But the unhurrying life, first in a coastguard cottage on the very summit of White Nose, and later at Chydyok, was best suited to his mood and his need. Next door to him lived his sisters Gertrude and Philippa, and for a time his brother John lived in an isolated cottage a mile or so away. His brother Theodore lived in Chaldon itself where Llewelyn also had devoted friends among the villagers.

In 1934 Llewelyn became involved in a libel action, and for the first time the 'dying author,' as a Sunday newspaper dramatically called him, became widely known beyond a restricted circle of discriminating readers. He lost the action—which occasioned a severe financial strain—and the necessity of attending the Court at Dorchester in January 1935 led to a further setback in his health. Yet, despite this, during the last six years of his life, in defiance both of illness and the apathy of the book market, he produced seven books, as well as many essays and articles which were subsequently collected in book form, or remain uncollected.

After a number of dangerous attacks it was decided in 1936 to try again what Switzerland could do, and early in December he looked once more, after twenty-five years, on the peaks above Davos Platz. With returning health, he was able to go on long expeditions into the mountains; and in a cottage owned by an old friend at Clavadel he spent three happy years writing, reading, learning the Swiss peasant life, and watching the seasons pass.

On the morning of December 2nd, 1939, he died. A few days earlier he had written: 'I have had a happy life for half a century in sunshine.'

Llewelyn Powys was actively engaged as a writer for less than twenty years, but by beginning comparatively late he was quick to reach maturity. Within a few years of commencing as an author he was writing books that contain the ripest expression of his faith. In 1931 he spoke of *Impassioned Clay* in a letter to John Cowper Powys as 'my most important book.' This long essay was actually completed during his visit to the United States in the last months of 1930, but it was conceived in Dorset and is full of the thought and observation of his walks along the solitary downs. Of another of these essays expressing his mature philosophy he says: '*Glory of Life* was written in a cornfield on the

Dorset downs under a cloudless sky and in full view of the English Channel.'

Just as Africa had taught him the terror, so Dorset confirmed his appreciation of the glory of life. And—everywhere he went —his surroundings, his neighbours, his circumstances were employed as material in his work. 'By day and by night no sight that we see, no sound that we hear, but has its own poetical burden.' This precept from *Impassioned Clay* he kept always before him, and how faithfully he applied it may be seen in almost any page, chosen at random in any of his books.

In Clavadel he completed his most ambitious work, the 'imaginary autobiography,' *Love and Death*. This was published a few months before he died. He began *Love and Death*, he tells us, in the late summer of 1933, at Chydyok, and he finished it almost two years after his arrival in Switzerland. During this time he was engaged with much other work, but the 'imaginary autobiography' must constantly have been in his thoughts. His prose always bears witness of a craftsman's care, but in *Love and Death* more than in any other of his books—except possibly *Impassioned Clay*—we are conscious that to every thought he has given the most accurate expression possible to him: and few contemporary writers have been more scrupulous in the exact use of words.

In *Love and Death* the perfect marriage between Llewelyn's impassioned philosophy and his mature prose style produces a love story at once disarmingly simple and disturbingly subtle. Read 'for the story' it is direct, sensuous and moving; read again (and more than once again) 'for the implications' it is found to be a rich and lovely collect, the stored repository of fifty years' memories and meditations.

In my opinion *Love and Death* is as certainly a great book—one of the great books of our time—as are his brother John's *Autobiography* and his brother Theodore's *Mr. Weston's Good Wine*. It is profitable to study these three books together, to note the differences in their manner, their approach, their scope; to observe the very different reticences, and the revealing similarities. Each book could have been written by no one else, least of all by the writer of either of the others.

My purpose in making the present selection from Llewelyn Powys is to give—so far as the limits of a volume allow—a fair view of his genius. It is, in a sense, a distant view; and my hope is that readers will wish to approach nearer to see him, not in selections, but in complete books. No choice of passages from *Love and Death*, *Impassioned Clay*, or *The Cradle of God* could sufficiently represent them, and every choice of essays must omit others as illuminating as those included. To Llewelyn Powys the actual, living world was enough, and no writer of our time has celebrated more willingly or more persuasively the recurring miracle of the Sun. He was a great writer—so have many been. For us to-day it is more important that he was a happy writer, proclaiming in the face of mutation and mischance the persisting loveliness of life.

KENNETH HOPKINS.

For a full account of Llewelyn Powys's life and work the reader is referred to The Life of Llewelyn Powys *by Malcolm Elwin* (The Bodley Head, *1946*).

ACKNOWLEDGEMENTS

The Editor and Publishers wish to thank the following for permission to use copyright material in this book:

Messrs John Lane, The Bodley Head, for extracts from *Dorset Essays*, *Earth Memories*, *Love and Death*, *Impassioned Clay*, *The Verdict of Bridlegoose*, *Skin for Skin*, *Somerset Essays*, *Henry Hudson* and *Swiss Essays*.

Messrs C. A. Watts & Co., Ltd., for extracts from *Damnable Opinions*, *Rats in the Sacristy*, and *The Cradle of God*.

CONTENTS

CONTENTS

LITERATURE

ILLUSTRATIONS

AUTOBIOGRAPHICAL

A SOMERSET CHRISTMAS

IT WOULD be a mistake to imagine that old people cannot enjoy the feast of Christmas. Many a grandfather and many a grandmother, seated close and quiet by the fire amid the revelries of children and young people, enter with their long, long memories more deeply into the true spirit of the night than do their light-hearted descendants for all their shining eyes, tossing curls, and merry mistletoe-laughing voices.

Yet Christmas remains, in its essence, the especial festival of the young. It is they who possess imaginations sensitive enough to respond with unspoilt eagerness to the glamour of the day. In my own case it has been most certainly so, and with the remembrance of half a century of Christmases held in my mind, it is to the first twenty that I look back with the most joy. My brother Bertie and I would begin to be aware of the approach of Christmas even before the end of the autumn term at Sherborne. We used, I remember, to walk to a certain holly tree growing in the field to the right of Babylon Hill from which we could look across the town of Yeovil to the leafless outlines of Odcombe, Montacute Hill, Hedgecock, and Ham Hill fretted in a miniature landscape on the wintry western horizon. This last-Sunday-of-the-term ritual we performed in a mood of exultant anticipation of the Christmas holidays.

No Christmas Day could have been passed more simply and innocently than ours was at Montacute Vicarage, and yet in retrospect every moment of it seems to have been full of an indescribable golden happiness. The celebrations had their beginning on Christmas Eve with the decorating of the horns in the hall and the pictures in the dining-room. All the day long my brother and I would have been busy collecting, in two large baker's baskets, moss and fir branches for the church, and holly and mistletoe for our own home. The best branches of mistletoe in the glebe orchard we had marked down at the end of the summer holidays when the ground was still thick-strewn with

over-ripe, wasp-eaten apples, but these we kept for our requirements at home, and in truth I do not think the pious ladies who
were so busy with the pulpit and lectern and windows and pews
of St. Catharine's would have welcomed the strange white-
berried plant, the very look of whose horned Pagan leaves is
remote from ecclesiastical sentiment.

At midnight, with the appearance of the carol singers, the real
Christmas celebrations would begin. The men—masons, farm
labourers, quarrymen, and gardeners—would stand with their
lanterns outside the front door to sing 'Joy to the World,' a
Christmas carol, the words and music of which had been composed by the delicate genius of Thomas Shoel. At the first notes
of the concertina, flute, and harmonium sounding along the dark
rambling passage of the silent house, we children would hasten
to the dining-room, and collecting on the sofa, wrapped in
dressing-gowns and blankets, would peer out into the darkness
to see what we might see of the dim dignified figures of old
Geard, of Mr. William Johnston, of Charley Blake, of Russ, and
of a score of other notable personalities familiar enough in the
streets of Montacute forty years ago. How strange it was to look
out upon the drive, with the tennis lawn obscurely visible beyond
the wicker-work fence, and to hear the ancient strains redolent
of man's desperate hopes, rise up from the secure Victorian
garden into the sky, into eternity! The nativity music would be
brought to an end at last with the words 'A merry Christmas
and a happy New Year,' and afterwards we would hear the
opening of the window upstairs, followed by the sound of our
father's voice giving the men his thanks and good wishes
for the season as he stood in his nightgown by the old broad
family bed.

Only a few hours would be allowed to go by in a dreamless
sleep and then my brother and I would light candles at our bedside
and would begin to examine our stockings—stockings that still
contained scraps of lichen from the trunks of the apple trees up
which we had swarmed the day before. With our cheeks
crammed, like the cheeks of monkeys, with sugar biscuits and
sweetmeats, we would occupy ourselves with our presents until
the moment came to hurry down to prayers in the dining-room,
into which the winter sun, half-way through breakfast, would
suddenly penetrate, shining between the naked beech trees that

surrounded John Scott's house, from a round ball red as a ruby. John Scott acted as huntsman for one of the Squires for many years. He is buried in the Montacute Churchyard. An epitaph on his stone reads:

> Here lies John Scott!
> It was his lot
> A huntsman bold to be
> He loved his can
> Like any man,
> And drank like a fish in the sea.

At the foot of this ribald drinking doggerel may be read these two curt lines, said to have been carved on the disreputable stone at the order of one of the Bishops of Bath and Wells:

> And now, God wot,
> He has got his lot.

The old house in Dunster's Orchard has recently, I understand, been demolished. The late Mr. Wyndham Goodden[1] could remember when it was inhabited, but it was in ruins when I knew it.

It was typical of those spacious, old-fashioned, genial decades that the first happy meal of the day should each year have been regularly interrupted by a card sent up to the Vicarage by the famous old liberal Baptist minister, the Rev. Henry Hardin, with greetings to my father. After breakfast we were free till the morning service, but on such a day, with the familiar chapter from Isaiah, 'Unto us a Child is born,' and with the singing of 'While shepherds watched their flocks by night,' even being in church was not irksome, especially if my brother Bertie and I, owing to the largeness of our family gathering, were allowed to enjoy the novel experience of sitting on the row of chairs by the Phelips' monuments, where we could whisper to each other and meditate upon Mrs. Hodder's turkey that had been hanging 'in the pride of its grease' head downwards in the larder for the last

[1] Son of the Rev. C. C. Goodden, whom the Rev. C. F. Powys succeeded as Vicar of Montacute in 1886.

week. After we were home again and the turkey, surrounded by sausages—Maynard's sausages, thin, crisp, bursted, and sizzling, such as I have never tasted since—had been devoured, with the mince-pies and a plum-pudding decorated with a spray of holly, red as a cock's comb, we would gather to have the contents of the Christmas hamper, sent by our Norwich aunts, distributed amongst us by our father, each of us holding out our hands with eager self-interest. Then in the late evening, after our turkey thirst had been thoroughly quenched at the family tea-table, where we all sat snug around the tall oil-lamp, warm behind heavy winter curtains, the hall bell would ring to announce that the Christmas-tree was ready in the school-room.

This was the most valued part of the whole day. It was on the Christmas-tree that we hung the presents that we gave to each other. The tree was dug up every Christmas and replanted the next morning, and seemed little the worse for its annual visit to the house. And how resplendent the spruce sapling would look, upright in its box in the centre of the school-room, in the centre of what in Mr. Goodden's days was called 'the servants' hall.' It is odd to remember that the Christmas-tree was practically unknown in England until, by the marriage of Queen Victoria to the Prince Consort, the custom was introduced from Germany, its kinship perhaps with unrecorded fire-worshipping practices rendering this primitive ritual easily acceptable, even in so conservative an island as England, used for time out of mind to the burning of a yule log.

In an hour the floor would be littered with tinsel paper and the coloured candles would be flaring low in their sockets, till, one after another, a feathered fir twig would fill the room with the incense of the wild forest. Then the moment would come when, with crossed arms, we would dance in a ring about the innocent tree, singing 'Auld Lang Syne.' I can even now, in my mind's eye, see the tall figure of my father, with child-like benedictions emanating from his good face, as our voices rose and fell loud enough to be heard out on the cold deserted allotment plots where parcels of roughed-up wintry ground were waiting to be re-dug for the planting on Good Friday of well-sprouted potato seedlings. As we swayed backwards and forwards about the tree with laughing voices, not one of us, I suppose, was cognizant of the calm processes of nature which were taking place around the house—the grasses on the lawn sparkling as brightly as the stars in the heaven, while beneath the comfortable slate roof of Montacute Vicarage the lives of old and young were passing away under the shadow of God's irreversible ordinance.

From *A Baker's Dozen* (1940).

OUT OF THE PAST

A RARE occupation it is to vex our minds with trying to recreate a living, visible background for events in our country's history, a rare thing to envisage with undimmed mental eye just exactly how the chalk cliffs of England looked, with thyme and viper's bugloss in flower, when Caesar visited our island; to recapture in retrospect the very smells of the great Hampshire forest on the morning of William Rufus' death; to hear across fields enclosed for hay the sound of the rebeck as the country villages rejoiced over the return of Charles Stuart.

But quite apart from such imaginative pastimes, which are, indeed, common to all of us; each family, however modest its origin, possesses its own particular tale of the past—a tale which can bewitch us with as great a sense of insistent romance as can ever the traditions of kings. The years lived by our father before he begot us have upon them a wonder that cannot easily be matched. Just as we feel ourselves half participant in the experiences of our children, so in some dim way do we share in those adventures of this mortal who not so long ago moved over the face of the earth like a god to call us up out of the deep.

Often it is the name of some particular place, some historic city with tilted roofs and clustered chimneys, some market town or wintry hamlet, that is associated with this transfigured world before we were born. We grow up with scraps of hearsay about the place for ever in our ears, the very repetition of the accustomed syllables creating presently an assured legend, a legend that takes soon an important part in the substance of our minds.

In the annals of my own family it is the Dorset village of Stalbridge that has held our imagination in fee. Ever since the days when our father would visit the nursery before going down to his tea in the dining-room, the word 'Stalbridge' has carried in its utterance a significance outside the commonplace. Stalbridge! The old china tea set came from Stalbridge. It was at Stalbridge that a cup of coffee used to be left in the oven over-night so that it might be warm for my father in the early hours of the morning when, as a boy, he set out to fish for pike in the still black river pools of the Stour. It was in Stalbridge Vale that my father had found all the rarest specimens in his collection of birds' eggs, in the collection which he preserved so carefully all through his long life in the three lower drawers of the cabinet in his study. It was to Stalbridge that he had gone, half across the county, in his great age when, rendered dumb as an animal by the merciless years, he had suddenly, without warning, left his servants in his house at Weymouth. Hour after hour passed and still he did not return, this aged, inarticulate clergyman, who was so old that he had almost forgotten how a man puts bread into his mouth. It was to Stalbridge that he had gone, to the beloved rectory where he had played with his brother.

What manner of call had he received, imperative and not to be denied, to return unto that place from whence he came? Far away over the seas as I was at the time, I have often wondered whether I could have borne to have found him, this old man, my father, advancing with deliberate intention, with intellectual intention, along the green leafy lanes of Dorset. Should I have had the temerity to divert him from his dedicated pilgrimage with the cry of 'Father!' as he went forward, this octogenarian who was lost and yet who knew every stile, every ditch, every shard, along the way he was taking?

It is exactly ninety years since my grandfather, who was born, indeed, but five years after the death of Dr. Johnson—came first to Stalbridge to take possession of the fattest of the Corpus livings, and in the circle of those years my father has lived to a great age, and to-day lies buried hip-bone to hip-bone by the side of my mother in Somersetshire clay.

For the first time in my life I visited Stalbridge last Whitsuntide. I set out upon my adventure in bright June sunshine. Hardly had I descended upon the deserted village platform when I felt come over me a strange glamour. Although for sixty years no member of my family had lived in the village, yet as I came up the street each crooked, mute paving-stone seemed to keep back a memory. I entered the churchyard, and there under the tall holly, with rose trees at its foot, was the flat stone marking my grandfather's grave. There he was lying, this other octogenarian, hip-bone to hip-bone with *his* wife. Presently I opened a side gate and entered

Stalbridge Park. It was noon. I found myself in a hayfield. As I ate my fruit, under the shadow of a group of West Country elms, ninety years seemed to me to shrink to the proportion of a day.

With the ancient timber standing in the mown grass, with the protecting wall of quarried slabs set up like tombstones about the meadow, familiar to me from many an old faded water-colour in the album at home, the prospect before me was exactly the same, and I knew it, as it must have been when, as a young girl, Queen Victoria sat upon the throne of England. Here through these sweet-smelling pastures my grandfather must have walked on many a summer evening; here my father must have come as a boy on many an early spring morning in search of the brittle eggs of the far-off ancestors of the birds which crossed and recrossed my vision in the trembling gnat-burdened air between tree and tree. Out of the stones of the old sheep-washing pool, now fallen into decay, grew herb-robert and silver-weed, flowers so familiar, so actual and inevitable to the experience of my own life, that it seemed impossible that these simple tokens of the country-side as I knew them could ever have adorned in the same matter-of-fact way the nooks of this rural structure on those occasions when my uncle and my father had stood to watch the busy activities that used to take place here in the old days.

I left the park and entered Wood Lane, a hesitating narrow lane which runs above the village. I knocked at the door of a thatched cottage. The woman who answered me gave me cool water to drink from her mossy well. She knew nothing of my grandfather, but told me to go to an aged woman named Maria at the end of the street. Old Maria had nearly lived out a century and yet her mind was still clear. She took down a book, a thin book on religion, kept carefully all these years, with my grand-father's writing on it. 'You yourself be terribly like to him,' she said. 'I can mind the old gentleman as though 'twere yesterday; I can most see 'en now come down the street with half-crown in flat of hand. On one of the young gentlemen's birthdays we would go up to the house and dance before 'en. I do carry the ditty in head to this day.' And this old woman, whose face had retained through all her years so much refinement, sang to me these simple words:

Children go to and fro
In a merry, pretty row.
Footsteps light, faces bright,
'Tis a happy, happy sight.
Swiftly turning round and round,
Do not look upon the ground.
Follow me, full of glee,
Singing merrily.

And as I gazed upon this frail human being, so purely winnowed by the harsh flails of life, I felt a deep love surge up in me for the old creature who still carried in her head the memory of the dancing days of her childhood under the mulberry tree in the rectory garden of Stalbridge eighty years ago. There she stood before me, backed by her cottage ornaments, her small head swaying a little as she repeated the words of the rhyme. When I turned to go, tears were falling down her cheeks and were in my own eyes. Had we not both of us been plunged into the deep waters of the past that are for ever flowing towards an ocean without marge and without bottom?

From Maria I went to the cottage of Mrs. Duffet, another old woman. She required no prompting. She remembered Mr. Powys. Had not her mother come to the very house in which she now lived so as to be nearer to the rectory? A duty had been required of her—the duty, namely, of twice a day suckling my father. Here, then, I was talking to my father's foster sister—this old woman and my father had been held up to the same fountain, had drunk from the same life-giving well. This was the daughter of the woman who had put wormwood to her dugs, sitting in the sun under Stalbridge Cross!

How would it be possible to catch, to hold for a moment, the quality of those magical hours of June sunshine, of June moonlight, down in that Dorset village? At night I wandered along Drew Lane far into the vale. On all sides of me recumbent cattle dreamed away their animal existence under hedges festooned with dog-roses already in bud. Barn-door owls with unfilmed eyes called to each other out of the hollow bodies of listening trees. One by one the lights of the village above the valley were put out. The old men dreamed, the old women dreamed, the boys and girls dreamed, and a grace, the solace of antiquity, sustained in Christian peace these ancient meadows.

The next morning I was waked by the treading of cows being driven through the street. All was once more astir. Above each little back garden, with its produce so neatly set out in rows, innumerable larks trilled. I left my hostess early and made my way in the direction of the next village. Often had I heard my father speak of a certain halter-path which led to Sturminster Newton, and I now had a mind to follow it. More like a lane than a path it turned out to be. Sturdy oaks flourished on each side of it. Presently I realised that I was overtaking a bowed figure, who, with a stick in her hand, was picking her way across the ruts. I spoke to her. She had lived in Stalbridge all her life, she said. When she heard who I was she laughed aloud. She remembered my uncle Littleton well. 'He used to run races along be I. He used to give I star cakes; they star cakes were as big round as a frying-pan and had currants in 'em.' And then as the old woman gathered her memories about her, it was as though in that ancient mind time became discounted. The bracken that was uncurling on upright stems in the ditches belonged to the year 1927, but to the old cottage woman it opened upon a world where death itself was forgotten. 'Tell him, tell him,' she cried with excitement, 'that ye met Nancy Curtis in the halter-path, the girl what used to run races for they star cakes—that will bring I back to the mind o' en.'

I asked for her blessing and hurried on. How could I explain that she had given me a message to a soldier who had been lying dead in the dry soil of India already for half a century?

From *Earth Memories* (1935).

Llewelyn Powys (1924). Taken during his hunting expedition to the Rocky Mountains with Dr. James S. Watson.

AUGUST

THAT SUMMER[1] was the hottest I have ever known in England. Day after day the sun rose over the horizon behind Vag farm into a cloudless sky. The pastures were no longer green. The cattle roamed over the brown grass-fields like famished eland on diminutive, scorched-up African veldts. There was so little water flowing in the deep river-bed of the Yeo that it was possible at almost any point in its long, winding course to paddle across it. The chub, fearful of being stranded in shallow water, kept themselves at the bottom of the few deep holes that remained. The stock spent long hours in standing about in places where the river was shaded by a group of alders, by an oak tree, or by the stone-work of some old bridge. The grass-hoppers skipped from bent to bent, the butterflies from flower-head to flower-head. The crust of the earth cracked and cracked, so that I was often able, right out in the middle of a field, to put my walking-stick into a crevice two or three feet deep. Many farmers were compelled to cut down saplings from the hedges, and branches from the trees, to save their cattle from starving. Not one of them but was short of 'keep.' As each Friday they came back from Yeovil market, they would do nothing but lament about the state of the country, as seen in panoramic view through the open window of a third-class railway-carriage.

On the hottest of all the days of that summer, when, as we learnt afterwards, the thermometer stood at one hundred Fahrenheit, John and I set out for a walk to Tintinhull. We approached this favourite haunt of ours by way of Marsh Lane. At the entrance of Captain Chaffey's drive we stood talking to Denman. This old labourer had been a quarry-man on Ham Hill for nearly eighty years. He had seen us from a distance, trailing along in white flannels through the Stoke Road dust. He accosted us. I began to think that the old man had already, early as it was,

---

[1] It was the year 1911.

been drinking cider, for presently he laid his toil-encrusted hands upon us and cried out in a loud voice: 'Sixty years agone to-day come two months I was trapesing along this here turnpike road to ploughing match. Yes, we know as much of life as they that cross the ocean, we *that live on the deep soil*. We have *our* waves as well as the rest of them, we quarrymen, ploughmen, shepherd-men, come fine, come rain, come cold, come het.' The old chap was so filthy and made such a din as we stood there under the decorous copper beech, that I was glad to escape through the captain's white iron gates.

Presently we came by Wulham's Mill, that ancient mill which stands by its stream completely lost in meadows. We leaned over a gate. The grey roof, sunken with age, cut an uneven line against the sweltering sky. The place seemed held under a strange noonday glamour. There was never a rustle in the long potato-rows in the garden, not one small purple flower stirred. Except for a pregnant tabby-cat stretched out under a currant-bush at the edge of the stone-flagged path, there was no sign of life. It was here that the miller's little daughter had been drowned in the mill-pond, her body being seen by her father floating against the old, rusty, water-worn sluice. It was here, also, that I was to come two years later with Marion Linton.

At last we reached the churchyard, which we two had been in the habit of visiting for so many years. Not far from the old seventeenth-century altar-tomb of the family of Francis, we noticed a new grave, covered with Madonna lilies, such as were then in flower in all the cottage gardens. Whom had they buried here so recently, in this hot July weather? We moved across to the church porch, seeking shelter from the sun, and pushing open the heavy door which held in its oaken timber great nails deep embedded, nails driven home centuries before by the hands of dead Denmans, long since crumbled to dust, nails still able to respond, after the limited fashion of iron, to the divine sudorific influences of that unequalled day.

We had some bread and cheese at the Lamb. We gave a drink to a postman who came in. He said he preferred frosty weather. Not so an old tramp, who had once been a ship's steward. 'I likes this het,' he kept repeating, as large, silvery beads fell from his forehead. He had come from Yeovil, resting often, so he told us, in shady places. The ends of his boots had been slit to make them easier for walking. We bought a celluloid hair-comb from him for half a crown. The tavern parlour was cool as a well. A wasp was beating itself against a window-pane, and John must needs catch it in his handkerchief to let it out. How different was the smell of this interior from the smell of the church! And how the atmosphere of such a place lends itself to philosophic discourse! In a tavern one touches life at its centre. Here is the heart of the bee-hive. Here, at any rate, no spiritual treachery is tolerated; here, at any rate, no deceitful idealism stretches out tendrils white and sickly. . . . He who sits down on a tavern settle must even take the world as he finds it. He must know what birth means, and that we come into the world in no very cleanly manner; he must know what love means, and wrath, and lust, and, above all, death. In a tavern, come winter, come summer, the blunt truth will out. I had walked not long before to a village situated behind West Coker, and had observed the grave of a former clergyman of the place, with the words, 'A little while,' carved on the headstone. 'A little while!' 'A little while!' It would be known under the smoky rafters of the Lamb Inn that the Rev. Launders' body was to lie there in the church-yard for a great deal longer than 'a little while.' These pretty texts survive best in a confined and pretty atmosphere, but grow faint and frail in these snug hostels, where simple, honest men gather, men who are disposed to speak good words of the old bawdy earth, and who, like so many Grangousiers, delight to sit warming their ballocks before a fair fire. We paid our reckoning to Mrs. Mary Yard, our hostess, who looked very prim and dignified in her white cap, and stepped out into the giddy, merciless sunshine of the little front garden.

We now wandered into Tintinhull Great-Field. The grass was dry and slippery. We were making our way to Kiss-Me-Down covert. On each side of us lay sultry orchards, with the trunks of ancient apple-trees, half fallen to the ground, like a host of tottering old men, which the sun had ensorcerised there. Lesser blues and gate-keepers flitted about our boots, the soles of which had been polished so smooth by walking over the fields. We found that the drove going up through Kiss-Me-Down was littered with straw. We trod silently. ''Tis as though the king of the owls were sick,' said John. Above Windmill we passed through a field of oats, the green stalks of which had already taken to themselves that amethystine tint characteristic of oat-straw when the grain is approaching maturity.

We were back in time for tea. In those days we were always wondering whether it was more pleasant to wash our hands before eating or to leave them still odorous of the countryside. Often, while we were still debating this nice point, we would hear the tea-bell ring, and without more ado would go downstairs, one behind the other, to find the rest of the family standing in their places, waiting for my father to say grace, before he began cutting up the two loaves of bread, which stood on their wooden platters before him, a brown loaf and a white cottage-loaf, the soft, crinkled crust of the latter being especially delectable when it came fresh from the ovens of the black-bearded baker.

When we had sat down, the old man, my father, rubbing his hands with delight at having his children around him, would ask us about our walk, and we would tell him that we had found the body of a dead heron down by Wulham's mill, and also a flower which we thought might be skullcap. And at that he would send my sister Lucy to fetch his 'Bewick' and his 'Johns Botany' from his study. He would then read out extracts from the two volumes. And afterwards, with a look of boundless benevolence, he would rub his hands and say that he was glad that we boys had had an interesting walk. And at this my mother's face would become lit up with a smile, at once so radiant, so sweet, and so *ironic*, that I would forgive her for being in love with the side of the moon which turns itself away from the earth, and which has never once been seen by Tintinhull tipplers, as they stagger out of the public-house past the village stocks, past the great elm, and past the duck-pond. And she would lean over to John and stroke his hand; for she always loved him, her first-born, the best.

Meanwhile, Lord Eversley, who, as our father used to tell us, had taken the side of our great-grandmother Shaw in some peevish quarrel with the first Lord Lilford, would look down out of his gold frame with the set, supercilious stare of a man of the world. And presently we would ring for more butter, which would be brought in creamy and freshly churned, and then we would ring for more milk also, and have the white china jug with tomtits painted upon it refilled with what was all 'top of the pail.'

From *Skin for Skin* (1926).

A STRUGGLE FOR LIFE

IT WAS in the month of November of the year 1909 that I first discovered I was suffering from pulmonary tuberculosis. Up till that time, although I had been conscious of feeling unwell, I had never suspected the serious nature of my malady. Probably it was fortunate that the disease so early in its advance broke a blood vessel. I was immediately examined by a doctor, who declared that I must leave England for a health-resort in Switzerland as soon as ever I was in a fit state to travel. Meanwhile the windows of my bedroom were removed from their frames and for three weeks I lay on my back contemplating the bare elms and misty autumnal roof-tops of the town of Sherborne, from, as it were, some open barn-loft unprotected from the weather.

Always of a nervous temperament, the doctor's diagnosis had been no small shock. As each morning I was waked from my restless dreams by the ringing of the bell of the convent in Long Street it seemed incredible that it was I, already so inordinate a lover of life, who had been selected as a victim to this terrible disease, selected almost certainly to die young.

I feel ashamed now when I think of how I dramatised my illness, talking incessantly of what it felt like to be dying, to be dying of consumption! My five brothers came to my bedside and with each of them in turn I discussed my fate. And as the rain drifted gustily in on to the bare deal floor, which in consequence gave out continually the curious chilled smell of a room where scrubbing has lately been in progress, they would lend their attention to the subject with philosophic detachment, treating it in a tone as frank as my own, for all the world like five disillusioned jackdaws gathering about one of their kind who has been winged by a sportsman's gun. I asserted emphatically that if I lived to be thirty I should be satisfied.

The excitement of going to Switzerland kept me in good spirits; though occasionally it happened, in spite of all my bravado, that I became conscious of a dull uneasy sense of lonely

37

apprehension as though I were about to set out upon a journey the length and weariness of which I could not foresee. For example, when a workman from the village at home who had come to visit me casually remarked that I had a 'churchyard cough' I felt myself immediately wide awake to the reality of my predicament, a predicament devoid of sentiment, bereft of drama, bleak, unpretentious, and *natural*.

The first few months of my stay in Switzerland saw me recovering rapidly. If I had had the wit to return to England then, all might have been well; instead I allowed myself to be persuaded to stay on through the summer so as 'to make sure of my cure.' Immediately I became careless and spent time diverting myself in the company of patients who were sick in bed. I believe by this means I reinfected myself, for otherwise I can in no way account for the fact that my sickness, quite unexpectedly, took a turn for the worse. The disease now advanced more rapidly than it had ever done. All the dreaded symptoms of consumption began to show themselves. I felt poisoned, listless, and would easily fall asleep only to wake up drenched with sweat. Each night my cheeks burned with an ever-increasing fever. Each time that I was weighed it was found that I had lost several pounds. In a few weeks I became so thin that I could easily enclose my thigh in the small circle made by holding my two thumbs and two first fingers together. My decline had been so rapid that it seemed certain I should be dead within a few months. I could tell by their discreet manners that the Sanatorium doctors thought as much. Every time I coughed, with a sickening sense of impending physical disaster, I tasted corruption, as though at its very centre my body harboured some foul mildew.

My attitude to mortality has always been childish. Invariably when I contemplate death my thoughts turn to the fate of my body, as though my timorous consciousness would still be aware of what happens to it after I am dead. Looking now into the future I shivered, my mind recoiling desperately from the thought that before the Christmas of 1910 I would be a member of that recumbent congregation of all nationalities who lie on their shoulder-blades, under the mountain snow, row upon row of them, to the right and to the left of the black-spired Protestant church of Davos-Platz.

Then on the night of July 11th I had a haemorrhage. The

shock of it caused me to tremble from crown to heel; but I believe, for all that, it saved my life, clearing away much diseased tissue and allowing me, as it were, to make a fresh start in my struggle for life. In the early part of the night the doctors were at my bedside constantly injecting me with gelatine. Later, they were called away to a neighbouring room to attend a young English boy named Burton who also had been taken suddenly ill. All through that night my abrupt fits of coughing, the particular significance of which could not be mistaken by anyone acquainted with the sickness, were answered by the abrupt fits of coughing of my friend, as he also gasped for breath in his small hygienic room on the further side of the white corridor. Towards morning the blood ceased to flow and I lay on my back not daring to move, watching a moth crawl up and down the flat impassive face of a large window-pane which already had received upon its surface the first pale indications of dawn. After the haemorrhage I remained in bed for four months. Throughout this time I was under the care of a Norwegian nurse to whose tireless devotion I have always felt I owe my life. Three weeks after the attack I was allowed to see my friend Wilbraham. I asked for news of Burton. 'Burton! Why, Burton has been dead and buried—three weeks ago.'

Slowly, very slowly, my temperature came down. For months I lay quite still looking out at the broken edge of a mountain-top on the other side of the Frauenkirk Valley. I looked at it in the morning when it was bleak and hard, I looked at it in the evening when, long after the setting sun had left the white roof of the hospital in which I was, its lofty clefts held fanciful rose-red shadows. The bare outline of this particular mountain suggested the exact shape of a woman lying on her back—her nose, her breasts, her knees, her toes even, limned against infinity. 'Queen Victoria "curing",' the more vulgar English patients called her.

I can well remember when I first, with the support of a serving-man, tried to get out of bed only to find my legs give under me like bent straws. The fact that my temperature was coming down filled me now with renewed hope. Slowly I grew better. I managed to get downstairs for the Christmas dinner. Each small advance filled me with exultation. So nervous was I, lest I should have another haemorrhage, that for months whenever I was dressed and moving about I would unconsciously be pressing my fingers against the right side of my chest, in an absurd endeavour to hold my damaged lung together as one might some precious fragile vessel. I wore a circular hole in a good serge waistcoat by this trick. An X-ray examination revealed that both my lungs were affected, but the right lung more seriously than the left.

By the end of January I began once more to take walks out of doors. At first a distance of a hundred yards would be sufficient to send my temperature up, but I soon discovered that such exercise-fever would come down as a rule after half an hour's rest on my *lieger* chair. This encouraged me to lengthen my walks, each day going a little further, but keeping all the time a careful watch on my temperature, which after rest would drop to normal. If it did not drop, then I concluded I had done too much and would in consequence reduce the length of my walks. Following this method I went first as far as the Kurhaus, then as far as the cattle shed where the crisp frosty air would be so pleasantly tainted; then, eventually, by the end of March, as far as the old white mill which stands by the river where the road winds its way down to the Frauenkirk village. Indeed, so proud was I of this last achievement that I marked one of its walls with my pocket knife.

It was now decided that I should return to England. My brother John came to fetch me. I well remember how impressed he was by the spectacle of the Davos 'main street,' every balcony of every house filled with prostrate human figures. An English clergyman passed us on his way to the skating rink. 'Aye!' my brother exclaimed. 'How one would like to see Our Lord come round that corner where the sleigh stands, with the twelve following behind him disputing among themselves over some nice theological point.'

We landed in England on May Day. I was overjoyed to be back again. After the snow-clad mountain landscape of the Engadine the fresh green of the Somerset meadows seemed wonderful. I found myself as sensitive to the sights and sounds and smells of the countryside as a brown hare in a field of sprouting corn. I remember one day meeting Fred Chant, the woodcutter, as I came out of the little back lane where the poplars grew and where Will Hockey's old grey mare used to graze. 'They doctors can mend ye, Master Llewelyn,' he said, 'but they cannot cure ye; patch ye up for the summer, maybe, but you'll soon *be wearing a green coat* for all thick there syrup ye sip.' The wearing of a green coat I knew referred to the grass of the churchyard which, so he anticipated, would soon be covering my bones.

It was not to be. To the astonishment of everybody my walks continued to lengthen, until I came to regard it as absolutely necessary for my health to walk at least ten miles each day, no less a distance being sufficient, so I considered, to bring about the required reactions. During that summer I came to know every lane and bypath around Montacute; the character of each field gate, whether it was stiff or easy to open; the places where there were gaps in the hedges; and the places where the banks of the deep muddy Somerset streams fell away so as to allow of a drinking-pool for the cattle. Under this combination of steady exercise and periods of complete rest my physical condition became extremely robust. It seemed that in a short time I would be quite well again.

The autumns in South Somerset are always damp. The woods at that time of the year give out the cloying smell of those small yellow toadstools that grow at the foot of decaying trees. My brother, T. F. Powys, realising this, asked me to stay with him in Dorset. He lived at that time, as, indeed, he does still,[1] in the small smuggling village of East Chaldon which lies hidden some three miles inland from the wild stretch of coast between Lulworth and Weymouth.

I remained well through that autumn. I continued to take enormous walks in all weathers, scrambling about the high chalk cliffs with the sea-blown rain lashing against my face. I came to know every rock, every high guillemot ledge, every projecting promontory. Sometimes on clear nights my brother and I would walk together to an old stone circle situated on the shoulder of the downs above the village called Poxwell, or Puck's Well, as it should more properly be written. And standing there in the centre of that grey Druidic ring we would listen to the surge of the distant sea, peering up, meanwhile, at the great Square of Pegasus, like two conjured spirits with red beards wagging.

As I still coughed it was now suggested that in order 'to finish my cure' I had better pay one more visit to Switzerland. This

---

[1] But not now (1952).

time I selected to go to the small winter resort of Arosa. On my arrival I found that I had a slight temperature and in consequence lay still for a few days. However, I soon grew impatient, and, excusing the fever on account of the rarefied air, once more took to walking. With the help of a pair of Canadian snowshoes I was able to leave the paths and climb along the higher mountain slopes.

Now, it happened one day, as I was carelessly looking at a map of Switzerland hung up in the hotel vestibule, that I was astounded to observe the word Davos-Platz almost touching that of Arosa and, on examining the map more closely, found out that, although by train the two places were separated by a twenty-four-hour journey, as the crow flies only some fifteen miles of mountain lay between them. Indeed, I realised that I had actually been looking at the other side of 'Queen Victoria "curing"' each afternoon as I sat taking tea on the hotel balcony. The discovery affected me like one of those dreams when familiar places, far distant from each other, suddenly merge; when the hard walls of a gravel school-yard, let us say, open unaccountably into the paddock of one's home. The mountain opposite now began to obsess my imagination. I found myself continually stopping in front of the map to study the minute topographical markings near the words Furka Pass. It was fascinating to me to know that I was looking at the other side of that range, every contour of which had been indelibly printed on my memory. I kept imagining myself coming down off the very slopes whose beauty, as seen from my bed, had so often beguiled the end of a long afternoon. I made up my mind to cross the mountain range.

The day I selected for the adventure was cloudless. I confided my purpose to no one. I took some sandwiches with me, and walking slowly and steadily soon found myself above the timber-line and confronted by smooth sheets of sparkling virginal snow. The crows in the dark trees below croaked a warning, but I gave no heed to them. The actual Furka Pass, as I remember, was about fifty feet wide, a steep slope of snow that went down into I knew not what abyss. However, by stamping I could break through the frozen crust and in this way secure a firm footing. Once across I found myself on a mountain plateau surrounded by rocky peaks. All was glinting white, all was silent. No track of animal traversed that high expanse, no flight of bird was seen

to pass across the blue ether. I did meet with one live thing—
a tortoiseshell butterfly! It came fluttering over those eternal
snows with the light carelessness characteristic of this particular
species, and which may perhaps account for the fact that one so
often sees them, with wings frayed, tragically imprisoned against
the dusty coloured-glass of church windows. I kept looking up
at the sky. I very well recognised the danger of being caught in a
snow-storm. On I went over that high mountain level, leaving
behind me a strange webbed track, as though some fabulous grebe
had waddled across the white plateau. I was very excited. Would
I ever reach the other side? I felt my pulse. It was racing. And
as each hour passed I became more and more conscious of the hot
flush of my sickness tingling under my skin. Had I undertaken
too much? And then suddenly I was rewarded! I had come to
the top of the last ridge and there, far down below, across the
valley, stood Clavadel Sanatorium, fretted with balconies, and
looking like a doll's house against that stupendous landscape. I
was exultant. I walked along in an ecstasy. Well I knew that I
was passing over those cusped slopes which a year ago had seemed
to me as remote as the furthest rose-tinted cloud. I found my
way down to the timber and before long came upon a chalet
where mountain hay had been stored. A woodcutter's path led
from this remote barn so that in half an hour I was in the Frauenkirk village.

I hired a room in the little inn and made my way slowly up to
the Sanatorium. The dinner-gong had sounded and the patients
had already collected in the spacious dining-room, each corner of
which had been made so neatly concave. My appearance seemed
miraculous, my story unbelievable. With my face burning to
an unhealthy blazing red I walked from one familiar group to
another; the young German doctor, in his white coat, following
me about and asking me to explain to him by what new method
I had cured myself. And all the time while I received their
congratulations I could feel my heart knocking against the walls of
my ribs. Before long I left the noisy hall and stepped out into the
cold moonlight which, with so curious an effect, was illumined
by those sad flaunting windows.

Once back in the little inn I went to bed. I flooded the room
with frosty air and lay down to sleep. I could not sleep. Nervous
thoughts kept scurrying through my skull like mice in a pantry.

Hour after hour went by, and then what I had been unconsciously anticipating actually happened. With a wretched sinking at the pit of my stomach I suddenly recognised the intolerable *bubbling sensation* in my chest indicative of a haemorrhage. I turned on the light, hoping against hope, I coughed, I looked, and once more I saw blood. Slowly the dawn came. News of my relapse was sent to Clavadel and a black sleigh arrived to carry me back to the Sanatorium, the greatest fool in all that dolorous citadel.

Over a month elapsed before I was strong enough to travel back to England. For a year after this I remained at home following out a rigid routine of life and in this way managing to hold my sickness in check. The summer of 1912, however, again found me on the Continent. This time I visited Italy with my brother John. We stayed in Venice. During those strangely exciting weeks I never for a moment was unaware of the presence of my dread complaint. When before breakfast I strolled out into the garden for the pleasure of watching the lizards chase each other behind the rose bushes trained to grow against the hot white wall of the hotel I knew of it. And again I knew of it when during languid summer nights we drifted along the canals with dark water, so startlingly evocative of the smells of an obscure antiquity, lapping against the bottom of our gondola and against the green-stained masonry of walls and stairways, the supporting piles of which had been laid in place on the muddy rush-grown bottom of an open lagoon, so many years ago. On one occasion I saw a young Venetian girl, her head covered with a black lace shawl, eating a bunch of red currants on the steps of a marble palace, and even then I did not forget; no, nor when, from the merciless meshes of a fisherman's net, I disentangled the hard crinkled body of a sea-horse, so exquisitely manufactured, and now left to perish on hot Adriatic sands.

Very well I remember, also at this time, sitting on a seat with Louis Wilkinson, listening to his wise saws about death coming to all of us and it being absurd to worry whether it came late or soon.

From Venice we went to Milan and put up at the Hotel Roma. Tired after the journey I took a hot bath, always an unwise thing for a consumptive to do. In a quarter of an hour I was once more coughing up blood. For weeks I lay on my back unable to move. To add to my misery I underwent a severe attack of kidney stone.

This was the first time I had been a sufferer from this disorder and I was amazed at the pain I had to endure. It was like having a rat gnawing at your entrails. Fortunately a most civilised Italian doctor was quite prepared to inject me with as much morphia as I wanted. He was the first doctor to say that I might live for years if, as he added, I gave up 'climbing mountains.' He confided to me that his own age was sixty-five. 'Sixty-five!' he said, 'that is not very nice for me,' and he gave me the dry look of a philosopher.

Apparently the houses across the street from my hotel were occupied by light women of the town. I used to watch them tiring themselves at their mirrors all through the hot summer afternoons. It was depressing to contemplate the shallow monotony of their existence. Sometimes one or other of them would come to the window and look out in the direction of the Cathedral, and I used to wonder in what manner they regarded that ornamental monument which had known so many of their kind pace backwards and forwards over the echoing paving-stones so far below its spiral pinnacles. I had no idea that the girls had marked my presence or troubled their dilatory heads about me one way or the other. However, when the doctor at length allowed me to get up they crowded to their window-sills like so many coloured birds in an aviary and began clapping their hands, overjoyed at my recovery. I waved and threw kisses at each one of them in turn. I don't believe I have ever received a demonstration of affection that has touched me more to the heart than this display from these daughters-of-joy, the tedium and frivolity of whose existence I had been witnessing for so many weeks.

We sailed from Genoa, calling at Lisbon. I wanted to visit the grave of Henry Fielding, but did not dare to go on shore, having caught dysentery at Tangier. I did not leave England again till 1914. Once more I concentrated my whole attention upon fighting my sickness, resting and regulating my walks and being nourished with bowls of fresh creamy milk, the rich produce of the half-dozen cows I used to watch each summer moving placidly about through buttercups and shadowed grass, as I lay on my boy-scout bed at the top of the terrace walk not far from the phloxes, the fragrance of which on sultry August afternoons, always seems to suggest, in its delicate luxuriance, the sun-warmed velvet-soft abdomens of peacock butterflies.

The farmer's wife across the lane used to give me every few days a basket of fresh turkeys' eggs. I must have consumed a countless number of these eggs. I would make a tiny hole at one end of their mottled shells and suck them with all the care and dainty precision of a punctilious weasel. In spite of my pains, however, my complaint seemed to gain ground. An old man in the village who had at one time been our coachman advised me to rub my chest with goose grease. I procured a pot of this precious ointment and my sister Gertrude every night would dress me with it as I lay in my bed under the stars. Often on these occasions we would remain quite still listening, listening to the distant barking of some dog who had heard the muffled footsteps of a traveller on the turnpike road, listening to the calling of a corncrake in the neighbouring field 'put up for hay,' listening to the singular sound made by a hedgehog in its prickly advance from one flower-bed to another.

Alas! Goose grease and turkey eggs proved of small avail. I grew worse. My brother Willie now wrote from Africa begging me to come out to him. It seemed risky, but not more risky than staying where I was. I left the port of London in September 1914, having spent my last week in bed with blood-spitting, a condition which at that time seemed to have become almost chronic with me.

I sailed round Africa by the Cape of Good Hope, my zest for life seeming to be keener than ever as I handled the flying fish which in the early morning would sometimes get stranded on the deck near where I lay. I used to stand at the end of the vessel and watch an albatross which followed our course, sweeping backwards and forwards with tireless white wings outspread. And then I would cough, and as the morsel of coloured spittle was caught in the dark rollers of that vast ocean over which the bird was flying, I would marvel at the tenacity of this sickness which it was my destiny to carry about with me to the ends of the world.

The altitude of the highlands of Kenya where my brother lived was 7,000 feet above sea level and the air in consequence, baked by the tropical sun, was very dry. My condition responded immediately to the change of climate. I was in Africa for five years and during all that time I never spent a day in bed. I still coughed, still expectorated, but in spite of all the hardships incident to a pioneer's life I continued, out of all reason, to remain well.

Once back in England I bought a revolving shelter. I had it hauled by a farm wagon up to the deserted overgrown garden of a ruined cottage situated on the crest of the hill called Jordan which lies to the east of Weymouth. Like a hermit I lived in this shelter for a year, walking down to the town each night for my dinner, but returning to my lonely habitation before midnight. In the early mornings I would wake to look upon a small still bay with rocks and rippling pools. Little hedge birds would begin to twitter on the grey stone wall near the empty nettle-filled well, while over a restless sea, behind the outline of a corn-field, black hungry cormorants would follow each other on their way to their distant feeding-places. I was in England for a year.

On the 13th of August, the thirty-sixth anniversary of my birthday, I sailed with my brother to America. The first winter spent by me in New York was encouraging. We lived at that time on Twenty-first Street opposite the Anglican Seminary in old Chelsea. Each night I would carry my mattress on to the roof. From first to last I have derived extraordinary satisfaction and consolation from sleeping on the roofs of New York houses. What a sweet restorative influence resides in those dim aerial spaces above the great city! How unspeakably refreshing after the racket of the streets, or after contact with shallow society people, to emerge through a trap-door into a dark inaccessible region under the stars! One comes to know the chimneys as if they were trees, sheltering now behind this one, now behind that, according to the quarter from which the wind is blowing. Rain would always wake me; but I found I often continued to sleep after it had begun to snow, opening my eyes to discover the roof and my own blankets hidden under a cold fleecy coverlet. Sometimes very early, in a faint grey light, sea-gulls would pass rapidly overhead. Indeed, I know of few things that I have found more liberating to my imagination than the sight of a common gull crossing the sky above a great city at the hour before dawn.

The following summer I spent with my brother in California. We stayed at Sausalito. A week after our arrival we walked over the downs to the Pacific Ocean. I was full of eagerness to dip my hands into its waters. It was a hot day, and although our walk was a happy one, with spring flowers thick upon the sloping hills, it proved too much for me. I began once more to spit blood. George Stirling persuaded me to take electrical treatments from

Dr. Abrams. I was conducted to this modern Faustus by the poet himself. The 'doctor' impressed me. I judged him to be half a charlatan and half a genius. I received ten treatments and was dismissed as cured. I suspected his verdict—you cannot catch old birds with chaff! But apparently the treatments did do me good. However, by the beginning of 1924 I was once more suffering from a slight evening fever. In the month of May I accepted an invitation to go hunting grizzly bears in the Rocky Mountains. I saw much that interested me. I saw a porcupine nibbling at the broad horn that a moose had shed and which was lying on the sun-warmed pine needles. I saw a bitch badger bringing her young down to drink in a mountain stream. I saw bears; I saw elk and moose and, indeed, received a hundred intimate glimpses of nature so refreshing to a countryman who for long months has been in a city.

I got back safely to New York, but as the days passed it became more and more evident that the camp food, the hard riding, and perhaps still more my immoderate love of walking, had done damage that it would take months to repair. I left for the country. Before I had reached my destination, however, I had a haemorrhage. Being unwilling to attract the attention of my fellow-passengers I kept as still and silent as I could. My eyes would look out at rock-strewn Connecticut meadows drowsy in the summer sunshine. On my birthday I sent a cable to my brother in England to show him that I had at any rate reached forty years. And I must confess as I lay in bed looking over the Norwalk garden trees, to where the masts of a schooner so unexpectedly appeared through green foliage, I found that my distaste for dying was as strong in middle life as ever it was in my youth. I want to live to a great old age like my father and grandfather and my great-grandfather before me. I want to live till 'the grasshopper has become a burden.' Indeed, if I could have my way, I would still be about on the 13th of August 1984, still able to look up at the great Square of Pegasus with all the unregenerate egoism of one who from childhood recognised that however prolonged his life might be, it would pass as swiftly as the flight of a gull crossing from horizon to horizon of a marine city in the hour before dawn.

From *Earth Memories* (1934).

A SHEEPMAN'S DIARY

MAY 28th.[1] The long-looked-for notice about my passage home came this morning, and I have been allotted a berth on the s.s. *Rufus Castle*, sailing on the third of June. I leave Gilgil for Mombasa at four o'clock to-morrow morning. At last, then, these years are over, and I shall escape, and shall be able to live again in the gracious cities and villages of Christendom. This is a most soulless and terrible country: the blazing sun—the fatal Gorgon's head of Africa—turns all hearts to stone. An incident, significant enough, occurred yesterday. Coming down through the forest I caught sight of an aged native hiding a sheepskin in some undergrowth: I at once took it for granted that he was implicated in the theft of the five sheep taken from the yard as week ago, and in a blind fury at being overreached so many times, I rode him down, cutting at him with my whip; when he was on the ground, I got off my pony, and kicked him, just as I would any dog, any dog *without teeth*—

At luncheon time my house boy told me that this particular old man, Kekwa by name, had bought a skin yesterday from those put aside by me for selling to natives.

MAY 29th. It was dark as I rode up to the station this morning. At the top of the hill I let the pony wait a moment, and by the light of the waning moon looked back at the dark, sinister, and well-known outlines of the Rift Valley. How it all came back to me!—the October lambings—the shearing time—perennial dipping—the places where I had buried natives, where I had trapped lions.

I could see the Eburu mountains away to the left, and I re-- membered the many days I had spent riding out to the far-away camp at Nagum; remembered them, almost with nostalgia, now that I knew they were over. Days in the dry weather, when all was dust and drought, and the sheep stood panting in any shade they could find, and attempted to graze only towards evening:

[1] The year was 1919.

49

days in the wet season, when a drifting rain would drench down, hour after hour, and the fifteen miles back to my house would seem so very long.

The train was punctual. It began to grow light at Naivasha. The line from here to Nairobi has always seemed to me depressing. The wretched station of Kijabi, where they provide breakfast, and miserable ill-tasting figs—the Uplands Bacon factory obtruding its modern presence and modern pork butchers—the dreary wattle plantations, so suggestive of our exploitations of the country, the sandy, washed-away roads of the reserve—the groups of naked children and over-burdened women—old Wardel's house at Kikuyu station, how unutterably devastating to one's spirits it all is.

Two tradesmen got into my carriage at Nairobi. An old Scotsman—a store keeper—bringing with him innumerable packages for his shop in Magadi, so as to avoid the freight on them, and a bald-headed, flushed, middle-aged man; drunken, sweaty-faced, stinking of whisky.

From Nairobi to Mombasa the line was all new to me. I had not travelled on it since I first came up country, five years ago. I sat looking out of the window. Suddenly towards evening I became aware of the presence of Kilimanjaro—silent, dominating, dramatic. I should think it was fifty miles away, across vast plains of waving, feathery red grass, but in spite of the distance I could see its high glacial slopes quite clearly. The sun was going down, and its sinking rays gave to the scene that particular wistful look which certain vast unchanging manifestations of nature take to themselves when illumined thus at the last brief moments of a fading day.

One could not help thinking of this mountain—here from the beginning—so aloof, so indifferent to the passing of the people in the plain-lands below, to the passing of the primitive negroes, to the passing of the Masai, with their spears, and buffalo shields, and tossing plumes, to the passing of us Anglo-Saxons with our commercial instincts, our whisky, and vulgar, unseemly conversations.

MAY 30th. Arrived at Mombasa at nine in the morning. No room in any of the hotels. At last I procured a sleeping place at the top of a tall Arab house in the native quarter, and made arrangements to have meals in the Savoy Hotel—a second-rate place kept by a Greek. After lunch to the sea; surely only English people could convert the finest part of their African coast into a suburban golf course. Escaped from it, and climbed down to the shore behind an old Portuguese fort. They cannot, after all, render the sea vulgar and provincial—the sound of it, the look of it—always the same: the same as when Columbus, standing at the mouth of the Tagus, scanned its horizons—the same as when Ulysses, battling against Mediterranean waves, felt its salt spray in his beard.

At twilight an Arab came on to the roof opposite, and cried to the sun as it went down over Africa. I was thrilled. I had no idea the house opposite was a mosque, and this calling to the sinking sun seemed to coincide so exactly with my obsession as to the importance, the almost sacred significance, of each separate day. From where I stood I could see spread out before me the white roofs of the old town, with here and there a palm-tree, grown up out of some far-away, delicious, shady court. I could see the fine coloured tropical sky, cut and cut again by swift gliding sister swallows; and over and above all was the voice of this priest, resonant as a bell, passionately registering the passing of each consecrated hour.

MAY 31st. In the morning to the Union Castle offices only to learn that the *Rufus Castle* is not sailing till June 19th. Afterwards, to the fruit market which I found to be an excellent place: I have seldom seen so bright and gay a scene. Indian, Somali, Swahili, and Goanese traders, jostling each other; and Arab boys, attractive and precocious, darting about as basket carriers. I had bought a basket, and filling it with fruit of every kind set out for the sea. I shall never persuade myself to eat lunch at the Savoy Hotel.

JUNE 1st. In the evening, coming back to my attic after dinner, I was accosted by a native pander. I followed him between innumerable native houses. He asked me in Swahili if I wanted a woman—a Swahili woman, or a Somali woman, or a woman from the Christian mission. He led me to houses not far from my attic; evidently I lived in the centre of the Mombasa brothels. We knocked at the door after door; sometimes they would be standing outside and I would strike matches to look at their faces; most of them wore nose rings and were painted under their eyes; they were seldom pretty, and the streets and houses and they themselves were heavy with a strange smell of spice, mingled with the curious unmistakable smell of black human flesh.

Presently, assuring my pander that he had shown me nothing of any interest, I wished him to the devil, and made my way back to my attic.

JUNE 2nd. I am now sitting under a tree away on the mainland. I got up early this morning, bought fruit, and crossed over to Freetown. The path up the hill from the ferry almost like an English lane,—tall grasses and overhanging creepers. The sun very hot. I passed a village with native huts and Indian shops and then along a straight white dusty road between coconut plantations, very gay and bright, and chequered with cool shadows. Presently I left the road and walked until I came to this shady place, where I shall stay reading the whole day. I nearly stepped on a long green snake coming here, and this put me in mind of mortality.

JUNE 3rd. Home yesterday just in time to hear my Mahomedan perform his offices. I shall always make a point of being back at this hour. I come to like Mombasa—except for a few scurvy clerks at the Savoy Hotel, I see no Europeans at all. I derive pleasure from finding myself every evening, at exactly the same time, walking along the shore under the town, and up the rock-hewn steps, and along the narrow streets, past the fish market to my attic. In the tropics it is the hour before the setting of the sun which is always the most enchanted.

JUNE 4th. All day on the mainland. Found L—— at dinner on my return. His conversation very refreshing after the chatter of these townsmen: we talked of country matters—of the after-births of cows, of scab, and of the cure for foot rot. I think if I had looked, I should have found dung from the cattle boma still on his boots.

JUNE 5th. Every morning when I go to the fruit market to buy my luncheon I walk through the old part of the town: continually I come upon ancient stone walls, very deep and beautifully constructed, and during the dusty, overheated hours of midday suggesting delightful reservoirs of coolness. One meets far too many Indians in the streets though, pallid, shifty people, wearing tight thin frock coats, followed by their degenerate children, with round red plush caps on their heads. After dinner to the public library and take out Dante's *Inferno* and sit and read amongst Goanese folk—all very quiet. I dare say these people are really far more cultured than most of us English with our clubs and golf courses. I discovered a splendid edition of Rabelais.

JUNE 6th. Across to the mainland and away to the right; passing stone quarries and vast sisal plantations. I made in the direction of the coast, and at last there before me was the sea; wide, and shimmering in the sunshine. Coconut-trees growing close down to the beach—growing out of silver-white sand. It was under these trees that I left my fruit basket, and emerging from their shadow stepped down to the very water's edge.

JUNE 7th. To the mainland and home along the shore. There is a sick Greek living somewhere in my house, I think on the second floor. I believe he is suffering from syphilis. If I knew of another attic I would desert this one. I passed him to-day sitting on one of the platforms of the staircase (the staircase is built outside the house); he looked horrible. I longed to crush him as I would a mutilated and unpleasant insect.

JUNE 8th EVENING. Explored the island: wandered down innumerable tiny paths with arrowroot cultivated on both sides and everywhere high slim-trunked coconut-trees. I grew tired and hot and coming upon a native hut, I knocked at the door and asked for food, just as a traveller in a fairy story would do, lost in a forest.

Two old natives came out and placing me under a tree hurried away to fetch coconuts; they climbed the tree themselves, and I noticed for the first time that every tree had steps cut in its trunk, so that they could be scaled without difficulty. The coconuts were excellent; they also brought me a gourd filled with coconut wine, but I saw too many ticks in the neck of the gourd really to enjoy it. They would accept no money. I found the Hotel a mile farther on, a very pleasant place, and managed to engage a room there.

JUNE 9th. Motored with all my belongings to this Hotel. There are several huts outside which are used as bedrooms: I have chosen one of these. The roof is thatched with palm leaves and I notice white ants keep dropping down, so I must keep an eye on my things.

JUNE 10th. Bathed last night with the husband of the Italian girl I noticed yesterday.

A lovely place for bathing, and they say there are no sharks. We swam far out. 'Do you notice,' he said casually, 'how the current has carried us below our landing-place?'

With panic strokes I made for the shore, chuckling afterwards, to remember how eager I had been to reach land.

I like to look at the wooded creeks opposite. One longs to explore them all. The colours this morning amazing. I have never seen such blues and greens—such painted scenery. The seashore covered with tiny crabs that dash about and sink into their holes, their eyes high above them after the manner of periscopes, and their shells and claws a wonderful red colour. Everywhere the roots of water bushes sticking out like countless slippery stalagmites. I talked with the Italian this evening. She also has suffered from the country.

JUNE 11th. A walk in the morning with the Italian along the winding paths—rested under the shade of a mango-tree, the sun glancing down between the broad polished leaves.

JUNE 16th. To Mombasa to blow the organ for the Italian while she practises in the English cathedral.

I was there before her, and for some time wandered about in the cool interior. I read the memorial tablets and noticed how many young men had died, scarce any over forty. It was interesting being in a church again after all these years. I opened a dog-eared hymn-book but what sentiment it contained! After she had finished her playing she wished to find the priest so that she could obtain leave from him always to practise in these heretical surroundings. We went to the Catholic church. A black coffin which was lying before the high altar made me feel how much more real a thing was their religion. We were led by a nun to the priest's house. I waited amongst the roses in the garden while she went in to speak to him.

JUNE 17th. Last night my cabin box was taken out of my room by native robbers. It was a fine night and I had dragged my bed outside and was sleeping by the door. My passport and note of credit I luckily had under my pillow. The box was taken into some bushes two hundred yards away and broken open there and rifled. The rascals had covered the ground round my bed with bottles so that if by chance I happened to waken my first movements would be impeded. This kind of thing makes one very bitter. Certainly in this case as I leave to-morrow the last retort was theirs. I remember G.C.'s wise saws: 'You will find no virtue under a black hide,' 'Fear rules the world—Fear FEAR.'

JUNE 18th. Paid my bill and away to the steamer—a hospital ship, everything under the military. Large wards for passengers, some with as many as ninety berths.

JUNE 19th. Precisely at half past four in the afternoon the s.s. *Rufus Castle* set sail from Kilindini harbour. Her siren made the whole boat tremble as slowly and silently she got under way. A fine rain was falling and it was growing dark. White horses were upon the open sea and it looked grey and ominous and desolately unfrequented. I did not forget my good fortune as standing by myself I watched the coast recede.

JUNE 26th. Arrived at Durban this morning. Walked with Lawrence Tooth to the sea front and was immediately made aware of the fact that I had not yet escaped. I never have seen such faces: without a trace of refinement, without a trace of sensibility, without a trace of distinction, of individuality, sharp, predatory, colonial, commonplace, no difference whatever; all exactly the same. Small wonder the true values of life have been forgotten and that an energetic preoccupation with the material world is their only real interest. It will require generations before these parochial, acquisitive minds can become even partially civilized. The very position of the chairs on their famous front proclaims their essential philistinism; rows upon rows of them with their backs to the sea.

JUNE 27th. To the Zoo with Tooth. Far the best place we have yet found. We saw a wonderful monkey. Its rainbow-coloured, lewd, bizarre appearance filled Tooth with horror. He declared that if he could, he would obliterate such creatures from the face of the earth. But I liked to see it. The more extravagant the creation the more in keeping with this brave fantastical Universe. Drank tea on the lawn outside, all very harmonious.

JUNE 28th. Sitting this evening on deck, suddenly we hear a roar of fog-horns, sirens, hooters. We knew at once that Peace had been signed. 'I am glad they have been done down,' said Tooth, 'they really were a frightful menace to civilization.' We remained silent. I could not get out of my mind the thought of the thousands and thousands of skulls in Asia, in Africa, in

Europe with the clay of the earth too tight in their ears for them to catch even an echo of all this—though the sirens bray never so loudly.

June 29th. By tram as far as I could go and then home by the side of a river which reaches the sea to the north of Durban. Lay on the sand dunes. Went to see some whales just brought in. They were the largest monsters I have ever set eyes on, larger than elephants—the surface of their vast skins shiny and smooth to the touch, like seaweed.

July 2nd. Set sail from Durban early. I never saw so gloomy a prospect as the sea provided this evening before it grew dark. The sky and sea were merged in a heavy grey, and in the cold desolation a single bird was flying—flying as though it was lost upon a forgotten ocean, which had never before known even the wings of a bird to distract the sad unconsciousness of its humming waters.

July 3rd. I take great pleasure in sleeping on deck these nights, lying in a sheepskin sleeping-sack, covered by a leopard skin, and in such a position that I can look up at the masts and rigging as they sway to and fro against the sky.

July 6th. We reached Cape Town last evening and sailed again at noon to-day. Dined last night in the town, a far more attractive place than Durban; its streets much older and the mountain giving the place some character of its own. A cheap but admirable dinner at the Silver Grill.

July 9th. I see much of Father Plunkett—an excellent old Irish priest—combining in his presence the culture of the Celt and the culture of Catholicism, very admirable, very gracious and consoling like old red wine.

He talks to me about 'inordinate desires,' about 'the soul of the Church,' about 'her offices,' and he also instructs me that the last sacrament is efficacious even an hour after death, the spirit, so it is believed, loitering near the body before taking its final flight. His berth is near to mine and I love to see him lying asleep 'in grace,' his little priest's hands crossed on his breast. He evidently very much dislikes the publicity of the ward. He is up and occupying himself with his toilet long before anybody else is awake, moving about with the furtive shyness of some bird, of a little tree creeper perhaps. In his pocket he carries an old stained Horace and we read much poetry together.

JULY 25th. Teneriffe sighted.

JULY 26th. Madeira at nightfall. Lights on the hillside impressive. The sides of the ship scaled by countless Portuguese with baskets and chairs and trinkets.

JULY 27th. Madeira not an attractive place; too much in the general track of tourists, too many villas. I liked much better a small island, apparently deserted, that we passed this afternoon. An island with green lovely uplands and a secluded bay. From my deck-chair I could see quite clearly delicate white-crested waves breaking upon its miniature beach.

JULY 31st. Woke to find that we were surrounded by many French fishing boats. There was a freshness in the summer air that made me know I was in health-giving northern waters 'Freshen'd by plunging tides, by showers.'

The sea quite still in the early sunshine of this last day of July. I could make out the tiny figures of the fishermen moving about under their sails.

AUGUST 2nd. Was up early and away to the prow of the ship where only the sailors and firemen go. Place myself on the deck here, looking across the sea, for the first glimpse of England. Gradually a faint white cloud-line separates itself, takes shape and form, and after a few hours becomes the familiar outline of the Dorset coast from St. Albans Head to the Island of Portland. And as I lay there on the sun-warmed deck while these simple homely cliffs became more and more clear, between the anchor and the ship's scrupulously white bulwark, I experienced, and I knew it, some of the most happy and most thrilling moments of my life. The sun was so hot that the very pitch in the interstices of the deck began to soften and melt.

We reached Southampton at 4.30 p.m.

I was at Montacute before it was dark. How delightful and yet how inexpressibly pathetic are our homecomings, when one remembers that, for all our tremulous joy at these reunions, death tracks the wayfaring of each one of us, to separate us, so soon for ever! As of old, my bed was prepared for me in the garden: but I could not sleep. How could I hope to sleep? Under that summer moon the beauty of the village seemed to me a thing so palpable, so positive, so importunate. After all these years to be once more 'where bells have knolled to church'!

I left my bed and walked about. I stood by the broad ivied wall which separates the terrace from the abbey fields—the tall tower of St. Katherine's Church, the mullioned moonlit walls of the Abbey, the fish pond, the monk's dove cot, the cattle moving slowly across the dew-drenched meadows—the trees known from childhood with shapes hardly altered—all were there, all were the same, unchanged, unspoilt. It almost seemed as though I had been permitted by some fairy intervention to look far back upon that older world of one's imagination, when Christianity was really true, when peace year after year was upon these country places, and when the simple manner of life, its true aim and purport, had not as yet been put aside.

From *Ebony and Ivory* (1923).

THE ROCKY MOUNTAINS

IT WAS in the spring of 1924 that I was invited by Dr. James
S. Watson, of *The Dial*, to join him on an expedition into
the Rocky Mountains. This man had always delighted me.
It used to amuse me to watch him drifting through life with the
unresisting adaptability of a long, drooping straw caught in the
current of a lively trout-stream. He was enormously rich, and
yet liked to appear poor. He was extremely wise, yet preferred
to be thought foolish. With a small black bag, held in the long,
sensitive fingers of an artist, he was to be encountered on a
perpetual drooping peregrination through the side-streets of
Greenwich Village. He made one think of those silent, evasive
eels one hears about, eels that find their way to the ocean from
remote ponds, sliding their sinuous bodies through night-
dusky, dew-drenched pastures. He possessed a subtle, cynical
mind, which he did all in his power to conceal. He was an extremely able doctor, who never practised, an extremely clever
writer, who never wrote. Whether one met him in the French
pastry-shop, or in the hall of his house, with its mullioned window and noble stone chimney-piece, he ever remained aloof
and uncommitted. Even the gracious presence of his beautiful
lady at the end of a lighted dinner-table was never sufficient to
overcome his embarrassed diffidence, a diffidence that seemed to
cover the most inconvenient reticences. In truth, as he knocked
off the grey ashes of his cigarette, between the courses, on to
the rim of the silver candlestick opposite the place where he sat,
he was capable of interjecting some whispered comment that
would completely destroy one's confidence and would keep
recurring to one's mind for days afterwards, because of its
teasing ambiguity.

To see Dr. Watson and Mr. Scofield Thayer together was
something to remember. It would have required a Henry James
to tabulate and record each interesting tarot card of this astounding association. And yet these two young men, in the face of the

sneering hostility of a score of pseudo-literary cliques, have managed to produce in America a journal which, without any doubt, is the most distinguished of its kind to appear in the English language since the publication of the *Yellow Book*. But how quaint it was to see these two working together for the aesthetic enlightenment of the Western world! It was like seeing a proud, self-willed, bull-calf bison, fed on nothing but golden oats, yoked to the plough with a dainty, fetlocked, dapple-grey unicorn, who would, an' he could, step delicately over the traces and scamper to the edge of the prairie, where, under the protective colouring of a grove of pale wattle trees, he might be lost to the view of the world.

The taste of Scofield Thayer was the austere aristocratic taste of a Roman noble, of a Roman connoisseur, who has filled his marble hall with the work of his Greek slaves; while the Doctor's taste was that of a super-subtle Nicodemus who has a mania for collecting at night, by proxy, images of unknown gods, put together by indigent artists whose lack of rice was never for long out of the mind of this generous young man.

A rare happiness it was for me to find myself once again heading for the wilderness, with a stout pony under me, and half-a-dozen crafty, long-eared mules following, one behind the other, between the dark resin-smelling tree trunks. The first day, we rode thirty-five miles and camped in an open place a few hundred yards from the banks of a mountain lake. I was tired and lay down to sleep early. Just before dawn broke, I was waked by the howl of a timber-wolf. He uttered a single yell; and the lone cry had scarcely died down when a dozen elk, with cowslip-coloured buttocks, came cantering through the ghostly white light. As the sun rose I was walking by the edge of the lake. I shall not soon forget its beauty, with its two sections lying there like the gleaming, outstretched wings of an enormous purple butterfly. In appearance and shape the lake was not unlike Lake Elmenteita, and I found myself instinctively scanning its surface for the head of a hippopotamus. Across the sky, against an outline of snow-capped mountains, flew three white pelicans, their pouched beaks giving them a gross look, very different from that of the flamingoes I used to disturb at such an hour in Africa, with their rose-red wings and serpentine necks.

The Doctor left camp early in his quest for grizzly bears, while

I, half an hour later, taking a rough stick in my hand, set out by myself. For some time I kept close to a river-bank. There were a great many willows growing there, but it was easy to push one's way through them. Suddenly I realised that some large animal was moving along on the other side of the stream. I sank down and waited. The creature was evidently working up my way. On it came, till, looking through the screen of narrow leaves, I could see a bull moose, with a cow behind him. If I had not seen their heads I would have taken them for rhinos, so massive and dun-coloured did their flanks look, as they slowly advanced, browsing upon the fresh twigs. Presently the bull stepped into the moving water. I thought at first that he was going to head straight for my hiding-place; however, to my no small relief, he selected for his landing a spot some twenty yards further up-stream. He looked very imposing as he stood in the middle of the noisy water, with his head half turned to see if his cow was following. I saw him lift his tail, letting his dung fall splashing into the water with the extraordinary aplomb of a large grass-eater who is untroubled and undisturbed. He looked to me about the size of a bull eland, though perhaps not quite so tall. The spread of his horns in the bright sunshine was wonderful, but what a weight for the animal's great head to support—for that huge, ungainly head, with its prehensile upper lip.

I was back in camp by the evening. The trapper we had with us was a small, wiry man, who had been living in these mountains for years. He had the wary, wizened look of a marten which had been caught half a dozen times, and half a dozen times got itself free. It was interesting to watch his face. It remained dull and unresponsive in ordinary conversation; but the moment his senses were assailed, its expression changed to one of intense alertness. Again and again I saw him stand motionless, snuffing the air long before the rank smell of elk was apparent to us; and I have seen him stop, with ears pricked, when he alone was able to hear a bear at work on a piece of ant-infested timber half a mile away.

The next morning I again set out alone. It seemed to grow hot, with an almost tropical heat; and coming to a stream in the forest, I took off my clothes and slipped into a pool. I felt as naked and unprotected under those great silent pine trees as I had felt naked and unprotected in Africa, when I bathed in a certain hot spring overshadowed with leaves large as the ears of elephants. And not ten yards away I saw my first track of a grizzly bear, tracks far larger than those of a lion, more like the footprints of a man, only with claws instead of toes. I was glad enough to leave the dangerous place.

On my way back I came upon some beaver-dams in the flat near the river. I examined them closely. They were so solidly constructed that I was able to walk across them, though there was deep water on both sides. I put up a wild grey goose that went sailing away over the stone expanses, over the heaps of white skeleton-like timber which the snow-floods had left stranded. I was fascinated to see how the beavers had contrived to bring trees down from a quaking-asp grove by means of a canal they had dug. I looked with awe at the marks of their webbed feet in the soft mud, the footprints of a warm-coated people possessing the ingenuity of goblins.

After some days we reached the Great Divide. Here was a river which separated itself into two halves, the waters of the one half being destined to reach the Atlantic Ocean, while the waters of the other would eventually flow into the Pacific. There were so many trout that it was possible to beat them on to the banks with sticks, and we spent an hour at this merry pastime. I tell you it was something to see our trapper Jones slit them up ready for supper! Their entrails he let fall on the dry, round pebble-stones at his feet; and Watson pointed out to me that their hearts still continued to flutter, even as filthy offal. I picked up a heart, a small, pink quivering morsel of flesh, that refused to die. It was like a baby skate.

When we next moved, we rode over the flat top of a mountain which reminded me of that part of the Aberdare range in East Africa where the elephant trails cross between the Milowa and Sugeroi Rivers. Coming down from the mountain we saw a brown bear. A little further on I caught sight of a porcupine absorbed in its own secret pursuits, and yet cognisant of our presence. What an infinite complacence its concentrated attitude seemed to suggest! And yet it is ordained that even a porcupine's composure is sometimes ruffled, as, for instance, when a bear turns it over on its back and gravely begins to rip open its un-protected, bark-filled, grass-filled stomach. The next morning I walked down a creek, and then along the foot of a mountain. I came upon a great deal of sage-bush. I kept picking it as I walked and crushing it in my fingers. How the plant, with its gnarled, lavender-like growth, its dry odour, health-giving and aromatic, must appeal to people born in the West of America, so redolent it seems of the dust, and prairie-dogs, and hot stones, and perpetual sunshine of their open plains!

I walked under a cliff clustered over with the nests of mountain swallows, which projected from the rock like so many Kikuyu gourds. Many of the nests were built so low that I found it possible to look down their funnels to where the small feathered mothers were sitting with sharp eyes full of apprehension. Meanwhile, a hundred screaming male birds flew backwards and forwards about my ears, a veritable hail-storm of darting arrow-heads. In the Rocky Mountains I was always impressed by the chatter and noise made by small creatures, the tiniest squirrel taking upon itself to shout after me. In Africa they would have soon learned better, would soon have learned that to make the world aware of one's presence is a privilege belonging to the carnivore, and not to little, thrifty nut-collectors. One day I climbed to the top of a mountain. I sat on a rocky ledge on its very summit, overlooking a wide, tree-grown valley. A thousand feet below me, and yet far enough above the tops of the trees, two eagles swept backwards and forwards in wild pursuit of each other. Aha! What a love-making was that! I began to retrace my steps; and there, right in the open, near a snow-drift, I came upon a bitch badger with three young ones. I tried to get close to her, but she faced me down with many false advances and ugly growls. The little badgers were round and very fat, and were covered with fur of a reddish colour. I came down the southern side of the mountain. For half an hour I rested upon a jack-pine at the top of a sloping shell-rock precipice. A moose-bird came and mocked at me; and a chipmunk, with tail erect, eyed me suspiciously, squatting upon its hind legs like a miniature kangaroo. These cloudy coloured streams above the timber-line, caused by the melting snow, are not much to drink at; and I was glad enough to come upon a spring of pure water, which spouted out of the side of the hill. I knelt down and drank at the earth itself, as though I had my lips to the udder of a monstrous, sweet-smelling, round-bellied dairy cow. The spring presently became a brown stream, which ran rippling through a grassy glade, green as the back of a green parrot. I lay down to rest, leaning over to look at the bottom of a clear pool, to look at the incredible activity taking place in its loose mud. Caddis-worms crept from mound to mound; and strange centipedes, with earwig tails, paraded over the shining subaqueous pebbles. I watched them as if I were looking into an aquarium. What did these creatures, with their remote, intense, intimate life, know about eagle love-making, or about bitch badgers, or about the moose that had dropped its flat horn not far from where I lay, a horn already nibbled out of shape by a porcupine? As I walked through these slippery pine-forests, I continually met with hot puffs of wind, pungent with the incense that rose from the sun-dried needle floor. But on the high lawns, where the lupin bloomed, the air was perfumed with the scent of flowers. If I shut my eyes, it was as though I were loitering in the kitchen-garden at home, between rows of divers-hued sweet peas. And how silent these uplands were, when the wind was still! Surely, if one had listened, one could have heard each tiny petal fall, could have heard the fanning of the butterflies' wings, as they flickered from one sweet-smelling blossom to another through the pollen-laden air.

One day I got to the top of the highest of all the mountains. Far above me I would see a waterfall sparkling in the sunshine, but when I reached it, there would be others still further up. Once on its summit, I followed along its razor edge, marvelling at the depths of the canyons that fell away on both sides.

The idea came to me that it might be possible to find another way down, and presently, looking over a banked-up snow-drift, I fancied that if I followed the course of a stream which, from where I was standing, showed like a thin strand of silver wire twisting between the rocks, I should have small difficulty in reaching the timber-line, whose slopes seemed to fall away in easy gradations to the valley below.

Down I went, down over loose rocks, down over mud-slides, down through ridges of melting snow, till I reached the stream I had observed. Below one of its waterfalls I came to a hidden, mossy bank, where heather grew. So enchanted was I by the lovely seclusion of the spot that I lay down and rested for a few moments. Presently the sky became overcast, and a distant growl of thunder reminded me that I had better be starting once more on my descent. With considerable difficulty I slid from pro-jecting rock to projecting rock, until I came to a place where the

Llewelyn Powys with his brother, John Cowper Powys, and their cousin, Father Hamilton Johnson, in the courtyard at Patchin Place, New York. (c. 1923).

stream, gathering itself into one swift, deep channel, disappeared round the slippery, blackened base of an enormous boulder. Obviously I must climb over this obstruction. I clambered up its side and found myself looking into the empty cleft of a shocking precipice! Fearful lest my very movements might topple the boulder down into the void gulf, I slid back. On every side ugly bastions beetled above me. The mountain had become darkened. Black clouds, ragged as the wings of misshapen ravens, were racing across the firmament, clouds that looked as if they had been torn and fractured by too close contact with the wild landscape over which they were drifting. Crouched behind the granite block, with the water racing past my boots towards the treacherous crevice, I became terrified. My kneebones shook. Above me, ledge above ledge, the mountain towered. The least movement I made seemed fraught with danger.

Then, just as when I had been caught by fire in a tropical forest, a deep animal instinct of self-preservation became fully awake. Step by step, I climbed back by the way I had come, up over the slide, up past where the heather grew, up over the ledge by means of a fallen tree, up over the shell-rock where the woodchuck had called to me. Often I was compelled to rest for want of breath, but I would soon be on my feet again, climbing higher and higher, with the persistent deliberation of a bear who knows that a trapper without pity is after him. And now the great forest trees on the slopes of the mountain had become suddenly articulate. Exhausted, and soaked to the skin, I passed between their stark trunks, nervous, impotent, while far above me they moaned to each other, as their stiff arms bent and swayed in the rushing gale.

When I woke the next morning I looked out on to rain-drenched mountains that smelt like Africa in the rainy season. Through the open door of my tent I could see a porcupine feeding, drawing into its mouth great, wet leaves with its right paw.

The next week we moved into even wilder country. On all sides of our camp, jagged crags projected into the sky, their shoulders cusped with snow, their broad backs covered with shell-rock. At the timber-line there were a few scattered groups of fir trees, which used to appear to me as I rode in the valley below, like cloaked women, like desperate female fugitives in tattered green capes, who, in an evil hour, had been caught on the bare hillside, as they fled from some unprecedented disaster, to be petrified for ever, with drooping shoulders and bowed heads. How many black, merciless blizzards must it not have required to bend this timber into such uniform dejection! Once more I scaled a mountain-side; and as, from the summit, I scanned the wild prospect of the Rocky Mountains, I felt rise within me a paean of triumph at seeing stretched out in every direction before my eyes this great ridged backbone of the world, which, sharp as the spine of a shark, each twenty-four hours in the diurnal revolution saws its way through the planet's circumambient atmosphere.

One night I sat for long hours over our camp-fire, the outlines of the distant mountains standing out clearly against the night sky, the trees that edged their slopes appearing like a growth of beard on a dead giant's chin. The red flames danced and the smoke drifted off into the surrounding darkness. I gazed at the glowing core of a burning pine-stump and tried to imprint the scene upon my memory. How emphatic and incontestable it all looked! The lively scarlet flames, the white snow, the encircling shadows! When I, at length, lay down in my blankets, I had a very curious dream. I dreamed that, as I was showing my brother Willie this country, we suddenly passed through a small door, and found ourselves back in the top orchard of our home in Somerset. My brother scanned the familiar fruit-trees in interested silence, the golden pippin, the russet by the terrace gate. He noticed the fresh gaps in their rows. I did my best to reassure him, though well I knew that time had done its work. Then it was that, while in my dream my heart sank with unutterable dismay at this new evidence of life's fatal instability, a long, low howl went moaning under the aged apple-trees, moaning across the lawns of the garden, moaning over the chimneys of the old house. It was a most singular howling, a howling such as one might fancy issuing from the contracted throat of a shackled god. It rang through my ears. Surely it could be no illusion. I sprang up from the ground wide awake. A coyote was making the creek echo with its barking, somewhere out in the darkness, beyond the smoulder-ing fire. For nearly half an hour I lay listening to its dolorous voice.

Our last night in the mountains arrived. We were camped in a meadow-like valley by the side of a mountain river. The moon was full, I could not sleep. Slowly she moved from behind the mountains across the sky. Hour after hour followed, and still the austere beauty of that midnight scene arrested my consciousness. There, far above the chill, black, ossified mountains, above the motionless spears of the pine-trees, paraded the passionless, treacherous, immortal planet. And as I lay with my head resting on the meadow lupin, already cool with night-dew, I became aware at last of the consolation that is to be drawn from silent communion with matter, with Eternal matter, bereft of divine innuendoes, but capable still of sustaining, after its sublime manner, the fearful and wavering soul of man. In the small hours of the night I rose up from where I lay, and with a blanket over my shoulder wandered along the river's shelving bank. To my left, in the centre of the drenched white pasture, I could see the dark shadow of the tethered mule, of the mule we called Ben, standing with ears forward, silently alert to all my movements, while before me, between the charmed forest trees, lay the silver highway of the river, as magical and uncertain as life itself.

From *The Verdict of Bridlegoose* (1927).

ALBERT REGINALD POWYS

Thou'lt come no more, never, never, never
never, never!

A FEW summers ago I was present at the re-dedication ceremony
of the little church of Winterbourne Tomson, which, with
money realized from the sale of one of Thomas Hardy's
manuscripts, had been restored under the personal care of my
brother, Mr. A. R. Powys. I well remember observing my
brother moving about amongst the officiating clergy and assembled people, a man easily distinguished by the sincerity and
vigour of his presence. He was evidently well pleased by the
accomplishment of the task he had taken in hand. To-day he
lies buried on the south side of this same church.

We had been warned that he was very ill and I dreaded lest I
should hear the tread of the man who brings us our telegrams.
When the message came the actual shock affected me in a way
that I had not anticipated. All that had happened to us during the
last thirty years seemed to fall into a fading distance, while with
the abruptness of a lantern slide every incident of my boyhood
we had spent together stood out bold and clear.

At the back of the kitchen garden wall of Montacute Vicarage
was a plot of pear trees and under their shadows we used to play.
My brother Theodore had been the first to take possession of this
section of the garden, and with characteristic originality had
occupied himself with digging deep holes and underground
passages in the firm clay a few feet below the surface soil. These
subterranean labyrinths I can only just remember. When he and
my brother John began to shoot with forbidden pistols, using the
apple trees in the lower orchard as targets, the pear-tree plot came
presently to be regarded as belonging to my brother Bertie, my
sister May, and myself. There had always existed a rough lean-to
shed against the high wall, and this we little by little rebuilt and
extended, giving it the name of the May-Ber-Lulu Castle.

During my life whenever I have wished to regain serenity it has been my habit to direct my thoughts to this playground of my childhood. Even when I have been in bed with a high fever I have been able to quiet my pulse by reviving my memories of this parcel of enchanted ground.

We were very fond of forget-me-nots, and our miniature borders were crowded with this lovely childish flower. It was an ordinary forget-me-not, except that each tiny individual head was larger than is usual and of a very light hue. As I came racing round the corner of the kitchen garden, past the July apple tree, and saw these pools of blue, the sodden Somerset soil might have been subjected to some airy transmutation associated with the sky above the outspreading garlands of the milk-white blossoms of the fruit trees.

My brother Littleton, long before I could remember, had devised a hole in the wall to serve as a nesting place for tits, and these bright little birds, with the faces of diminutive owls and a plumage almost tropical, would be for ever flitting through the patched sunny shadows on some dancing quest of happy spring-time discipline.

At Sherborne, my brother Bertie used to save all his money for buying posts and matchwood-boarding and tiles and bricks for our Maberlulu 'improvements.' My own nature was never as stable as his and I was never very good at saving. While he would spend hours in the school workshop carpentering I would be eating chocolates at Ford's as shamelessly insatiable as a yellow guinea-pig over a saucer of bran. He was never one to care about dress and I can see him now standing by a chess table that he was making, his waistcoat covered with sawdust, his trousers baggy at the knee, gravely concentrating with brown, long-fingered, sensitive hands upon his work, and yet glad to see me also, even though he was well aware I had only appeared with ingratiating manners to beg pennies from him. This chess table was a master-piece of carpentering skill, the squares formed alternately out of ebony and boxwood, but, alas! when it reached Montacute with our other luggage and was unpacked by us *it was broken*. I was a very small boy, but I remember as I saw the tears suddenly begin to flow from the eyes of my brother, always so proud and re-served, my very marrow bones melted with a longing to be able to comfort him. We sat, I recollect, side by side on the drawing-room sofa, with the singing of the birds coming in to us through the wide open sash window so loud that the familiar room might have belonged to a summer bower in a Sultan's aviary at Nisha-pour rather than to a Victorian vicarage in England. A few days before he died I experienced the same desire to protect him when he ended a letter with the words 'My whole love. A.R.P.'

How tender he always was of me at school. At Wilson's House he shared a study with a rather conventional boy in whose presence we never dared to be demonstrative. Many a time I have loitered in the boot-room at the end of the narrow passage outside the studies waiting for this worldly-minded athlete, with his grand velvet caps, to come out, so that I might slip silently into the little room knowing that my brother Bertie would take me upon his knee and we would talk of home, sitting on a dusty cushion-padded cane chair in front of his fire. With what competent conscientious thoroughness he used to plan out every detail for our return to Montacute at the end of each term! To gain a few hours he would ask leave for us to get up early on the long-anticipated morning, and we would walk to Yeovil with our black school handbags, packed with our home-made night-gown and brush and comb, swinging in our hands.

On one of these occasions a worldly London boy took it into his head to see us off. He walked with us across the field be-hind the Preparatory, my brother keeping up as best he could the 'hard talk' of the school world, and I followed behind, silent.

He left us at the field gate where the girls' school now stands, quite unmindful that his departure, straw hat nonchalantly tilted on the back of his head, marked the real beginning of our holidays, with freedom to kiss without being laughed at, and with freedom to talk about our sisters without fear of being overheard.

As we trudged up Half-way Hill and along by Col. Goodden's palings, released at last to plan eagerly together about the new Maberlulu roof, how happy, how happy we were, with the small birds singing in the hedges, and the lords-and-ladies unfolding in the ditches, and with the scarcely credible prospect dancing before us in our minds of being home so very soon, with our mother leaving her sewing to welcome us, her face illumined, at the front door, and our father coming out of the study into the dining-room to listen to our excited talk; with Rogers mowing the lawn for the first time, and one or two hyacinths already out in the round beds. I remember that the new roof of the Maber-lulu had become so important to us that when the wood we had selected with such economic foresight from the timber yard of Mr. Drayton came we were up long before dawn to begin the work, my brother driving in his three-inch nails with the precision of a capable carpenter, but I, less expert, adding the anguish of hammered fingers to the unexpected discomfort of sunless un-warmed winds.

We kept an alarm clock in the 'end room' where we slept, and often before the bell rang for family prayers we would have already enjoyed many hours of an April day. If there was no particular work to be done on the Maberlulu we would go for long bird-nesting walks, following one behind the other beating the green hedges, bright and shining with dew as the level sun rays touched each leaf of the shrouded West Country trees. How fresh-created the coverts and woods would seem as we stole into them long before the keeper Parsons had left his lonely house surrounded by kennels of fierce fast-chained black retriever dogs; and how they smelt of cool-shadowed mossy swards, and rang with the songs of the newly awakened birds. With our boots soaked and muddy we would sit very hungry waiting for the servants to come in for family prayers, and our father, doubtless remembering early morning expeditions of his own through the Stalbridge meadows, would say, as he rubbed his hands together with a look of extraordinary good nature: 'Well, my boys, I see you have been out early.' On one of these walks we actually went searching for the sources of the River Parrett in fields that my father did not even know, in fields far away beyond the Chin-nocks. These long, long walks by the side of my brother left on my mind a peculiar glamour so that the sensation of extreme physical exhaustion when walking in the open country has never since been disliked by me.

It was my custom in the summer holidays to spend all my birthday money at Miss Sparks's shop. I would buy pots and pans and crockery for the Maberlulu, selecting with the utmost care the mugs and plates I liked best, and then run all the way back, so eager would I be to present my purchase to my brother and sister whom I would perhaps find enjoying the refreshment of some of our home-made ginger beer which we used to drink out of teacups sitting on the seat of our new bow window. Or perhaps as I came round the corner I would see my sister in her red overall stirring a mess of Quaker oats for my birthday feast on a wood fire in the little yard, Bertie kneeling at her side selecting the exact, right-shaped sticks to put under the pot. The smoke would be mingled with the smell of the flowers lying upon the air of that sheltered spot, as the heat of the midday sun increased. In after years whenever I have smelt burning wood, whether from the bonfires of broken boxes that the little boys of New York love to build on the kerbs of Greenwich village streets, or from camp fires in Africa where the tree hyraxes call, or from black Bedouin goat-hair tents near the Lake of Galilee, in a single instant my spirits would be freed from ordinary time and space restrictions to be transported, swift as any Ariel, back to the Maberlulu.

By the first week of September the wall-fruit would begin to ripen. In early days it had been my mother's custom at this season to appear in the nursery with an apricot or peach and to gather us about her like little birds with wide open mouths to receive in strictest turn portions of the sun-sweetened food dipped in dessert-sugar and transfixed, all dripping, on the end of a silver ivory-handled fork. As we grew older, we learned to pick the fruit from the trees ourselves. I can remember doing this on Sunday evenings with Japanese anemones in the button-holes of our dark suits, and with the church bells just beginning to chime, their silver sound hardly noticed by us as we searched for hidden greengages, with hollows of sweetness edged brown by the maws of wasps, wasps which at the first sign of being disturbed would, with yellow-striped abdomens curled towards their heads, drop from leaf to leaf, hopelessly inebriate and yet still apt to mischief.

These were the weeks when we all would play at 'Jabberwock,' a game invented by my brother John, with the acacia on the top lawn as 'home.' With what fleet feet, tennis-shoe shod, we would race along the terrace-walk and up the narrow garden path by Willie's wood, and across the lawns slippery with dew; while every moment the garden grew dimmer and dimmer, an incense-breathing garden populated by creatures fabulously fitted with goblin eyes for seeing in the dark, owls that flew silently out of the leafy obscurities of the sycamore, bats that flickered with high-toned cries to and fro above the drive, and nectar-sipping moths with back and wings fur-covered, sumptuous and soft as silk, exploring with fixed stare each lavender spike and each yellow cavern of the evening primroses now no longer limp. In those laughing hours it was impossible to think of life as ever ending, so reassuring was the sound of tittering lovers at the back gate, and the trit-trot of horses' feet growing fainter along the dusty Stoke road; and with the light of the lamp, its shade painted by my sister Gertrude, shining steadily from the drawing-room window, where our mother sat reading to our father as he worked quietly at his netting, a string firmly looped over one black slipper.

In the Christmas holidays all was different. We scarcely visited the Maberlulu then. Always we were eagerly waiting for it to freeze or snow, looking up continually at the cowl on the top of the 'end-room' chimney so as not to miss the very first indication that it was swinging round to the north-east, a cowl that was more dented than the helmet of Achilles by our lucky idle hits with leaden slugs from the catapults that my brother was so good at making out of forked sticks chosen from the tall privet hedge surrounding the out-of-door earth closet. When the frost did come at last we would race round the garden in the early morning along the banked-up celery mounds as hard as iron and stand first on the ice on the tank, and then on the ice on the butt, so that at breakfast we could report how hard the frost had been.

Then after Bible-reading we would rush off to the Montacute Hill ponds in the hope that they might already bear. When the night came we would be running out of the back-door every few minutes to look at the thermometer hung up by the study window and to put more and more water on the slide, which we always made in the yard above the tool-house, so that it would be ready for the next morning. How cold it would be in our room at the end of the passage on such nights! My brother had been given a large flat red candlestick which was kept on our dressing table, and the last in bed had to blow it out and get himself safe under the clothes before the glowing spark of the wick was no longer to be seen. What pleasure there was too in getting our skates out from the schoolroom cupboard in order to sandpaper them and see that their leather straps were in order! They were the old-fashioned skates with great rusty screws protruding, which when Pitt Pond was reached the next morning would be affixed by the help of a gimlet into the heels of our boots.

Gone, gone, gone, my brother who shared with me my childhood memories and forgot nothing! Who is able now to tell me whether the apple tree in which we found our hawfinch's nest is still standing? Who can now explain to me why it was the kites we used to make with long paper tails never flew properly, hold them against the wind and run as fast as we might? Who now could go to the beech tree that overlooks the Trent valley from where the best view of the Montacute and Odcombe range of hills is to be got, and from the white part of which we used to dislodge the little excrescences called by us 'eyes,' taking them away as tokens of the lessening number of school weeks?

When he was lying sick in what proved to be his deathbed I sent him my essay on the Montacute poet and musical composer, Thomas Shoel. In the essay I explain that the village of Montacute is sheltered on the west by Ham Hill. 'This,' he wrote, after his abrupt manner, 'is not true. *In fact it is a lie.*' This roughness in the interest of truth was as characteristic of him as it was when, at the end of his letter, he described Shoel with singular imaginative sympathy as being 'like a rare autumn crocus crushed in the print of an ox's hoof.' It was the last communication that was ever to pass between us, and it was in this letter that he ended with the words 'My whole love. A.R.P.'

I remember as though it were yesterday when he first decided to be an architect. We were sitting sketching in Stoke Churchyard surrounded by grey tombstones. And now he who always had so deep a regard for the past lies himself buried, all his exceptional knowledge of wood and stone stored up during his life utterly lost, of no more avail in man's economies than the dust of a buried stock.

The first work in his profession he supervised was the repairing and enlarging of a little schoolhouse at Longload. He had then been in Mr. Benson's office but a few weeks, and I remember the expression of supreme satisfaction on his boy's face as he watched the Ham Hill stones being lifted into their proper positions. It would be difficult to calculate the number of walls belonging to every period of human building that have since received the informed and dedicated attention of 'this giant of quiet good works.' That afternoon marked the beginning of a career of great value to the country. It was perhaps his obstinate sincerity, a sincerity never to be budged, that gave so much weight to his judgments as secretary of the Society for the Protection of Ancient Buildings. All the views he held were integrated by a single individual attitude of mind, a vigorous philosophic attitude of mind that was continually directed upon the whole stream of his sense-impressions.

From *Somerset Essays* (1937).

PHILOSOPHICAL

Two passages from

IMPASSIONED CLAY

I

*I begin to write this book on Sunday, June the first, nineteen
hundred and thirty. May power come to me through my
belly, from the earth, and from the sun.*

STEPPING out of my coast-guard cottage on the top of the
White Nose, I raised my eyes to the heavens. It was a clear
night in spring. No cloud obscured the vision of the universe
outspread above the earth. The stars were shining as brightly as
they do in Palestine. In my room upstairs a peat fire was glowing.
All was snug and secure and actual there. The glimpse I now had
of the outer spaces beset my imagination. It was not possible for
me to rid my mind of this infallible review of matter. As an
animal gathers its limbs to its body in the fastness of its den, so
did my consciousness draw in upon itself. I began to take my
bearings, physical, spiritual, and intellectual. What could be
made of my case, an eager living organism alone on the top of this
sea cliff, while the planet, with the deliberation of a process
endlessly repeated, turned the protuberance of Europe slowly
towards the light of the sun?

Shut fast your lips, close tight the lids of your eyes, from the
super-universe upheld upon an ocean of primal darkness to the
invisible atom with electrons revolving about it, all is uncertainty,
all is mystery. Astronomical space is infinite, time but the child
of an incomprehensible eternity. What though we are taught that
at the ultimate borders of the universe space is found to re-enter
upon itself, what though we are instructed to conceive of time
as a mathematical conception unreliable and relative, it still remains an indisputable fact that the human mind is confronted by
the inconceivable. Each animate creature that for a moment
receives quivering life from the matrix of matter takes its breath
over an abyss that must remain for ever unplumbed. Though

79

audacious imaginations touch dangerous and ambiguous areas, allowance must yet be made for possibilities beyond and outside the apprehension of telluric vision. The physical limitations that are imposed upon our scope must always, even in these realms of matter, leave room for vaster outer edges. Our wise astronomers tell us so themselves. Their stellar time calculations from a human point of view presuppose eternities within eternities, their stellar space measurements enfold infinities within infinities. With the best will in the world it is impossible for the grey brain contained in our skulls of bone to envisage the simplest facts of the sidereal heavens. These speechless stars move under a discipline, this is all we know. In the words of Lucretius, 'the most solid bodies of matter fly about for ever unvanquished by the ages.'

From a womb, dark and obscure, we take our life, and no testimony of our five awakened senses can elucidate the vision given us from the sun-warmed harbourage of the earth.

The bright stain of the universe did not come from the hand of any God. No son of God shouted for joy over the vast oceans of evenly dispersed matter out of which the nebulas were formed. No conscious eye noted those first indications of gravitational instability which quickened the endless throe. Under the compulsion of the same immutable laws that we observe in the workings of nature upon earth did the constellations themselves find a beginning. The resplendent peacock-tail expanse of the uncounted stars, steadfastly obedient to a rigid conformity, had, we can hardly doubt it, a secular origin. Again as Lucretius puts it, 'Nature is seen to do all things herself, and entirely of her own accord without help of the Gods.' The first cause is the last cause. It is unconscious, unending movement eternally transforming itself and innocent of purpose. If we wish for a hint as to the manner of the workings of all things, we have but to observe rain falling, we have but to watch red fire burning. It is extraordinary how the human mind relucts at the idea of such a sublime indifference. Was it not Nature herself who brought us to birth? Surely she must conceal somewhere in herself a tender regard. No favouring direction, however, is apparent. Every manifestation of the universe is regulated by certain fixed primal laws, and from these laws there is of a certainty no appeal. It is against a background of rigid determinism that our own ephemeral beings live and move. During those forlorn aeons of primal energy there was no mind to contemplate the process by which the stars drifted to their posts; no eye to envisage the rushings together, the outburstings, the spiral revolutions; no brain to contemplate the utter loneliness of those wastes between the stars, those ultimate voids of material, immaterial, godless space-tracks. 'For not by design did the first beginnings of things place themselves each in their order with foreseeing mind . . . but by trying movements and unions of every kind, at last they fell into such dispositions as those, whereby our world of things is created,' writes Lucretius.

We step out of our closeted parlours and forthwith our way is lit by the torches of a timeless empire. It is impossible to exaggerate the inconsequence of our lot. There is a rising and a setting, a bringing to birth and a decay.

It has been suggested that matter is capable of destruction, that every atom is destined to be dissolved away in radiation. The possible annihilation of matter, the possible annihilation of the ultimate elements of the universe—here indeed is an hypothesis upon which to found the philosophy of our lives.

Long ago in my home at Montacute I used to attend a village meeting in a room at the upper end of a blind passage, at the top of the Borough. It was here that a number of men assembled each Sunday for the purpose of discussing religion. I remember that on one occasion the village clerk spoke to us of the evidence the stars gave as to the existence of God. My brother John, however, who would not be convinced by this manner of persuasion, emphatically declared that in his opinion the stars were profoundly melancholy. If the ultimate issue really lies in the annihilation of matter, how justified he was! Yet to many minds, below and beyond the immediate mood of melancholy in such a thought, what a release is to be found in this sequence! What a blessed deliverance! When one contemplates the restlessness of life upon earth—its purposeless strivings, its laborious unsuccessful adjustments, its frenzy, its disorder—when one considers its age-long suffering, the anguish of body, and the anguish of mind, what a boon is here offered! Peace, peace, eternal peace and nothingness, a flat plain of undisturbed space, oblivion reaching out to oblivion. To the right and to the left, above and below. For there is a weariness in the stir of the animate and the inanimate. Star beyond star, nebula beyond nebula, universe beyond universe, and everywhere this same unsubordination. Here is a plan for a double oblivion; the certain oblivion that overtakes the universe at the death of each contemplative mind will now be made doubly sure. Not only shall the dream universe of each man's separate conception disappear, but also the actual objective material universe will have an end, a complete and utter end, as when ripples subside upon a glassy surface.

It is strange how particular moments in the development of one's understanding are preserved by the memory. I recollect when walking one winter evening through Odcombe, that village where Tom Coryat had so often sat kicking his heels, questioning my father about the movements of the constellations above our heads. In that brief conversation I realized the gap that must always exist between human-made creeds and astronomical science. The accent of displeasure in my father's voice as we walked like two phantom shadows, white head and yellow head, revealed only too clearly to my boy's mind the danger latent in such a juxtaposition.

Yet the Jews were right. No sight that the human eyes can look upon is more provocative of awe than is the night sky scattered thick with stars. But this silence made visible, this silence made audible, does not necessarily give rise to a religious mood. It may evoke a mood that neither requires nor postulates a God. On frosty January nights when I walk over the downs I feel myself to be passing through a lofty heathen temple, a temple without devil-affrighting steeple bells, without altars of stone or altars of wood. Constellation beyond constellation, the unaltering white splash of the Milky Way, and no sign of benison, no sign of bane, only the homely hedgerow shadows and the earth's resigned stillness out-stretched under the unparticipating splendour of a physical absolute.

'Concerning the Gods,' answered Protagoras, 'I cannot say that they exist nor yet that they do not exist. There are more reasons than one why we cannot know. There is the obscurity of the subject and there is the brevity of human life.' In spite of these wise words, throughout the ages there has been one God, glorious and apparent, before whom it is no dishonour for a man to fall down in prayer. It was from the mere glance of this God, full of an invincible magnetism, that dead matter was first moved to give birth to life, and this God remains still the means of our

salvation and the strength by which we are sustained. O unvanquished and visible sun, from whom we draw the very sources
of our being, give me the strength this day to repeat with heedless
daring and true understanding after my own fashion thy eternal
doctrine! For to those who worship the sun there come moments
of rapture that can never be gainsaid. This is no dream-God that
rises each morning into the sky. Before his steadfast affirmation all
our misconceived timidities, all our morbid preoccupations,
vanish. The sun shines upon the just and upon the unjust alike,
and is concerned with nothing but the dance of life. Here is a
glory that lightens our hearts, that convinces without argument,
that justifies without a word said. In summertime how happily
the sun's light will lie along the small gravel of a road at noon.
The shadows of the wayside trees are beautiful, but their beauty
may not be compared with the beauty of sunlight, with sunlight
flat and common, with sunlight that shows us *for certain* that the
earth is actual and our existence no fantasy. Our imaginations
balk in the contemplation of the fox-eyed stars uncatalogued in
number, yet from a human point of view the duration of the sun
is also eternal. It has been calculated that eight million million
of our poor fleeting years would scarcely measure its life. When
we are born we are born into a world without end, and when we
die we relinquish our momentary apprehension of such a world.
We must adjust our philosophy to this. Like ephemera our
dalliance is over in an instant. We look up at the sun once, twice,
and a moment after we are gone. They come seeking for us, and,
behold, we are no more!

Sitting at this second of time in a cleft of the White Nose, I find
it no easy matter to envisage the wild flight of the solar system,
the sun like a strong-winged gannet leading on and on through the
cold illimitable deserts of space. A fly explores for a second the
elder-leaf at my side, an uninsurgent bee murmurs behind me, in
the mid-air between the white chalk and the glittering water the
herring-gulls wing their way. Each creature fulfils with content
and confidence the imperative of its being, and yet for all the
rigidity of the shining cliffs dotted with flints incorruptible and
indestructible, fly and insect, gull and man, are being carried after
the sun in its headlong aimless rushing. Portland looks solid
enough, its oolite rocks deep-rooted in the bed of the 'race'; the
sun looks stationary and reliable as he pours forth his triumphant

bounty; yet now, very now, samphire and seaweed, bone and stone, are being carried forward and ever forward in actual physical images through an actual physical universe. Small wonder there have been found those to mistrust the senses. Yet grossly as our senses may mislead us they must remain for ever the basis of all our knowledge and of all our appeals.

How my imagination as a boy was roused by reading a book upon the nebular theory! How the pennants of those whirling spirals seemed to me a fitting beginning for the high passion of life! It was my lot that same afternoon to entertain a Christian missionary. As I walked by his side through the winter woods, this hypothesis affected me as though I had been permitted to hear the music of the spheres. I knew that the values of the man at my side were false values and that I had been initiated into a secret dangerous and haughty. The mud over which I trod, with tiny larch-tree needles sprinkled upon it, was actual; the black gown of my elderly companion was actual; but these, and all the other familiar objects, with common day following common day in use and habit and custom, had an existence, so I suddenly discovered, in a universe more fortuitous and more desperate than I could possibly have imagined. The youth and life in my blood called back to the life and youth of the stars. I knew it. There was no foresight, no support, in our origin, only an exultant cast of chance in harmony with an original chaos. To this day my mind responds to the accounts we have of astral cosmology as though men were speaking of God: these momentous rushings together, these centripetal and centrifugal movements, these elliptical swervings, these dissipations and condensations, these rotations of the elements out of which in a veritable spinthrian ecstasy life is begotten.

They tell us that the planets of our solar system were drawn out of the body of the sun by the too close approach of another star which went on its wild way unmindful that its masterful proximity had wrenched from the solar matrix nine heavenly children. I have seen gnats upon the surface of a river unite in just such a mad saraband of a second's duration and then be parted for ever. The gnat dances and brings to life, boys and girls dance and bring to life, the suns dance and bring to life. And it was out of that swift momentary meeting of inanimate matter, out of elements not even in solid form, that a provision as unexpected, as tender, and as heart-breaking as human tears came into being.

It is extraordinary how casual a consideration we give to the sun, to this prince of our allotted days. Noons come and go, and scarcely twice during the week do we look up at our great master who with never a word spoken floods with his blessing the alternate flanks of the planet. Yet what a sensible mystery is here! In the hour before dawn, when the stars are cold and the breath of the morning is blowing, every living thing that flies, or swims, or creeps, is cognizant of an obscure physical relief. Once again the dreadful regimen of darkness has been defeated. Once again an unsurprising day is ours, offering to us fresh occasions.

In the Rocky Mountains the grizzly bears press the earth with their clawed pads as they move along high slopes grown thick with dew-drenched lupin; in Africa the spur-fowl with sharp voices call to each other with glad, reiterated insistence; across the Dorset sea-coast downs jackdaws dash themselves in rushing flights, sweeping over the undulated mounds covered with swaying blades of reserved and wakeful grass. Fearful spirits imprisoned within the boundaries of our own limitations, we men invent for our comfort fanciful differences, and hardly vouchsafe to uncover our heads in the presence of this living God potent to cause even an unnoticed July poppy-bud to straighten its frail stem.

What a delicate thing is this affinity between the flowers and the sun! Consider the dainty movement of the petals of flowers, the dainty and definite process actually taking place each day as we walk inattentive through the pastures. Maybe our talk is of the gods, is of our meat, is of our loves. With sly self-interested words we disguise our slanders, pausing with one boot upon the step of a stile, and all the time, behind and before us, an imperceptible disquiet has taken possession of the gilded edges of a myriad buttercups. In a world of such wonder, in a world where there is deceit in our very sense-impressions, we may well cling with justification to symbols. A crooked cross has sufficed for many. A weed is my badge. An ordinary dandelion in full flower offers me an absolute assurance that good hope lies at the bottom. Each one of these sun-images reaffirms that life is to be trusted. Examine this flower at close quarters and what gay matters are revealed! Behold, its round jocund shield is made up of innumerable sceptres, sceptres that are shining and bright as gold. It is as impossible to look into the eye of a dandelion as it is to look into the eye of the sun and harbour treasonable thoughts. Indeed, to be ever aware of the sun as he moves from horizon to horizon is a form of prayer to us who are ignorant of other Gods. By such secret religious glances are we taught to number our days. We cannot look over our shoulders too often in this way, nor can we commend ourselves too often in princely adoration to this resplendent lord of the heavens, for the oldest man has had time but to take a few glimpses of this majesty whose sovereign rein has given life to all that breathes.

From *Impassioned Clay* (1931). The second passage from *Impassioned Clay* begins on page 119.

THE CRADLE OF GOD

THE PROPHETS! What images of terror, of old men covered with mantles, of monstrous lean men with loins girded up and eyes flashing, does this word evoke! They appear, these terrific forms, now here, now there, like beings possessed, like whirlwind spirits. Nothing could quench their flaming belief in Jehovah, who more and more came to represent for them the omniscient, omnipotent God, not only of Israel, but of all the nations. Although to begin with their prophetic zeal confined itself to maintaining the purity of their Hebrew worship, yet, as the generations passed, it widened its range until such qualities as justice and compassion came to be included amongst the attributes in harmony with the divine purpose. Many of us believe this faith to have been a delusion. Many of us deny that the finer impulses of men and women are under the divine providence of a transcendent God, those impulses that tremble so shyly amid the ferocities of life. That a certain path of conduct, a personal way, should be followed, irrespective of rewards and punishments, and, indeed, with complete indifference to every form of conventional morality, was, and is still, far from being received as sound doctrine. Many years have yet to go by before it will be understood that a virtue which derives its strength from incomprehensible assumptions, is, in its essence, a sorry, unreliable virtue, and that any real delicacy of spirit, any true perceptiveness and understanding, must be purged of the least taint of 'moralic acid.' The most treasured goodness in this world is not unselfish goodness, not Christian goodness, but that selfish, unoffended, imaginative sympathy, that princely, heathen goodness, which, in well-bred spirits, is as sensitive as the lovely waving feelers of a sea-anemone. This simple goodness, sometimes miraculously evident in the houses of tinkers and tailors, kings and cobblers, causes tears of joy to start in the eyes of men. A soul cannot be saved by following the laws of Moses alone. These rudimentary regulations answered their purpose well enough in their day. Yet a finer tenderness remains, a more discriminating moral susceptibility, which their discipline does not satisfy. By taking away 'the sodomites out of the land,' the soul of Asa was not sufficiently justified. His heart was perfect with the Lord all his days. 'Nevertheless, in the time of his old age he was diseased in the feet.'

As we read the sonorous pages of these great chapters, it is impossible to remain unaffected by their power. The insolent claim that the children of Israel were brought up out of Egypt by two golden calves presently presents itself to our minds also as an intolerable travesty of the truth. A few chapters read, and we are in a fit mood to welcome the sudden appearance of the most terrifying of all the ancients. Let there be an end, once and for ever, to this halting between two opinions. Like a clap of thunder, Elijah, the Tishbite, bursts upon the scene with a magnetic violence that can cause the very elements to bend to his will. 'As the Lord God of Israel liveth, before whom I stand, there shall not be dew nor rain these years, but according to my word.' The prophet had spoken, and the Lord commanded him to hide by the brook Cherith, himself instructing the ravens, with their understanding round eyes, to abandon their daily occupation of scouring the hillside for the afterbirths of sheep, and to concentrate all their ingenious, far-seeing purposes upon fetching food for the prophet.

Three years pass, and Ahab and his steward have themselves been reduced to searching for grass for their mules, 'that we lose not all the beasts.' Then Elijah suddenly reappeared to the God-fearing Obadiah. 'Go tell thy Lord, Behold Elijah is here.' Obadiah hesitated, and immediately the prophet answered with haughty foolhardihood: 'As the Lord of hosts liveth, before whom I stand, I will surely shew myself unto him to-day.' It was a daring resolution. Search had been made for him far and near, and he was now welcomed by Ahab with the significant words, 'Art thou he that troubleth Israel?' However, the personal power of the hirsute man 'with a girdle of leather about his loins,' who had started up out of the highway, was sufficiently strong to dominate the weak-willed king, and he obeyed his orders. A decree was issued that all Israel and the four hundred and fifty prophets of Baal were to gather upon the eastern ridge of Mount Carmel.

'I, even I only, remain a prophet of the Lord.' There it was that the great trial took place, and there below, by the banks of the river Kishon, Elijah, like David before him, making use of the uncertain temper of men's minds at a period of universal disaster, caused the unfortunate rival priests to be massacred. 'The Lord he is God; the Lord he is God.'

When, in the month of May, we sons of a righteous father, sons of Eli, used to read the magnificent passage at the brass lectern, I never imagined that it would be my lot to visit the stony terrace where Elijah had mocked the false priests. It has happened so. I carry with me my memory of the historic mountain, with its glens and honey-combed dongas, with its sage and black-berried bay trees, with its slanting dew-damp rocks gleaming like plates of copper in the early sunshine. It takes over three hours to reach the place by a wild mountain-road; and from its high crest, which was once 'black with clouds and wind,' a man can look down upon the Promised Land, upon the hills of Samaria, upon the hills of Nazareth, upon the slopes of Gilboa, upon the snow-capped head of Hermon, and the lofty mountain-ranges on the other side of the Jordan.

Out of the blazing heat of noon I sought refuge in the cool, whitewashed interior of a vaulted monastery cell; and there, as I lay meditating, with a incipient fever in my blood, my attention was caught by a single picture in the room, a tawdry-coloured Catholic print representing Elijah, sword in hand, standing with his foot upon the neck of a false priest. I regarded it at first with an interest entirely detached. Then suddenly I recognized in the narrow, bigoted, fanatical countenance of Elijah the very expression that I have seen upon the limited faces of the people who are my natural enemies. In a flash I realized that I was, and ever would be, on the side of the fallen victim, on the side of this renegade worshipper of the sun, with his shifty intellectual head and beaver-brown beard. These honest priests, who took their meat at the table of Queen Jezebel, were surely of my kidney. I could very well understand the queen's prejudice. If the truth is to be blurted out, it offered as great a release for the human spirit as did the unreasoning superstitious loyalty of the obsessed old man.

What a woman she was, this daughter of Ethbaal, priest of Astarte, dwelling in her 'ivory house'! A word from the painted lips of this 'imperious whorish woman' sufficed to send even the Tishbite going for his life, like a long-winded cantering kongoni over the hills. There is also something attractive to me about the personality of Ahab, the son of Omri, who 'did evil in the sight of the Lord above all that were before him.' I commend his weakness in sparing the life of his conquered enemy, Ben-hadad, the king of the Syrians: in calling him brother and causing him 'to come up in to his chariot.' I like him very well for his pithy utterances 'Hast thou found me, O mine enemy?' and, 'Let not him that girdeth on his harness boast himself as he that putteth it off.' I like him for dressing in sackcloth after the matter of Naboth's vineyard, and, indeed, for wanting to have a garden of herbs at all. The guilt of this affair was not his, except in so far as 'he turned away his face and would eat no bread.' From the day of his birth, even unto the minute when the arrow 'shot at a venture' pierced the joint of his armour, he remained an amiable tool in the hands of his resplendent Phoenician spouse. It was she, as the Scripture tells us, who invariably 'stirred him up.'

How these bitter-tempered, provincial Jews hated this woman of high fashion, gloating over every detail of her misfortunes! When the chariot of her husband was backed into the pool of Jezreel, and the dogs collected to lick up the blood that was washed out of it, they rejoiced; and when her own terrible fate came upon her, they put it on record for all generations to read. 'And when Jehu was come to Jezreel, Jezebel heard of it, and she painted her face, and tired her head, and looked out at a window. And as Jehu entered in at the gate, she said, Had Zimri peace, who slew his master? And he lifted up his face to the window, and said, Who is on my side? who? And there looked out to him two or three eunuchs. And he said, Throw her down. So they threw her down; and some of her blood was sprinkled on the wall, and on the horses; and he trode her under foot. And when he was come in, he did eat and drink, and said, Go, see now this cursed woman, and bury her: for she is a king's daughter. And they went to bury her; but they found no more of her than the skull, and the feet, and the palms of her hands. . . . And he said, This is the word of the Lord, which he spake by his servant Elijah the Tishbite, saying, In the portion of Jezreel shall dogs eat the flesh of Jezebel: and the carcase of Jezebel shall be as dung upon the face of the field in the portion of Jezreel; so that they shall not say, This is Jezebel.'

Different enough was the destiny reserved for her rough enemy, for the solitary holy man who had spent the days of his life in cabins and in cock-lofts, for this worthy, with but one idea fixed in his head. It was in keeping with the imagination of the Hebrews that his fanatical spirit should at the end be translated in glory, that God should transport to heaven his stark, ferocious soul by means of a miraculous equipage. Down to the sandy banks of Jordan it came, the flaming carriage, causing Elijah's bucolic disciple, fresh from the plough, to explain in startled stupefaction, 'My father, my father! the chariot of Israel, and the horsemen thereof.'

From *The Cradle of God* (1929).

JESUS OF NAZARETH

JESUS was born when Augustus was emperor and was executed in the reign of his successor, Tiberius, that man of 'mud mixed from blood.' Rome, partly by the accident of opportunity, partly by the ability of her people, had come to dominate all the nations of the known world. A materialistic view of life was natural to the Romans. Their values were cash values. This statement may be supported by the fact that their greatest contribution to Western civilization is found in their highly-developed sense of justice. They had a genius for dealing efficiently with everyday affairs. They had the highest sense of organization. Their gift for government can find an analogy in their great roads which stretched themselves forward to the ends of the earth, regardless of obstacles. Yet on any other plane but that of the work-a-day world they were artless vulgarians. No sooner, therefore, had they won the kingdoms by the strength of the sword than they themselves were spiritually vanquished by the prevailing cultures of those kingdoms. Every philosophy, every religion, found its way to Rome. Like rooks in autumn gathering to a king rookery so did these phantom insubstantial creations of the human mind close in upon the victorious city. Generations passed, and presently that ghostly flock of superstitions infected the natures of these men of action with a deep and unsettling restlessness. They in their turn began to worship strange gods. The sensuality of the East sapped their vigour. Gone for ever was the harmless gaiety of the Greek Eros; it had been replaced by what was heartless and gross and commercial. There is something singularly repellent about the Roman attitude to these things. How destructive to the grace of the sex illusion are the great clumsy phallic signs to be seen to-day over the common stews in the streets of Pompeii! The Romans ordered their pleasures wholesale without restraint or discrimination. Their pleasures were rich men's pleasures; sensuality was rendered worthless by satiety. They never learned that the rarest delights that mortal can experience are not to be bought or sold. I recollect seeing in a house of Pompeii a coloured representation of a huge, heavy, half-erect, drooping, uncircumcised cod-piece weighed in a pair of scales against a heap of golden coins. No pious sermon against the abuse of primitive impulses could have been more persuasive. Looking at that mural picture it became apparent to me as never before that the true secret of life does not lie in unrestrained sexual indulgence.

Herod the Great, that Idumaean slave, represented in his jurisdiction and in his person a fine example of Roman brutality. He philandered with Hellenistic traditions, but at the same time never forgot that his sovereignty ultimately depended upon the Roman rod. Yet any estimate of his career would be one-sided if his peculiar individual genius were to be overlooked. He had in his veins strange blood. He was driven by the passions of his desert ancestry. He was froward, superstitious, cursed. Firm and frightful in his outward dealings with men, his inner being was hunted and haunted. There can be no doubt that Herod the Great ploughed the soil for the spring corn of Christianity. No restharrow impeded that terrible coulter until all was ready. It was his ferocious administration that drove the spirit of the Hebrews back upon itself. Material values, a material conception of life, ruthless and without restraint, were predominant, and it was inevitable that a reaction would set in. The body had conquered, but the oppressed soul was not dead. The times were ripe for a new subversive revolution. There was a power abroad more insidious than money, mightier than the sword; a secret, lively power that, although it had been crushed and crushed again, still lived on with the tenacity of a worm cut in several parts.

The Jews saw majestic Pagan buildings rise up in all directions upon the sacred soil of the land God 'sware unto them'; they saw their new temple, 'Herod's building,' as they grudgingly called it, dominating their Holy City. They were massacred, tortured, pestered with tax-gatherers; yet all this suffering had the effect of driving them back for nourishment upon their own secrets. They bowed their heads and brooded upon their lore. They remembered God, their own God, more powerful and more merciful than any Pagan deity, they remembered the mad murmurings of their own possessed prophets. All the banked-up traditions of their theocratic reliance surged through their obstinate beings. The world was 'out of joint.' Deliverance must be at hand. A miracle would happen, must happen. If they waited long enough upon the Lord, if they repented and exercised with still greater fervour their moral preconceptions, then the Messiah would come and with him salvation. Their desperate necessity caused them to elaborate their irrational hopes. A whole literature sprang up having to do with doctrines of last things. If they could hold still to the secret paths of their ancient teachings, then surely the very heavens would crack! To all appearance the province of Jewry was developing as other tracts of land under the suzerainty of Rome; in reality the dwellers upon its surface were quick with unsubjugated premonitions. Throughout the length and breadth of the country, from Hebron to Jacob's Well, from Nazareth to the Dead Sea, the minds of this peculiar people were preoccupied with impossible hopes.

Jesus was born some time during the last years of the reign of Herod the Great; was born, perhaps, in the house of a common carpenter high up in the hills of Galilee; was born, perhaps, at the very time when the sinister king was dying at Jericho like a leopard grown foul, panting at the back of its cave.

The two great influences that went to form the character of Jesus were the sacred Scriptures and the simple sights of the country. It is abundantly evident that He applied Himself to the study of the Psalms and of the Law and of the Prophets with the greatest diligence. He had a quick intellectual apprehension, but what was more important still was His spiritual responsiveness which made it possible for Him, with the unstriving sureness of genius, to understand the religious divination that lay beneath the emotion of the ancient words. Driven back upon Himself by outward circumstances He assimilated the inner wisdom of the scrolls He read. His soul took shelter in the writings of His ancestors, yet they did not cloy His mind. He did not acquire knowledge of them as did so many erudite Pharisees for the sake of that knowledge. He drank from those words of exalted assurance as a thirsty man drinks from water springing freshly from a fountain. All this wealth of blessed utterance He made His own, and applied it without artifice to the everyday world about Him. In doing this He was helped and influenced by the simple environment of His upbringing. Close contact with natural scenes is a mighty protection against the conceit of pedantry. In later times the strength and beauty of His teaching were dependent to a very large extent upon these early impressions. It was because He Himself had seen and heard and touched the perishable objects of the natural world that His lessons were so convincing, as convincing as only the pure poetry of the senses can be. Coming out of His habitation as the sun went down He would mark how the circuit of the clouds glowed with the red over Mount Carmel; crossing a slanting place of dry mud He would observe the anxious concern that His neighbour's hen would show gathering her chickens to her and outspreading her wings over the littered ground. In the mornings He would follow that lovely upland track that runs above Nazareth, and as He picked His way over the ruts, would observe how the tares were entangled with the tall, thin barley of those cultivated acres; He would watch the small wild birds with eyes of consideration for their individual existences, the sheep and goats He would observe, and the tethered wayside asses. He noted the water bursting out of the village spring, so cool, so transparent, and so *living*. He was acquainted with the taste, with the smell of the fruit of the vine. He meditated upon the personalities of the people about Him until He had learned to discount the outward presentation, and with a single glance, or a single word, could reveal the inner hidden being. His perceptions were unfailing, His insight certain. Whether it was Herod or an harlot who stood before Him, nothing was hid. He comprehended the grace of spirit that lay behind the blandishments of the girl just as readily as He understood the pathos of the Tetrarch's portentous presence. There are many dreams that can only exist in temples, churches, and libraries; His dreams live on in squares and thorough-fares and market-places. They have to do with life, they are made out of life, and considering the general bent of His teaching this thing is a great anomaly.

It was His meeting with John the Baptist that first put into the mind of Jesus the dangerous and audacious belief that it was He Himself, and no other, who was the long-expected Messiah. We can never tell what exactly happened at that river bank, what passed between those two remarkable Semitics as they stood knee to knee in the sacred stream. Did they know what they were doing? Did the older man, the rude, rough prophet, caught up in a whirlwind, look for one hesitating second with significant suspended consciousness into the eyes of the other? There had already been Jews who had taken upon themselves to be the worldly champions of their race, and the fable of the Temptation would seem to suggest that for a short period something of a like purpose came into Christ's mind also, soon, however, to be discarded for this other plan of His own devising. He had studied the Scriptures in such a way that He not only understood, but actually *felt* their meaning. He had pondered over these great chapters of Isaiah which symbolized the sufferings of the Jews in the form of a servant who through willing endurance wins for the nation a state of blessed redemption. In some obscure way this idea may also have been associated in His mind with the notion of sacrifice which the long centuries of temple worship at Jerusalem had made so familiar. At the beginning of His mission He does not seem to have been very clear as to what He intended, yet it is evident that in the more illuminated moments of His life, when He was alone, or when He prayed, He knew of a surety that He was the 'Blessed one' who by preaching repentance and a return to righteousness would hasten the coming of 'the last days,' and who, so He eventually came to believe, would be chosen when the heavens opened to sit on the right hand of 'Power.' Whatever explanations may be given for what happened it cannot be disputed that the mind of Jesus, with all its mysticism, was singularly childlike. Indeed, the tragedy of the Crucifixion was the direct outcome of a reasoning as irrational as it was magnanimous.

The fifty-third chapter of the Book of Isaiah would seem to have especially inspired Him. These oracular verses have fascinated the commentators of successive generations. Their very obscurity is provocative of interest. In these lofty words we find consciously developed the idea of vicarious sacrifice, the idea of the redemption of the guilty through the anguish of the innocent. They had been begotten of the old theory that the misfortunes of the Jews as a nation had been imposed upon them for a moral purpose. By such a winnowing could the golden grain alone be separated. Brought to birth out of a reality hard to be explained, this idea of deputed punishment presently took the form of a despised and rejected person who in some mystical way, under no compulsion except a secret, silent, heroical impulse, voluntarily offered up Himself as a lamb upon an altar. Though the notion in its inception was essentially barbarous, yet an attempt to make practical use of it postulated a spiritual altruism that in the history of the

Llewelyn Powys (1928). Taken in New York by Doris Ulmann while he was "Visiting Critic" for the *New York Herald Tribune*.

world can never be regarded as anything but startling. The seed
of the idea accorded with the alarmed superstitious impulses of
the Neanderthal man 'in his dark cloud making his moan,' but its
practical application drew near to the sublime.

It is extraordinary to think that these Christmas words, so
familiar to us, must have been considered and reconsidered by
Jesus—words caught out of the air and borne down the ages from
mouth to mouth.

'Who hath believed our report? and to whom is the arm of the
Lord revealed? For he shall grow up before him as a tender plant,
and as a root out of a dry ground: he hath no form nor comeliness;
and when we shall see him, there is no beauty that we should desire
him. He is despised and rejected of men; a man of sorrows, and
acquainted with grief: and we hid as it were our faces from him;
he was despised, and we esteemed him not. Surely he hath borne
our griefs, and carried our sorrows: yet we did esteem him stricken,
smitten of God, and afflicted. But he was wounded for our trans-
gressions, he was bruised for our iniquities: the chastisement of our
peace was upon him; and with his stripes we are healed. All we like
sheep have gone astray; we have turned every one to his own way;
and the Lord hath laid on him the iniquity of us all. He was
oppressed, and he was afflicted, yet he opened not his mouth: he is
brought as a lamb to the slaughter, and as a sheep before her shearers
is dumb, so he openeth not his mouth. He was taken from prison
and from judgment: and who shall declare his generation? for he
was cut off out of the land of the living: for the transgression of my
people was he stricken. And he made his grave with the wicked,
and with the rich in his death; because he had done no violence,
neither was any deceit in his mouth. Yet it pleased the Lord to
bruise him; he hath put him to grief: when thou shalt make his
soul an offering for sin, he shall see his seed, he shall prolong his
days, and the pleasure of the Lord shall prosper in his hand. He shall
see of the travail of his soul, and shall be satisfied: by his knowledge
shall my righteous servant justify many; for he shall bear their iniquities. Therefore will I divide him a portion with the great, and he
shall divide the spoil with the strong; because he hath poured out his
soul unto death: and he was numbered with the transgressors; and he
bare the sin of many, and made intercession for the transgressors.'

We are justified in conjecturing that Jesus in some secret understanding of His own, identified Himself with the heroic subject

of this chapter, and this was especially the case probably when the initial success of His mission had been succeeded by the period of humiliation. He was the traditional Messiah, the consciousness of this was His life illusion. Such a conception, probably ill defined even in His own mind, formed the fortifying background to His life. Whatever might occur this belief could not be threatened. It was in its nature to give sustenance to His spirit in the face of the most appalling disaster. Not by the might of the spear would the old dragon be conquered, but by the impossible power of love.

Jesus was no great philosopher. He had no wide vision of life. He interpreted the human situation as viewed from within the confines of Palestine. It would be difficult to systematize His teaching, so full of contradictions is it. Its strength lay in His personality, a personality possessed with a disarming innocence, but at the same time alive with an unaccountable passion. Ordinary values, the values of this world, never influenced Him. His 'innocence' set Him apart in some curious way. There was that in Him that could not be contaminated. All those material anxieties that pester our minds like twilight gnats did not exist for Him. Till the hour of His death He was immune from all those ephemeral preoccupations that perplex and beset us. He treated only with matters which had the truth in them, yet no homely incident occurred but He saw in it 'eternity in an hour.' Those that came in contact with Him could never rid themselves of the love that He roused in their hearts. The simplicity of His genius held them enthralled. No homage could make this man vain who throughout His life remained vulnerable to each new turn of events, and yet who never, not for a single moment, lost the integrity of His inner being; no homage can be great enough with which to honour Him. It was the intense personal adoration provoked by His unique individuality that rendered the rise of Christianity possible.

When He was dead and could no more look over His shoulder at the sun, when His life had been taken from Him, and the particular tone of His voice could never again be heard, the power of His mysterious person still remained unabated. All that was tender, all that was sensitive and nervous, all that was opposed to the harsh claims of triumphant matter, rallied to the rumour of this unlikely prophet. From the first the spiritual assurances that He himself had felt were communicated to others. Was this the hint, the word, that the hungry generations had waited for? Immediately upon its presentation a restlessness was observed and there appeared in many places and in many manners that strange myth, simple, subtle, dangerous and sublime.

Yet though so large a portion of the human race has believed in Jesus, few have been able to put His preaching into practice. There is indeed something essentially impractical about it. Taken literally it is not applicable to the rude workings of the world. Perhaps Jesus Himself realized that life is wavering and blind, and that truth is to be found in a comprehension of opposites. Certainly, in the account we have of His sayings we can be sure of no consistent or accurate doctrine. We receive the impression of a certain temper of mind, that is all; a temper of mind radical and yet at the same time deeply spiritual.

> *What was the sound of Jesus's breath?*
> *He laid His hand on Moses' law;*
> *The ancient Heavens, in silent awe,*
> *Writ with curses from pole to pole,*
> *All away began to roll.*

If we try with complete honesty to make stand out the more important disclosures of His attitude we shall find that He vigorously admonishes us to be unreconciled to the world, deliberately to court misfortune and suffering, in so far as the true values as He sees them are endangered by such worldly considerations as desire, ambition, and success. No teacher has ever laid down a narrower way for his disciples, and none from the first has been less obeyed. Yet even this general drift of His teaching can be contradicted, and it may well be that the strength of His gospel lies in its latent power of infinite interpretation. The intellect can get no coherent sense out of these pages, and yet in these accidental sayings it is possible for even the heart of an atheist to respond as though he had been permitted to hear, against all expectation, divine words. The soul, the soul of man, was all His care. His hatred of hypocrisy was an obsession with Him. He had a prejudice against anything that was strict and formal and subservient to the copybook laws of society. A mean soul He could smell from afar off like a bad fish. He definitely preferred a fornicator, an adulterer, a good bad man to the sanctimonious self-righteous. Have no doubt of it, He was not

unconversant with the existence of 'heathen goodness,' that goodness which looks for no rewards and fears no punishments, but
which blesses the fields of the earth like sunshine. 'The publicans
and the harlots go into the kingdom of heaven before you.' How
it has come about that in these times we associate the name of Jesus
with unpleasant people of 'stupid being' I know not. They have
taken Him by perfidy; and by force they have locked Him up in
their churches.

From the beginning Christianity has been perverted. Theolo-
gians and priests and conventional householders have given many
an ill term to its doctrines. Down the ages it has been their constant purpose to appropriate these free words to their own usage.
The values of such people are transitory values. They are at pains
to preserve society as it is. The deeper, more dangerous intima-
tions that have to do with eternity they consistently ignore. Like
carrion birds they grow fat out of the commodities of death. The
strength of the priest lies in man's fear of mortality. He is not concerned with any daring or dangerous state of heightened
consciousness. He endeavours to enclose men's minds within the
compass of his own vision. Nothing could be further from the
purpose of Jesus. The thing is apparent. It has been apparent to
the saints. Jesus hated dead estimates. All those depressing surface
standards of the commonplace, unillumined world He could not
abide. What such 'home-guards' extolled He hated. The only kinds
of people He execrated were the strict moralists, the petty-minded
priests of His day, the sly, conventional oppressors. He turned
from them. He showed openly that He preferred the company of
whores to theirs. 'The sins which occupied the attention of Jesus
were hypocrisy, worldliness, intolerance, and selfishness: the sins
which occupy the principal attention of the church, as everybody
knows from experience, are impurity, murder, the excessive
drinking of alcohol, swearing, and the neglect of the church
services and ordinances.' Ridding our minds of the traditional
priestly teachings, it is possible to catch the true tenor of Christ's
mood. A hundred chance utterances confirm our opinion. What
does He say to the woman caught in adultery? 'Neither do I con-
demn thee.' What does He say in defence of the harlot? She is
forgiven. 'For she loved much.' Even in the prayer that He made
up, He bases our plea for forgiveness, not on any atonement that
He was about to make, not 'for Jesus Christ's sake,' still less because

we have taken advantage of the mystery of the church sacraments, but simply on the plea of natural human goodness. 'Forgive us our trespasses, *as we forgive them that trespass against us.*' What has He to say to the spiritual authorities of His time, to the men who everybody acknowledged lived strict, punctilious lives after the exact letter of the law? He called them deceitful depositories of dead men's bones, adders, and I know not what else. His attention was ever directed toward the soul of the individual and its place in the eternal plan, and He was never weary of showing that to live according to the law was not enough. It is true that He said many ignorant and foolish things. No one who contemplates our earthly existence with an emancipated mind can possibly believe that men and women, still less the sparrows in the spouting, live under the benevolent care of a human-minded God. We touch just here what good churchmen call one of the mysteries. They use the word advisedly. The fact is that the mind of Jesus was full of mis-conceptions. Life is not ordered by a loving father. A sucking child can see that it is not. We would all like it to be so, but that is another matter. Actually, what do we see?—dim uncertain shadows moving across apparently solid margins of beauty and terror, with below and below again, a cold and dispassionate causation transforming and retransforming all matter. A kind of underground law of gravitation is everywhere at work and no white magic has at any time altered its direction. It is absurd to believe that it has. The more we study mind and matter scientifically the more we see that all things follow a natural sequence, a sequence as liable to work for our disadvantage as for our advantage. It flows like the water of a river, it falls like rain, it is as impartial as the sea. It is as innocent of malice as it is of compassion. It is deaf to our prayers. The tender love in the heart of Jesus caused Him to believe that this was not the case. He boldly challenged the empire of matter. He insisted that eventually victory would lie with the spirit. It is stated that the question still remains open. In order to justify His confidence even Jesus found it necessary to appeal to a future existence. There can be no doubt that He constantly made use of His belief in a future life to strengthen His teaching. This belief also remains to-day a matter for controversy. The corn lands of Christianity from the first were sowed with seeds from a mixed bag, seeds of truth and seeds of falsehood.

Yet, say what we will, Jesus was no common messenger; He whispered a secret that cannot be forgot. Words like forgiveness, compassion, innocence, will always be associated with His name. With all His hasty speaking against the lakeside villages, and against the sanctimonious, He represented in a peculiar way the emotion of pity. He put into God's heart what He found in His own. Christianity is based on several illusions: the illusion of a beneficent God, the illusion that each individual soul lives after death, the illusion that Jesus Himself rose from the dead, the illusion that the world is shortly to come to an end. But yet truth remains in it.

No man has been less blinkered than Jesus, less spiritually blind-fold. His reactions were always undirected—swift, sure, and un-expected. He saw life with imaginative sympathy as a poet sees it. He revealed a mystery which has never grown stale or out of date, and it is upon this spiritual mystery deriving direct from Jesus rather than from St. Paul that Christianity in all its manifold forms is ultimately founded. It grew out of truth, but it has prospered upon lies. In any rational consideration of a religion it is not only the hidden immortal seed of the faith that should command our attention, but also the dogmatic, objective claims that have sprung from that creed. Here we come upon certain legends that explain the phenomenon of what we see to-day. St. Paul was not slow to appreciate the essential value of these, and especially emphasized that absolute credence should be given to the report that Jesus had risen from the dead. This seemed to be to him the pivotal fact. 'If Jesus did not rise from the dead, then is your faith in vain.' Against all reason a portion of the human race has clung to this fancy. The evidence supporting it is childish, yet the continual existence of the error gives perennial proof of the eagerness with which mankind in its predicament is disposed to embrace any hope. We are like sheep who find themselves in a butcher's pad-dock. If one of our number has ever got through the fence there is at least a chance that others will be able to do the same near the elder tree where the brambles grow the thinnest. Certainly, if it could be absolutely proven beyond any possible doubt that the story of the resurrection was true, then all the stored industrious knowledge of humanity would weigh lightly indeed. We would have a sure demonstration that anything was possible. We would enjoy a large sense of freedom. We would know that at any time the crass circumstance of things could be reversed. We would be justified in relying upon arbitary interventions. At any hour, in any year, our situation might be relieved by a fresh interference, a fresh illumination. A swallow might carry a message to us brushing the wind of its whisperings against our cheeks as it swept by in the open fields. Prayer might be potent to save us. The unendurable sequence of cause and effect might be considered to exist on sufferance only; to be firmly planted only as long as the miraculous did not cut through the thread of sequence. There is not evidence enough to justify such a supposition. There never has been. Too prone are we to invent such subterfuges.

The story of the crucifixion as we have it in the Gospels is written with such naïve realism that it is difficult to doubt the veracity of its main outlines. The account we have of it is certainly taken from actual recollections of that dolorous afternoon. Seldom is it possible to suspect the hand of any religious manipulator. 'My God, my God, why hast Thou forsaken Me?' The deep impression that this last desperate cry made upon those who stood about the cross is proved by its preservation. One would scarcely have supposed that these were words to found a religion upon. Yet how convincingly they testify to the authenticity of the secret convictions sustaining the suffering man up to the very last moment of His life.

From *The Pathetic Fallacy* (1930)

THE GRAVE OF A GOD

THERE is, perhaps, a certain simplicity in the desire we have to visit the burying-places of great men. Century after century the earth has gathered them into her belly and it is possible, we imagine, to catch from these cradles of treasured dust moments of high meditation. We used to be told when we shivered in a particular way that a goose was walking over our graves; the adage, even in our childhood, jerked our minds into an awareness of the inevitable fate of our mortal bodies. In a transitory moment of disturbing consciousness we recognized that the hour would come when our skulls also would break asunder like earthenware pots, and our ribs also would give in, and our bones also settle themselves for their long-drawn-out dissolution. No son of woman, however blithe, however taut with damaging self-counsel, can evade this final culmination. It is part of a universal auditing and in the end the worms are our scriveners. If we incline to indulge this passion for visiting the burying-places of great men it should be no matter for surprise that the perplexed and pious generations should have laid such store upon seeing the burying-place of a God. How should it be otherwise? The planet continues its even, uninterrupted flight round the sun. As though in a supernal trance it preserves its mesmerized revolutions. Light from an infinite distance gilds its round grass-grown flanks, illuminating at dawn the underside of the sea-gull's wing. Darkness falls in diurnal repetition, and once more the body of the earth moves with blinded unobservable sureness through the haughty night. On high moorlands, in hay-growing valleys, carefully constructed human habitations project like tiny worm-hills on a downland; and at intervals on the banks of rivers the lights of great cities stain with their radiance the dimness of the outer atmosphere. And everywhere men, minute and brittle as grigs, go about their occupations, thoughtless and bewitched, each one of them presently to be wrapped tight in a shroud. Only at long intervals are men born capable of understanding. Small wonder therefore that we should be easily persuaded to gape over their sepulchres.

The religion of Christianity is in itself so startling a departure from the normal that the most obstinate among us can but contemplate it with astonishment. When we consider the other so reasonable Gods before whom human beings have prostrated themselves, Gods free, powerful, and untraduced, or Gods malignant and given to malfeasance, it is a matter for surprise that the abused generations of the last two thousand years should have raised up out of their unconfessed longings so tender a figure as that of Jesus. For it is to no Apollo—gleaming, arrogant, and God-like—that the religious bend the knee in our time. Though obscured by the grossest sentiment, the praying populations have found expression for a yearning deep as consciousness itself. It cannot be doubted that there is a morbidity in the Christian notion, and yet what an interesting portent it is, how unexpected, brought into existence by nature so that half the world without difficulty has been persuaded.

The words of Jesus, the life of Jesus alone, have made this strange interlude possible. A few scattered sentences of sure insight, of childlike illumination, carry forward the sublime fable. His thoughts, preserved by the ignorant, have had a power not dissimilar to that exercised by radium in the physical world. They slide sideways, they are inevitable, irresistible, struck as it were by a miracle out of nothing.

From my youth the mysterious figure of Christ has puzzled and allured me. The tales that were told me about him projected themselves into my vision of existence. They were hard to assimilate. As the years passed I came to understand that the faith sprung up about his name was but a product of the deluded preconceptions of the Middle Ages. Yet what a curious epoch it marks in the history of the conscious thought of the Western world! Childish chat though it must seem to any intelligence of tempered wisdom, yet it was derived spontaneously enough out of the world's suffering. It was a subtle method of escape from pain and the intimidations coincident with the conclusions to be derived from the massive grossness of matter.

To those of us who rely upon the senses for the appreciation of life's dispassionate mystery it would be hebetudinous not to let this chance command our utmost attention. We open our eyes upon the earth. On frosty winter nights when duckweed ponds bear, we look out at an unpartisan universe; in the twinkling of an eye our winter moons and our summer moons are gone and all is darkness for us again. Would it not be addle-headed in us then not to turn over a stone or two, not to lift up a rhubarb leaf, not to examine the fir cones at our feet, before we depart hence?

Fortunately in the nature of things we have been given every opportunity to indulge such pastimes. For say what the Berkeleians will, from a human point of view matter is stable. It is subject to ordered laws. It is impotent to vanish. Throughout my life this simple fact has been a cause of increasing surprise and satisfaction to me. Life under observation is found to be so feral, thrown up out of causes neither to be explained nor understood, that one would have expected its physical manifestations to have had a bias toward the untrustworthy. This is not so. Where the tree falls there does it lie; though our honeysuckle lanes are thronged with phantom faces, only the autumn can pilfer the sweet fragrance of the flowers.

From the first the human mind recognized in matter a trap. It twisted and contorted itself to find an escape. It confused the issue with words. It left facts and trusted to fancies. It bent itself backward, screwing its head upside down like a paralytic canary. Its conclusions have been false. This is no dream within a dream. There are no miracles because *all is a miracle*. There is no magic because *all is magic*. Yet whoever we be, or wherever we be, on the earth's surface, doubt it not, we have an actual objective position in time and space. At any instant it would be possible from the ultimate borders of the universe 'finite and unbounded' to discover in the flesh our actual bodies; a yellow-haired gipsy swarming up an apple tree after mistletoe *could be found*, an aproned grocer selling a paper bag of flour in an atmosphere of paraffin and pastry has a positive actual existence and *could be found*.

It is a fine spiritual exercise as you sit in a turnpike ditch at night time to drive your imagination out into the void of the firmament. It will return to you, come back to the familiar nettles and rusty blotched dock leaves, a creature more courageous by half. It will have learned a new scholarship from the night. It will approach with more confidence the room of death, the room of birth, the bed of delight and love. More than ever will you be aware of your own identity, of your own mobile body light with blood and breath, and under the instruction of such a heightened consciousness you will be alert to look around you with new eyes and to listen with an improved pair of eland-long ears. In an instant your congenital drowsiness will have left you and you will know that your hour is here and now.

It was under the influence of just such a mood as this that I first decided to go on my pilgrimage. Amid all the tumult of the years, tradition has preserved safe the exact spot where that far-off sepulture took place. What madness, then, not to visit before I died that 'rock of white colour and a little meddled with red'! What use to be alive under the sun at all if one did not take advantage of such privileges? How do I know that Jesus was not actually a God, and if so I should indeed be a fine dolt never to trouble to look for traces of his earthly sojourning. Why, in such a case a dinosaur's egg in the Gobi desert could not have half the interest of the Holy Sepulchre.

From A Pagan's Pilgrimage (1931)

WHEN I CONSIDER THY HEAVENS

Look how the floor of heaven
Is thick inlaid with patines of bright gold.

HOW DELICATE and delightful is that dim vague illumination known as 'starshine'! The phrase is seldom used now except by labourers and fishermen and simple people of that kind who are often out after dark and therefore of necessity have come especially to value this uncertain half light which makes it possible for them to go about their business even when there is no moon in the sky. Moonshine in comparison with sunshine is a lovely and evasive thing, but starshine, that concentrated reflection from many thousands of remote fires, is infinitely more dainty, infinitely more magical, than either.

It may be that its associations with human history have much to do with the imaginative thrill which we feel in its mere mention. In the daily experience of our earliest ancestors, the punctual movements of sun and moon, on account of their very simplicity, must soon have been taken almost for granted. Not so the complicated procession of the constellations advancing in an unwavering circle across the zenith! It was undoubtedly this phenomenon and no other which first piqued their sottish, barbaric animal-brains into making cunning and curious observations. Night after night, as they peered out of their darkened caves, or looked up through the leafy branches above their heads, they would see moving across the sky in regular order, the same fantastical shapes that we look upon to-day. It would be interesting to know the exact occasion when for the first time these stellar revolutions were remarked upon by a sapient mind, struggling to indicate with inarticulate gestures the fact that it had recognized this or that zodiacal sign rising silently in all its beauty above the primeval horizon.

As the ages went by such early astronomical scrutiny rapidly developed. 'Look now towards heaven and tell the stars if thou be able to number them.' The task became a congenial pastime of all the races of mankind spread broadcast over the face of the earth. On cloudless nights in many a far interior, yellow-jowled Mongolians squinnied with slanting, meditative gaze at the spheroidal universe; Babylonians in rock-paved courtyards were employed at the same occupation; while from the confines of a thousand deserts vast and unsurveyed, intractable sun-tanned nomads scanned the earth's rim with fearless falcon eyes.

After protracted labour and monstrous travail matter had given birth to a child greater than itself, a child whose intellect was capable of scrutinizing with calculated detachment the very womb from which it had sprung. From that miraculous hour the awful panorama of cosmic energy was witnessed by crafty, infinitesimal spectators. Man had become conscious, and the universe had been looked upon, had been recognized at last!

How suggestive are the names given to the stars in those early times, those queer Arabic names! Algol, the eye of the demon; Aldebaran, the follower; and that other one which denotes in its original meaning the brand upon a camel's neck. Could anything be more reminiscent of smoke-stained tents, of proud men walking together over wind-ribbed sand, in sight and sound of animals munching their fodder by flickering camp fires in the grateful coolness of the desert night air?

Then the Greeks made their sudden appearance and like free artists, transformed the complex science into pure poetry, peopling the heavens with gods, and giving ready attention to Hesiod when he instructed them to pluck the purple fruit from their vines at the time of the year when Arcturus was visible at dawn, and fall to the business of pruning when his light showed at the time of the setting of the sun. The Jews also arose and after their dedicated manner, drew strength to their souls from contemplating these impressive manifestations of the power and the glory of the living God. It may well be that their attitude is right, though throughout the centuries there have continually been found minds of quite another temper, minds that hold that there are few things more profoundly provocative of melancholy than to look into these indifferent and yawning gulfs of space. Old Kant, looking up from Potsdam at the Milky Way, felt his spirit sink within him with a sense of insupportable insignificance and misgiving. This would seem to have been the general feeling of the human race; for how otherwise can we account for the fact that the mythology of the sky was so little influenced by mediaeval legend? The early Christians were at pains to have the Great Dipper known as 'Lazarus's Bier', and there has always been a disposition with them to appropriate to their own ends the cruciform shape of Cygnus. Such nomenclature has not worn well, perhaps because it has seemed inapt when applied to these pagan figures which for so many aeons before the coming of our Lord, nightly strode across the firmament.

There is a fitting simplicity about such names as 'King Charles's Wain,' and the 'Swan,' a simplicity perfectly in accord with the rough innocence of the people who are most apt to cast meditative eyes up towards them. How well Shakespeare understood this. We know few passages in his plays that seem better to express the very essence of his homespun imagination, at once natural and philosophic, than the one wherein he describes the drowsy ostler of the old Rochester hostel looking up from the cold, cobbled courtyard, to tell the time by the position of the Great Bear.

> *Heigh-ho! an' it be not four by the day, I'll be hanged!*
> *Charles's Wain is over the new chimney, and yet our horse is not packed.*

To know the constellations is no hard matter, and yet in these latter days many of us remain quite content to let them pass aloft, above the towers of our cities, unheeded. We are content to go down into the grave in vulgar ignorance of these stellar forms which with their deep eternal calm have performed their functions from the earliest times, and will continue to do so long after the nimble little brain of man has passed for ever from the scope of their 'sweet influence.' Not to know Sirius or Procyon or Altair, not to recognize the great Square of Pegasus, is a sad loss, especially since it is no trouble to know them, but not to be familar with the splendour and magnificence of the giant Orion as he rises in all his strength over the wintry horizon, is nothing short of misfortune. How restorative, how wonderful it is to catch a glimpse of such a nebula as Coma Berenices, in its enviable remoteness, as we pace the strident street of some modern town! 'The hair of Bernice' owes its name to the ingenious resourcefulness of a certain Egyptian astronomer who mollified the wrath of Ptolemy for the theft of his wife's hair—which had been placed in a temple as a sacrifice to the gods for his safe return from warring with the

Assyrians—by declaring that it had been transported into heaven. Indeed the study of the stars offers an infinite field for such quaint historic recollections; much lively romance being concealed, if we but knew it, in the delicate web of golden light that each night is stretched across the sky. An interesting example is seen in the presumptuous audacity of the old royalist astronomer who at the time of the Restoration in England, asserted roundly that 'Cor Caroli' had appeared in the heavens to denote that the Almighty shared with the English shires their boisterous enthusiasm at the return of Charles Stuart.

To those of us who are given to wandering, there is something full of reassurance in seeing always above us the same well-known constellations. It is certainly with a curious sense of planetary security—as if we were still home, so to speak, on the grain-bearing earth, however far we might journey—that we recognize above the eucalyptus trees which fringe the Sausalito downs over against San Francisco, the identical celestial shapes that we have so often observed reflected in the great central lakes of tropical Africa. What mattered it that the foundering and snorting of hippopotami along the rush-grown stretches of Lake Elmenteita gave place in California to the splash and croak of frogs on the cold fern-sheltered pools? Far up in the uncircumscribed darkness the Pleiades in all their chaste loveliness were still there. How well, too, the natives in those far-off countries know the stars! The aboriginal bushmen in Australia, time out of mind, have called Corona 'Womera,' or the boomerang. How many passengers travelling by night on a Fifth Avenue 'bus look with as much intelligence at that sparkling coronet?

Blind we live and blind we die, scarcely having wit enough in our feckless crania to raise our eyes towards that infinity which forms the background to our pretty and trivial employments. We may make, I suppose, one exception, for it is probable that even the most earth-bound of us, high-brows and bone-heads alike, can scarcely be altogether oblivious of the appearance and occultation of that stupendous star of stars, the sun itself, whose emphatic glance brought us into existence and still sustains our life, and at whose gleaming runaway heels, whether we will or no, we are carried forward through unexplored space at so headlong and incredible a speed.

From *Honey and Gall* (1924)

THE POETIC FAITH

What could be more extravagant than the various religious notions that have got into our heads? They can each one of them be discounted. They are all utterly false—chimeras, delusions, dreams. The actual movements of matter, secret and indefatigable, have no concern in them. In the outer spaces cosmic adjustments are consummated in all their perfection, beyond and apart from man's mind. The indifferent dance of our solar system would continue unchanged were there no erect glass-eyed mammals intent to watch. If there were no living men abroad upon the lucky fields of earth, yet would the snow still fall after its lovely fashion of wavering uncertainty; yet would red fire still burn, and water still gather to its level.

To understand the true rhythm of life, so beautiful, so heartless, it is necessary to accept with conviction the accidental irrelevance of our kind in such an astral pasture of cold energy. The mind is the apex point of all our senses. Without our senses it could have no existence. Just as a large garden poppy opens the glory of its scarlet petals, blotched with black, to the June sun, so we in our hour expand our consciousness in trembling reciprocity to the wonder of existence, and fade as soon. Yet we cannot, we will not, be content. With fretful minds we grudge at the mystery, striving with pitiful expedients to subordinate an Absolute, unpartisan and withdrawn, to our own advantage. Our religions, our metaphysical systems, are all of them projections of our misdoubts, of our deepest instinctive wishes. It is impossible for us to regard our predicament objectively, and it is for this very reason that such fantasies as the Christian religion thrive.

Yesterday I sat talking with a farmer's wife in Owermoigne, and as I looked out of her parlour window at the village street I understood well enough the terms of life. There in the churchyard lay my old friend, Tom Baxter, never again to snare a rabbit or mark upon a downland path the blackberry droppings of a badger. Not far from him, deep buried, was the body of the boy who shot

himself last autumn, pushing down the trigger of his gun with a
forked elder stick; and close to his mould the gravestone of a girl,
dead now sixty years, who was drowned in Ringstead Bay as she
was rowing back from Weymouth, her wedding dress in the bow
of the fishing boat. Through the parlour window I could see a man
cutting down the leaning grass of the village hedgerow and a hay-
maker bringing in his horses. Observing their preoccupations,
their entire absorption in the activities of a common day, I could
hear the long, deep sound of the wave of oblivion bringing forget-
fulness to all that lived.

It is a mistake to imagine that religions spring up to offer a wider
scope to any form of contemplative consciousness. This is not
so. They exist in order that men and women may employ themselves in the ordinary affairs of life undistracted by the awful
mysteries that encircle their foreheads and lie like dangerous
radium below their homely shoeleather. Religions offer a refuge
from thought, and it is for this very reason that they have been so
damaging to human happiness. Deep in the hearts of all men and
of all women is lodged a suspicion of their falsity, and it is because
of this that they have always been defended with such ferocious
intolerance. Insecurity breeds anger. It is when we are in doubt
that we show emotion.

'Out of Egypt have I called my son.' So besotted have we
become with the legacy of Egyptian priestcraft as represented by
present-day Christianity that it is difficult for many of us to understand that there is no truth in any religion depending upon the
supernatural. Such religions are the hearsay of barbarism, rumours
of rumours handed down to us from the earliest times—from the
times of the Neanderthal man perhaps, when first his brow above
his famous orbital ridge became corrugated with confused trouble
over the unexplained sounds that he heard, over the dreams that
he had, and over the obscure dread he felt that some dead man
should become again ambulant among forest shadows. The
ancients were right; it is fear that first gave birth to religion. It is
fear that has given such pernicious power to the priests. It would
seem that the simple message of the sun is too strong for us
unless it comes through the veil of a temple, prosperous and occult.

Yet how exciting, how dramatic to envisage life upon earth
at its lowest terms, to recognize the intellectual and spiritual subterfuges of our race, as subterfuges and nothing more. Here is an

incredible tale to meditate upon; a tale full of exultation, yet blessed with the heartbreaking tenderness of human tears; a tale that has in it the passion of a keeper boy, who, for the sake of love, presses down the trigger of a shot-gun with a forked elder twig cut from a churchyard hedge.

Christianity teaches us to despise life. Say what its adherents will, the earliest central doctrines of this morbid faith are all of them associated with a subtle attempt to disparage the visible world that we know.

Let us not lend our ears to such talk. It is refuted every hour. Walk by the seashore, observe how the spray-splashed rocks gleam and the cool green samphire shines against the white chalk. You will never, never open your eyes upon so unsurpassed a vision again. Lie flat on your belly on the high downs; listen to the wind whispering over your bones. You will never hear again so plaintive a breath, nor see again a beauty more fragile and profuse, as the dew-drops show on the bright downland flowers, hidden an inch high among the grass. Our fairy-land actually exists upon this Middle Earth. Here is our lane of ferns, here our circle of enchanted stones.

When one thinks of our modern churches with their godly smell, with their punctilious decorations, with their masquerading priests—priests of a made-up religion ever fearful of honest words spoken out from the heart with sincerity, it is impossible not to feel ashamed. These new altars are not even in the open air. They are under cover, altars of pretence.

Oh, let us get out beneath the cloud-driven sky; let us hear the sound of the free sea; let us stand to pray godless prayers before summer vegetation, growing up by summer streams. Let us fly; let us escape so we get well out of earshot of such shifty and ignominious mumblings. This is a neurosis alien to life. There is something wrong here. It is, if I may be allowed to use an objectionable word favoured by the 'pure in heart'—'unwholesome.' It is the plaint of a people whose spirits have been broken. It is the ingratiating whining of pet dogs in the presence of the hand that strikes them. There is no good reason why men should kneel to worship in these dim habitations of necromancy shut in from the sunshine of the day. Is it the rotting bones lying so close under the flags of the aisle that drew them to it? Has it always been the presence of this whoreson terror that has caused the sons of men to look *outside of nature* for salvation? What the generations have wanted is a sense of safety in eternity so that they could pursue their daily occupations without fear. Ever since man learned to till the fields, to domesticate animals, to weave, to employ himself with ceramic arts, the possessive impulse has gained more and more in strength. It has become the most important purpose of life, and this has been the chiefest cause of our misery. More than ever to-day the true purpose of life is in danger of being forgotten.

The true purpose of life is personal happiness. It is a state that can be entirely independent of any external accessories. Good governments, instead of devoting their energies towards designs of imperial pomp, should concentrate their attention upon organizing their commonwealths so that each individual should be free to develop to the uttermost the inner springs of his nature as revealed to him by the senses. It is greed and gluttony—it is the itch to get —that is our damnation. Oh! but how dull our palates are to the wine of life! To dip our hands into the salt sea is nothing to us; nothing to walk at the hour before dawn over curved hills. Swift, wayward, never-returning moments of contemplative rapture we have come to prize no longer.

To make matters worse, those in authority, people for the most part too mean-spirited to think of anything beyond worldly affairs, have managed, with the help of their accomplices the priests, to inject into our consciousness the suspicion that simple happiness derived from the indulgence of the senses is wrong. In this way the very living waters of life have become soured. It is for this reason that the delights of the body have been so degraded that emotions of sex springing fresh and fair in the hearts of boys and girls, as brown sprouting bracken fronds shoot up in a wood, have been driven to find sorry expression in covert pornography.

It should be an open secret that all ethical imperatives are man-made. They represent tentative human methods of organizing with propriety human groups and assemblies. Their roots are not in nature. No more should be required of anybody than an acknowledgement that to have senses is to have rights, and this tentative assumption has been strengthened by the necessity of curbing the ferocity of the individual for the sake of the horde. The knowledge of it is in our heads and in our hearts, and the conduct of every well-descended spirit, however profane his detachment, is regulated as far as his nature allows by the acceptance of the belief that happiness cannot be had at the cost of the unhappiness of others. We believe that the only sin is cruelty. Yet even against cruelty there is in the universe no arbitrary absolute *law as from the Gods*. There is no pity in the clouds, and if we do make concessions to this discipline of grace we can justify our purpose with no better foundation than with such airy words as taste, sensibility, and love. Below the feet of every living spirit there is always the cold impassive indifference of nature. It is childish to persuade ourselves otherwise. The motive of a generous action is entirely fortuitous. To retard in any way the unfolding of so rare and irrational an attitude would be to offend against the most secret destiny of our race. We may boldly challenge or slyly deceive every regulation of the conventional world, but wilfully to torture a man, a beast, a bird, a fish—nay, an insect—is truly to blaspheme against the very life-illusion of our kind.

How does it come about that under modern conditions the majority of men and women are so unhappy? Walk along any street in an industrial centre, and how pinched and peevish are the faces one sees! These people are like ill-tempered mules with galled withers. They are being given stones instead of bread. They are taught by those in authority that the purpose of life lies in a fretful utilitarian activity, with a half-satisfied acquisitive instinct as its high reward. Ignorant though they are as to what is taking place their very natures rebel, and upon their clouded forehead is the protest registered.

The conditions of a man's happiness are circumscribed by the senses only. His love for another has its sole existence in the rush of the blood through his veins and the quivering of his navel. No possessions of the objective world beyond food and drink and raiment are essential to his own spiritual life-ecstasy in his moment of time. The senses, the senses, the senses—hold to the senses. They alone will not betray us. The careless prodigal impressions they transmit present the nearest approach to an absolute reality that we shall ever know. And it is through the senses that we become initiated into the deepest secret of all—the secret that recognizes a poetic vision of life as the highest guerdon of each passionate intellectual spirit.

With each one of us it is the simple poetry of our hours, with their joys and their sorrows, that will count at the last. It is through an ardent allegiance to the leap of life, and through such secret moments of heightened awareness, as when alone upstairs we stand to watch the curtains of some summer bedroom move backwards and forwards in the breeze of a garden twilight, that we can realize our gratitude for having been allowed to breathe at all in these coasts of light. The more we overcome our congenital apathy, our lumpish disposition to take for granted the deep mystery of existence, the more do we fulfil the design of being alive.

Not only should our poetic vision irradiate each scattered moment of our own days, taking every single leaf, every single grass blade, as a symbol of an utter mystery; not only should we surround those we love with a religious concentration, counting, as it were, the miraculous beating of their hearts, and treasuring, as though for a basil in a flower-pot, the morsels of earth mould that have ever felt their tread; but also we must accustom ourselves to contemplate the whole long drama of the earth's history in this way—the cataclysmic conflagrations that begot our solar system, the unexplained movement of life, the triumph of man with his mystical yearnings in a godless universe, the pathetic, ironic, tragic delusion of Christianity with its moving appeal so expeditiously subverted by the rude promptings of nature into arbitrary self-interested ecclesiastical tyrannies.

The ultimate justification of life in earth, air, and water is to be found always in the simple primeval happiness of the immediate experience of being alive. It is this very experience that we hold cheap in these depraved modern times. We have forgotten how to respond to the poetry of life. The hollow, tinkling façade of life put up by noisy and trivial people stands between us and our deepest wealth. We give scant heed to the earth murmur, to the sound of the sea breaking against solid land, to the sound of wind passing over corn, to the sound of rain upon a roof, to the sound of fire burning. We look at the coulter of a plough, and no race memory stirs in our hearts; a shoal of fish darting through clear water is to us no exceptional glimpse. There is nothing extra-ordinary in the light from the sun touching a girl's wrist; nothing uncommon in seeing moonlight on the flesh of her hand as she gathers her frock about her out of the dew. Yet the very substance of happiness, the delicate hoar frost of happiness, is made up of nothing more stable than an intense awareness of such things.

The reality of such happiness, the reality of this heightened awareness, descends upon our spirits like small rain, like sunlight through the veined leaves of a forest of enchantment; and it is in its presence that our poor lost souls, faithful still through lonely betrayals, touch for a moment the linnet wings of the eternal.

From *Damnable Opinions* (1935).

Two passages from

IMPASSIONED CLAY

II

I APPEAL to youth, to boys and girls with senses uncorrupted, with senses fair and fresh. Do not be deceived, do not listen to the foolish talk of envious old women and of fearful, defeated old men. The days of your youth are yours, the hours of your youth are yours, so few, so few. 'For our life has not now any place for irrational belief and groundless imaginings, but we must live free from trouble.' With concentrated purpose follow the deepest inclinations of your being, and snatch, snatch at happiness with passionate eagerness. Do not be satisfied with any vulgar or sordid existence. As Bertrand Russell has said, 'Freedom consists in realizing the extent to which we are governed by forces other than ourselves.' It is better to live recklessly and dangerously and even disastrously than not to live at all. Remember that all who surround you are conspiring to subject your own imperious actions to their own convenience. Awake, open wide your entranced eyes. Let your limbs be fleet and your silver spears of joy never far from your hands. Many a boy and many a girl have had their lives stolen away by the slow poison of words, and, with precept upon precept, here a little and there a little, have had their cheeks against the cold clay of the grave before ever they have lived. 'I spit upon virtue and its empty admirers when it gives no happiness.' We must be understanding and with expedition free our minds from these stifling mists of traditional beliefs to which each one of us is exposed from the day of his birth. Much of the misery of the world is sustained by canting talk, enormous villainies by the preachers. Have a care, you have only one life, one little life. It is yours, entirely yours, to spend as you like.

The fact is we are too fearful, we too easily submit to pressure. 'It is an evil thing to live in necessity, but there is no necessity to live in necessity.' If that station of life 'to which it has pleased

God to call you' is not to your liking, escape from it, get up from your desk, walk away whistling. Alter your manner of life ten times if you wish. What deters you—worldly ambition? Look well at the ambitious, the time-servers. We see them today as Lucretius saw them of old, 'sweating out their life-blood, worn away to no purpose, battling their way along the narrow path of ambition; inasmuch as their wisdom is but from the lips of others, and they seek rather through hearsay than from their own feelings, and that is of no more avail now nor shall be hereafter than it was of old.' Escape, escape, escape, it is better to be a free footpad than to lose your precious hours without reward. With Epicurus let us 'give thanks to Nature the blessed, because she hath made necessary things easy to be obtained while things hard to be obtained are not necessary.' A great deal can be done if one has the spirit. No man or woman has the right to be unhappy except it be from a tormenting sickness. If you are unhappy find out the cause and in God's name remedy it. The greatest freedom and the greatest control are both required. To live wisely we must emulate, not only the abundance of Nature, but her severity as well. Of whom are you afraid—your neighbours? They are nothing more than a flock of silly sheep shut in on a patch of half-rotten turnips by a few wattled hurdles that the grey backside of any modest donkey can push over. 'Yea, but I am ashamed, disgraced, dishonoured, degraded, exploded: my notorious crimes and villainies are come to light, my filthy lust, abominable oppression, and avarice lies open, my good name's lost, my fortune's gone. I have been stigmatized, whipped at post, arraigned and condemned. I am a common obloquy, I have lost my ears, odious, execrable, abhorred of God and men. Be content, 'tis but a nine days wonder, and as one sorrow drives out another, one passion another, one cloud another, one rumour is expelled by another, every day almost come new news . . . thy father's dead, thy brother robbed, wife runs mad, neighbour hath killed himself; 'tis heavy, ghastly, fearful news at first, in every man's mouth, table talk; but after a while who speaks or thinks of it? It will be so with this and thine offence, it will be forgotten in an instant, be it theft, rape, sodomy, murder, incest, treason. . . .'

We used to be told that it was our duty to conduct ourselves in this or that way because we feared God. There is no good reasoning in this. Reality is from first to last dependent upon man's sensations. All ethical considerations are man-made, and ultimately rest upon some civil convention rather than upon Nature. It is the first principle in a good life for a man, woman, or child to be happy; and to be happy, mark you, is to do the will of God. Make no doubt of it, to have had an unhappy life is to have failed in life. It is the one consummate error, and around the death-bed of such a one the very angels weep.

Leave all free. It should be an open secret that nothing really matters, that once in a graveyard all is at quits. When the death-agony is once over, the illusion of the world, the dream of the world that the skull of the dead man so lately entertained, has entirely and utterly vanished. To believe otherwise is to believe a vanity. The wicked apprentice who squandered all in riotous living was justified if that was the way in his opinion to spend his life best. I remember a harlot I was with as a boy saying as she turned her head upon the pillow, 'I believe in a short life and a merry one,' and I daresay according to her nature the generous creature was correct in directing her life to so simple a tune. To drink yourself to death because it is your chosen manner of enjoying yourself is a perfectly rational procedure. There are many worse graves than a drunkard's grave. The pox? You got it, I trow, in a good cause. You are a victim by chance, by your temperament, of unending days of misery? Very well. 'Why dost thou not retire like a guest sated with the banquet of life, and with calm mind embrace, thou fool, a rest that knows no care?' Cultivate always understanding and more understanding. 'Life offers most to one who, though he never denies himself a pleasure, at every moment continues master of himself and of circumstances.'

It is the ethical people who blaspheme the worshipful sun with their timidities. This November day I walked home through the wintry woods, through woods that are wintry as only American woods can be, the bare bones of the earth showing up between the naked tree-trunks, and I saw the sun going down with detached sobriety in all the glory of his round red form. Through the illumined floating cloud-mists of the heavens the planet was visibly turning, the disobedient and forgotten planet whose trowel-deep soil has brought such wonders to birth and spread over her fair surface so incomparable a burden of many-imaged life. Consider it, consider it, consider the plumage of the jay; the scales of gold on the back of the little fish in a glass bowl; the mouse in the cup-board, with bright pin eyes, dainty fore-paws, and elegant tail; the bee-orchis in her June perfection; and there below the painted clouds, man, man walking erect through the hardhack scrub, man with his frantic skeleton surmounted with a skull thick as a pot, and still under provocation given to war, with his slippery eyes full of ferocity.

Yet there have been found many to distrust this word happiness, which by its derivation is so fittingly to be associated with the word chance. This mistrust is no worthy mistrust. Surely happiness can be won against odds if we possess wisdom and imagination and a passionate unregenerate allegiance to the leap of life.

Of all the enemies of human happiness none is so destructive, none of so cursed and forward a disposition, as is Death. Oh, how to be abhorred! All though our lives, taking one here and another there with his startling unexpected strokes. When least we look for him, there he is at our elbow, selecting us alone among so many, as a black dog might, let loose in Manchester and not content until he is upon us, all unaware and at our ease in a yellow cornfield. Though death is our common lot, his malevolence is apparent. When he has us then only have we lost all. It would indeed seem a thankless task to those who are fully alive to his intention, who comprehend without mitigating hope his shocking plan, to find any rewarding circumstance in his terrifying and ubiquitous presence. Yet as he is abroad and likely enough to enter any door left ajar, it may be wise to say what can be said in his favour. While he is still upon the open road, crookedly leaning against a weathered sign-post, while he is still in the winter woods, or loitering by sea-coast fens, we may venture to speak out our word. We are by nature of so sottish a complexion that we require just such a marauder to be about in the night *to keep us awake*. It is the know-ledge of death that gives an especial tang to the taste of life. Death may be regarded as a scurvy condiment of excellent service as long as our reins are sound. He is the sour vinegar to our dish. If we did not know our days were numbered, then the water that we drink and the bread that we eat would lose something of their flavour. It is because we know that we must die that we can watch each dawn spread its light over the face of the earth with so deep a satisfaction. With such a shadow across our counterpane the most lethargic of us welcomes the light of day; under the menace of such a threat our quick senses shiver with incredible reciprocities to the visible world. When we walk through fields of yellow flowers, when we tread over the shining pavements of the world's great cities, when we look into the eyes of those we love and take note of their steadfast gentleness, the presence of death's face over our shoulders causes us to tremble with new trembling, a new tenderness. It would not be so if life were rid of this treachery. Impermanence is beauty's attribute and the attribute of our rarest emotions. Yet because nature has included anything as lovely and as unlikely as human tears for the mitigation of the earth's rudeness, there is no reason for ingrate reproaches. Sorrow is inherent in the hap of all human life. Every hour, every day, it is to be observed. This fact, however, should not deter us from our purpose. Life upon earth would be shallow and unredeemed indeed if it were not an affair to move our very bowels to pity. Without woe there could be no cry of exultation. It is a rhythm sorrowful and sublime. The possibilities of life are infinite. We enter its garden to play with no harlot, but with a child as sad and sensitive as a murdered king's daughter, and always there is a feeling of rain upon the air.

For the rest, though we fear to think of our hemstitched shrouds, though we hesitate so much as to pick up a bone under a churchyard wall, though we would and we could fly to the ends of the world from this whoreson, let us take what comfort we may. Eighty generations have passed since the old school-teacher of Samos sat concealed in his little garden at Athens and wrote three hundred books, perhaps out of rage and ambitious envy of Plato, and yet the wisdom of his stout sentence still holds. 'That as before we were capable of sense, it was not grievous to us to have no sense; so likewise when we shall have lost it, we shall not be troubled at the want of it as when when we are asleep we are not concerned because we are not awake; so when we shall be dead, it will not trouble us that we are not living. . . . Death which is said to be an evil, hath this belonging to it, that when it hath been present, it hath never troubled anybody. . . . Death is nothing to us; for that which is dissolved is without sensation; and that which lacks sensation is nothing to us.'

We must courageously face the fact that there is no pity in the clouds, and that the law of the universe is one of indifference to our lot. We are taken from our mother's womb scot-free of supernatural observation, and we are buried under the same enfranchisement. All this talk of a stream of righteousness not ourselves has no foundation in good sense. It was invented to contribute to man's self-importance and is repeated in season and out of season for the same purpose. What the generations do is of no significance whatever; what each individual does in his life of no lasting consequence. We are free men; and if we conduct ourselves with propriety, with generosity, it is our own affair, and done at the bidding of no categorical imperative. All ethical codes have arisen out of man's attempt to subject the errant, truculent, individual will to the discipline of society. All cultures, all civilizations, are sustained by this agreed-upon interference. They did not grow up naturally. They do not accord with our instinctive life. They represent an intellectual effort to relegate what is stiff-necked and wilful. The burden of some of these restrictive disciplines has been hard to bear, and to many the sacrifice required has seemed to be too great. Why should harmless gratifications be forbidden when the only purpose of life is to live and to live as richly as possible? 'An excess of social control results in interfering unduly with the spontaneous expression of human nature, which is civilization.' These sacrifices that we are asked to make have no sanction that could be called absolute, they merely represent certain arrangements necessary for human comity. 'The individual retains his freedom by a compact, and for his own sake respects his neighbours.' To a degree we are now dependent upon the rulings of tradition and our nation's laws; and it becomes all well-descended spirits to give a kind of deference to them, remembering always, however, the artificiality of their origin. What concessions we make to the morality of our time should be pressed in just here, should have a small but acknowledged place, a matter merely of upbringing and discretion. Our personal conduct should principally be regulated by the natural response of our being to each situation as it arises. Every action of ours should be directed by one aim, the happiness that will result from it. Imaginative sympathy is sufficient as our guide. These herd-inhibitions that hedge about conventional people are as often as not mean and harmful. 'A wise man is he who has acquired the habit of wise action.' Many of these moralities are the products of a rude experience out of an age that is past.

'Custom does not breed understanding, but takes its place, teaching people to make their way contentedly through the world without knowing what the world is, nor what they think of it, nor what they are.' Often, if carefully examined, the roots of these ethical exactions are found to be deep-set in a very gross mud, are found to be derived from an imprudent desire to preserve at too great cost the semblance of a stability in an existence where all is flowing away, where there can be no stay to that 'precipitate sinking of things into the past.'

Let us once again repeat the actual truth of the case, that hopeless, dangerous truth which the human race is everywhere, and at all times, so reluctant to acknowledge. All religions, all metaphysical systems, all cogging theories of life that claim for human polity any foundation outside the ramparts of the visible world, are the veriest counterfeits. They are the sea-frit, the flying foam blown hither and thither over the face of a salt, unplumbed ocean. They are believed to-day and disbelieved to-morrow, they are here to-day and gone to-morrow. Only the dark, strongly moving gulf-stream of our instinctive emotions remains unaltered. It is the satiety or hunger of our sexual life, that has been the cause of the uprising of these strange creations of the human mind. The scarcity of corn-grains will alter them. They can be just as easily adapted to suit the victorious as to suit the vanquished, will take themselves any colour, like cloud-shadows on the waters of Weymouth Bay.

As a spider suspends herself by ropes from her own body, so the human race has created out of its head imaginary meshes that through a kind of hallucination of mass-faith acquire the appearance of substance. With these bonds of illusion we bind our natures. Except in times of war, in times of famine, they serve well enough. Every day, every year, we are entangled in these ghostly nets of finest mesh. Our nurses and our mothers show them to us. We grow up to know them as real, for do not all people see them plainly? Now, no real lover of life is deeply concerned with the stability of society, or with the stability of property. It is reassuring to live in countries where such advantages exist, but we would also be happy with savages in wild woods. Italy or Soviet Russia, it is all one to us as long as we can eat the bread of life and drink the wine of life and love and be loved. These are the things that really matter. To live happy in the sunlight without thought of material advantage or personal ambition, content with existence on its lowest terms, content to see the earth solid and actual about us, and to know that we are alive! alive! alive! More scrupulous than the common people in not adding to the sum of the world's misery, we can then live like Gods, free of care.

From *Impassioned Clay* (1931).

THE COUNTRYSIDE

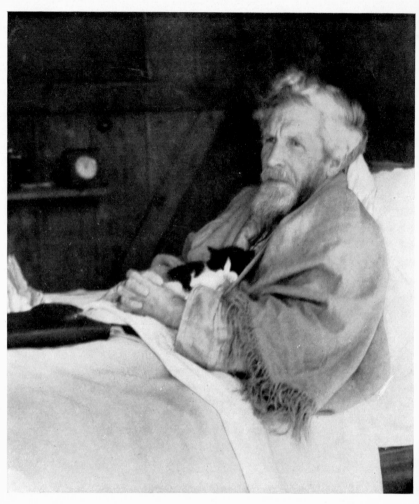

A photograph of Llewelyn Powys in his shelter at Chydyok during his illness in 1935, taken by Professor R. H. Mottram.

STALBRIDGE RECTORY

I REMEMBER once at Montacute asking my father many questions about his boyhood at Stalbridge. From my earliest childhood every scrap of information about my grandfather or about my father's life at Stalbridge had been cherished by me. The mere mention of the name of the stately old Dorset market-town had the power of stirring my imagination. My grandfather, who was born in the eighteenth century, only six years after the death of Dr. Johnson, held the living of Stalbridge from 1837 to 1867, and was buried in the churchyard there at the age of eighty, the same age reached by my father who died in 1923.

With the burial of my father in the Montacute Churchyard it seemed that the family memories of Stalbridge must be for ever at an end. This has proved far from the truth. Recently I happened to meet a native of Stalbridge, Mr. Henry Habershon, whose passion for the village and all that is connected with it, amounts to an obsession. I have never known anyone with such an infatuation for the place of his birth, anyone who husbands with such tenacity, with such depth of emotion, his long, long memories. The trees, the very stones of Stalbridge are sacred to him. As my grandfather was the Rector of his natal village for the first quarter of Mr. Habershon's life the Powys family is closely associated with his youthful illusions. Here therefore against all chance I had discovered someone who preserved in his melancholy head an inexhaustible store of ancient rememberances, capable of being transmitted to me as clear as if they had happened yesterday. He described to me my grandfather's carriage, recollecting even the precise livery of his postilion, so that I was able to see as plain as in an old print the coach starting away from the Rectory gate for my grandmother to take the air through Marnhull, 'passing by little Charley's favourite oak-tree,' or for her to pay a call on Mrs. Yeatman at Stock House. From an absolute oblivion he could snatch back the very name of my grandfather's dog, and tell me how when he barked the echo could be heard by those walking in the street. He told of meeting my father and my Uncle

Littleton one winter on the Sherborne Road 'beating the snow off the high hedges with their sticks,' and this casual reference, dropped without premeditation, seemed to give me a glimpse of my father's boyhood as though I myself had witnessed the incident with my own eyes, so convincing in its naturalness, and yet so difficult to connect with the dignity of my father's later years. He told of how my uncle challenged 'the worse poacher in Stalbridge' to a boxing match behind the tall wall of the Rectory garden, and how the men were astonished at the number of rounds and the amount of punishment that my uncle, a mere youth, had taken, and how when in the end he was 'knocked out,' Mr. Habershon, who was bringing water from a near-by cattle trough, heard him say: 'Don't let the old man know.' In a letter to me this survivor from early Victorian times records the first occasion that he ever saw my father and uncle, and for me, a man of fifty, this recollection seems to penetrate into a past age beyond calculation.

'The first time I can remember of seeing the two young gentlemen was when I was a small lad going past the old Cross I looked up Gold Street and I saw a large donkey with panniers on its back and one young gentleman in each and a man in charge, Sam Shepherd, who was living then in one of the Powys cottages on the top of Gold Street known as the Knap in those days.'

I came upon a reference to this very donkey—under what exact parcel of Stalbridge turf are its long bones even now turning to dust?—in one of my grandmother's note-books, describing how my uncle when he was still unable to speak, would pull at his own baby ears so as to emphasise to my grandmother his satisfaction in the exaggerated length of those of the tall beast. She tells too with pride how my uncle before he was twelve months old would recognise my grandfather's step coming down the fine old staircase of Stalbridge Rectory, and would cry out: 'Papa! Papa!'

Among some old family letters I came upon one from Dr. Harper, the celebrated headmaster of Sherborne, the moral tone of which, as much in advance of his age, matches some of Dr. Arnold's communications.

King's School,
Sherborne.

My dear Sir,   *May 10th*

I am always at home of sheer necessity, and it is part and parcel of my daily work to talk over such matters as those now concerning your boy. I am very sorry that he has chosen the army. I am always sorry for every boy who does so, not only because it is no profession in reality but also because of the temptations into which he is so thrust. However, in many points your lad is fit for a soldier and will be a straightforward brave fellow under any circumstances. . . .

 I am, dear Sir,

  Yours Sincerely,

           H. D. Harper.

It interests me to remember that while my grandfather was at Stalbridge, Lord Sidney Godolphin Osborne, whose character I so much admire, was the Rector of Durweston further down the Stour. There could scarcely have been two men more different. In spite of his academic honours, for he won 'a first' in both the classical and the mathematical tripos at Cambridge, my grandfather had an extremely simple nature, and I do not suppose ever had the slightest misgivings on the score of the social injustices of his period. Along with most of his contemporaries he seems to have taken the existing order of things as inevitable. He was, however, of a generous nature and gave a great deal of money away, never, so one old village woman told me, stepping out of the Rectory gate without a purse full of half-crowns to meet any unexpected call upon his charity.

While on a visit to London he met some of his Cambridge friends on their way to present a University address to the young Queen. He hired appropriate robes and went with them to the palace.

We went to Buckingham House about two o'clock and were in due time ushered into the Throne Room, where sat Victoria having at the left hand Prince Albert with divers other notables. I was fortunate enough to get a good place and saw the Queen and Prince well. The Prince is good looking much like an English gentleman, as for her Majesty, I cannot say that her personal appearance is very engaging or imposing, but Pipsey will utter one of her indignant *grunts*, if I speak with less admiration than she deems fitting. The Duchess of Sunderland sat apart, retired, and looked a Queen, aye, every inch a Queen.

The Ministers of State were present and on the whole it was very well to have for once been present at such a Spectacle. The Yeomen of the Guard and Beefeaters in the ancient costume were arranged in a picturesque manner in the Halls and on the staircases. The rush of the carriages was most awful, and the pressure through the gateways quite dangerous, reminding me forcibly of the contending crowds in my Proctorial Days at Cambridge.

I suppose I shall stay to Friday and shall hope to find my way back to the good old Rectory by dinner time.

I am your most attached and affectionate

L. C. Powys.

On the occasion of my father taking his honours degree, he wrote:

My dear Charley,

As the intoxication of success has now subsided a little, you can perhaps bear with the humble congratulations of the Old Folks. We are both very thankful to see you in so respectable a place in the Honours and we doubt not that this will be the beginning of a happy and prosperous career. . . . Littleton crosses to Ireland this evening from Plymouth. He takes with him the brown mare, by way of shewing her a little of the world. . . . I hope your purse held out against the University fees. I shall soon expect a letter from Mr. Perowne—

Ever your affectionate father,

L. C. Powys.

But there are more intimate scripts that used to be preserved in the tall study desk at which it was my father's custom to stand when he composed his sermons, and these writings show clearly that my grandfather possessed a deeply religious mind. All through his long life he never for one single moment doubted that he was under the care of an attentive deity. As a young man he had a bad fall from his horse at his home at Achurch in Northamptonshire and he puts on record his gratitude for his escape. Again as a man of forty, when he was a Fellow of Corpus, he had a serious misadventure. Sitting in his spacious rooms in the Old Court of the College—rooms which in my time were used by the present Bishop of Derby—he makes this entry:

Another providential interposition. Much bruised by the wheel of my gig crushing me against the wall but thro' Mercy not materially injured. While I live will I praise the Lord. May I have grace to use the life which Thou so frequently preserves to My Glory in Christ Jesus.

Lastly at Stalbridge in the cold winter of 1864 he mentions falling outside the house of a certain Mr. Lewis, and inscribes these words at the end of the old service book that he used all through his life:

Jan. 20. Thrown down heavily on Pavement and stone step at Mr. Lewis but providentially preserved from serious injury; all thanks and praise to Him who watches over His servant both in body and soul. He keepeth all our Bones so that Not one of them is broken.

To my mind, however, the most interesting of my grandfather's papers is a small parchment on which in the year after the Battle of Waterloo, at the age of twenty-six, he makes a formal dedication of himself to the service of God. 'So that I may become a blessing to my generation,' is one of the simple phrases he uses. As a schoolboy at Winchester he had spent 'idle and unprofitable days,' and steadfastly resolves to live for God's glory rather than 'for my own selfish ease and gratification.'

This document, sealed with the Powys crest, seems to have represented in his mind a kind of testamentary declaration of the spiritual purpose which was moving him at that period in his career; and which, in truth, was to direct his life for more than fifty years still to come. To me the devout words on this faded paper, already one hundred and eighteen years old, seem infinitely affecting. It is as though I were permitted to look at, to handle even, the scroll that had served as my grandfather's passport across the Delectable Mountains to the very gates of the Celestial City!

In these days, when the hazard of life becomes every year more apparent, how restorative to take sanctuary in the sound pastures of such a village as was Stalbridge in Queen Victoria's reign, when, under the persuasive influence of age-long human usage, every cranny of life was well caulked with the honest clay of wont and habit and bright polished with the shining resin of an unquestioning Faith. Those long slow years knew no treachery. Clearly I can see them pass into eternity. I can see my aunt Philippa, my father's half-sister, the Pipsey of my grandfather's letter, at the age of eight holding in her nursery at Christmas time a reception for the 'poor old women of the village,' like a silver-slippered princess enjoying the pleasing sensation of presenting

each one of them with a new shilling out of her savings. I can
hear the footsteps of my grandfather punctually every autumn
evening going up the broad staircase, flat silver candlestick in
hand. I can hear my father's very voice calling to his brother
from those old rooms, and can see him in the pantaloon trousers
of the day bringing in the first primrose for my grandmother,
a service of grace which in after years he never failed to do for my
mother. I can see him running along through the hay-seed
meadows of midsummer to inspect his eel lines laid by the bank
of some dark pool of the Stour, careful not to disturb the corncrake on her nest. Where was there opportunity for treason in
such a life—son following father, son following father, in long
generations of easy circumstance, with the confidence of an
endless sequence of happy reunions beyond the grave? What
perfidy could there be in the agglomerate atomies that made up
the yellow and black stripes of the September wasp's abdomen as
it hovered with drowsy murmur over the last King William pear
at the bottom of the silver fruit basket? It was my grandfather's
habit in winter and summer to dine at three in the afternoon,
a custom he had retained from his bachelor days at Cambridge.

There were no misgivings, no uneasiness of conscience about
society as it had been ordered under Providence. Year after year
my grandmother continued to fill her precious albums with
spatterings of seaweed, with delicate paintings of spring flowers,
of sea-shells; never, however, forgetting to see that Maria, the
cook, put the tea-leaves that had been used in the beautiful
drawing-room teapot out upon the wooden settle beyond 'Dash's
kennel, so that poor people, by merely opening the back gate,
could fetch them away.'

In his old age at Weymouth when his mind was beginning to
fail my father one day mysteriously disappeared from his house.
My sister remembered afterwards that he had said good-bye to
her with unusual formality before setting out for his morning
walk. Actually he had gone to the Weymouth station, and
procuring a ticket to Templecombe, had walked from there to
Stalbridge presenting himself for tea in his old home where he was
entertained with courtesy by his host. He settled himself in the
parlour looking about him with a benevolent expression but spoke
no word. In the late evening, thanks to the efforts of the station
officials, news was telegraphed that an aged clergyman had been

sitting for several hours on the Templecombe platform. He seemed to be in no trouble, his mind quiet and at peace, a happy old man who knew he was lost, but who was content to wait in benign confidence for the moment when he would again be looked after, again be found—perhaps by his daughter, perhaps by his wife, perhaps by his mother. I have often speculated as to the exact nature of the impulse that prompted my father to undertake so unexpected an adventure. Did he simply wish to revive in his mind old memories of his childhood, to remind himself for the last time through the sense of sight, before he entered the realm of dust and darkness, of the exact look of the mulberry-tree, of the chestnut-tree whose every bough he knew from climbing them as a boy? Did he wish to see again where his baby garden had been at the end of the nut walk, with its well-watered mignonette and large grave-faced pansies purple and yellow? Or as he approached near and nearer into his power, had Death, like an enchanter, cast a glamour over my father's faltering imagination so that he really came to believe that he had only to go back to the house where he was born to be welcomed once more by his brother, by his mother, and by his father, past all expectation clothed again in the sweet flesh of life, united and happy in those dreaming rooms of the ancient Rectory of Stalbridge in Dorset?

From *Dorset Essays* (1935).

THE FIRST FALL OF SNOW

THERE is not one of us, I suppose, who does not experience a curious sensation of romantic interest at seeing each winter the first fall of snow. There is something about the appearance of these delicately congealed, feathery morsels descending so uncertainly, so lightly, from the sky that is ever provocative of attention. The most stolid citizen upon noticing white flakes on his sleeve is disposed to raise his eyes and for a moment at least to contemplate with a vague, uneasy interest the clouds above his head.

So must our ancestors have regarded the same phenomenon when, leaving the languid security of warmer regions, they wandered forth in the direction of the poles. For snow has ever about it a suggestion of those chilled, flattened acres where for centuries upon centuries black waters have been enclosed by measureless layers of ice.

Is it, after all, but an old race-memory astir in us still that causes us so inevitably, when we hear that it is snowing, to cross our fire-lit rooms and glance between the curtains out of the window? Do we retain in our round skulls, in our square skulls, in our narrow hatchet-shaped skulls certain subconscious recollections of the appalling struggles of our race in far-off glacial periods? Do we to this day, when these dainty fragments of frozen moisture float downwards between the high walls of our houses, become aware of an ancient menace?

Walter Pater used to mark with pleasure the faint reflected light that snow-covered lawns cast on the white ceiling of an interior; and which of us cannot remember our own amazement at waking up after a storm to find the familiar landscape outside completely transformed? What elation to walk along strange, muffled roads, under trees whose gaunt, naked branches are illuminate to their topmost twig in the bright, winter sunshine! On such occasions, if one wanders for a few steps into a forest, what a strange initiation one undergoes into the secrets of nature, into its faculty for negation, for complete rest! Mutely, patiently, the boughs of the green firs bear their burdens. A kind of majestic audience would seem to be in attendance. It is as though every upright piece of sentinel-timber were waiting, waiting for a voice to speak. How dare the irreverent squirrels emerge from their clefts even for a moment; how dare those sharp-eyed, thick-furred creatures mark with delicate filigree the crisp, unruffled surface of the forest floor? Even to pray were a desecration in such a place, a place articulate of timeless eternity, of ineffable, sublime cessation. Small wonder the tiny shoots that survive against all reason, still quick under fallen autumn leaves beneath the snow— small wonder they hesitate to disturb by the slightest pressure that august stillness.

The influence of snow has in it a magical quality that cannot be gainsaid; an influence entirely different from that of rain. In the tropics I have known what it is to see a parched and thirsty land awake to life at the beginning of the wet season. I have seen the buck come gambolling down to the valleys to nibble impatiently at the few first blades of green grass, have heard the winged fantastics that in Africa are called birds, fly screaming through the forest branches whose flat leaves are dripping with round drops of lukewarm moisture. I have felt the earth, our ancient mother earth, beneath my feet, tremble and quiver in an ecstasy of child-birth under the sweet persuasion of those torrential down-pourings; but never once did she attain to such mysterious power as when, at rest under a covering of snow, she lies with the appearance and potency of a sepultured goddess who is in truth dead and yet retains that upon her ivory forehead which is equivalent to immortality. How strangely children understand the enchantment of snow; watching with shining, excited eyes the dun clouds gathering about the distant horizons while the weather-vanes on housetop or shed-roof resolutely predict colder weather; realizing the latent power in those clouds so grim and solid, a power that can confound the best-laid plans of their elders, can choke the progress of enormous iron locomotives and set every township agog with spade, shovel, and steam-plough! And afterwards, from the nursery window, how delightful to watch it falling—like bees, we used to say—falling, falling, falling this way and that, wavering and uncertain as life itself!

Each winter what delight to snuff up through our nostrils the unexpected, unmistakable odour of snow! There is a fine privilege in that. For snow does smell. It is indeed odorific of the empyrean, of the actual tract of space across which we speed at the heels of the sun. Not only does it smell, but it can take to itself also a thousand incredible colours. It is a mistake to imagine that snow is always white. I have seen fields of it in the high Alps of the colour of a red rose-petal; and in the dark northern forests, where the wolves howl under the pines, its shadowy levels towards evening resemble stretches of charcoal. Thrust a stick deep into a snow-bank and one discovers to one's amazement that the interior of the aperture made is blue, is, in fact the precise colour of the inside of a wave as it stands, for a single second, motionless and curled before its final breaking into lineal froth against the wild sea-banks of pebble or sand.

But just as freshly fallen snow gives one the impression of absolute virginal purity more than anything in the world, so, after contact with the baser matter of the earth, does it seem to typify that which has been degraded. There are few things more depressing to look upon than a heap of soiled snow, several weeks old, banked up against the sidewalk. It is then, when one's eyes light upon scraps of human refuse projecting from the soiled mass, that one's imagination conceives with a shock the vision of the planet so radiant in itself being rapidly disfigured by the presence of an importunate, restless animal who, for all its upright stature and brave brainpan, is unseemly in its habits and continues with appalling thoroughness to litter the surface of its winged prison-house.

Small wonder that the great English poet in contemplating the birth of God upon our planet conceived it as having occurred when the wilful, unregenerate land was concealed as with a winding-sheet. It is with Christmas that most of us associate the curious, evasive beauty of this strange white substance. Nobody wishes the ground to be green at that hallowed time of the year. A uniform whiteness seems more in accord with that most daring of human fancies which represents to our reason the assumption that, in very fact, a divine messenger from the other side of the flaming ramparts did actually in the latter days become incarnate.

Previously unpublished in book form.

THE ROMANCE OF RIVERS

IT IS small wonder that the Greeks imagined every stream, every river, to have hidden in its recesses its own tutelary deities, for rivers quite apparently do possess separate and distinct atmospheres which often enough seem to take to themselves individual and personal tones.

What a sense of strength, for instance, of power, comes to us with our first glimpse of the Hudson! It is a river formidable, but at the same time adventurous and liberating, and as the sun goes down behind the jutting promontories of the Palisades, behind the Giant's Forehead and the Eagle Rock, one feels falling upon one, with the crying of the wild birds that haunt their frowning ledges, something of the spirit of those gallant pioneers who first, with tiller resolutely held, steered inland on its broad waters.

One gets a different impression from the vast winding rivers of the South. They do not inspire or invigorate; rather do they fill one with awe, lying with their irresistible volume stretched out across the States, unabashed, lethargic, self-confident. They are capable, on occasions, of inundating whole districts, of leaving little behind them but a sodden, desolate landscape of debris and stark trees garlanded with river-weeds. At other times, when they are content to be complacent, the tall corn sways with its heavy grain up to the very brinks, and, without fear or thought, Negroes gather in the fluffy cotton all day long about their sultry tributaries. Such rivers are like great, drowsy giants, sprawling upon their bellies asleep; and it is best when they do sleep.

Not so with the rivers of California. There is a peculiar gentleness about all streams that flow into the Pacific. How smoothly, how graciously the Sacramento offers its shining waters to the golden Bay of many Islands where the sea-lions sport, and where black cormorants, each evening, with yearning necks outstretched, fly past the white sentinel-house of the Golden Gate toward the open sea.

How infinitely pleasing also are those smaller streams, those diminutive water-courses, that wind down to the ocean from the soft, rounded hills of Marin county; streams which spring to a sparkling sunlit life in some cool ferny bed at the foot of Tamalpais and, after winding under oak and eucalyptus, soon find their way to the grey sands of the Pacific.

Of European rivers, perhaps the Rhine remains for Anglo-Saxons the most romantic. The Tagus is indeed lovely as it glides past the long yellow stretches which lie this side of Lisbon, but he who has seen the tumbling, slate-blue, swirling eddies of the great German water-way, even as far up as Basle, can never forget the peculiar thrill that comes with the memories of its vineyards and ivy-grown Gothic castles.

Fortunate is the man who lives to see the Nile. The human race has wandered far since it was first generated on those steaming mud flats filigreed so curiously by the feet of crocodile and the delicate pointed claws of the sacred ibis. The Ganges also has its peculiar fascination: the mist that rises from it in the hot noonday is like a priceless incense mingled with the breath of a myriad Oriental prayers.

Who is able to catch the mystery of the Amazon, with its fold upon fold of undulating tree-tops, its green heaped upon green over valley and mountain, and everywhere flocks of screaming birds whose plumage challenges the brilliance of the rainbow. But perhaps even more bizarre, even more ambiguously suggestive than any of these are the great rivers of Equatorial Africa. There is the Uasin-Nyro, whose thick, matted jungles are frequented only by black men, by the Wonderobo, alert and silent of foot, who, with their primitive weapons ready at hand, are ever on the lookout for food. Punctually each evening at six o'clock the sun goes down behind the waving red grass of the limitless veldt; and it is perhaps after this event that the Uasin-Nyro presents herself in all her original strangeness. Far off in the unsurveyed depths of the bamboo forests, elephants with flapping, extended ears trumpet shrilly to one another; rhinoceroses move silently about on their mysterious quests; and the hippotami, weary at length of their submerged life in the darkened pools, go grazing through the open glades, brushing away the dew from the quivering grasses with their round four-toed feet and enormous, bristling mouths. For countless centuries along these far, undisturbed stretches, water has given place to water, as the river rolled on toward a lukewarm ocean. Nightly since the world was created, its slippery drinking-places have quenched the thirst of how many zebra, of how many buck, and of how many flesh-eaters whose heavy jowls have turned its lapping ripples into eddies of black! It matters not whether the southern stars shine clear, or whether the night be murky with the clouds of the heavy rain, the Uasin-Nyro remains unperturbed, offering the beauty of its shimmering waters to fierce, furtive, unobservant eyes.

How different from this is the happy quietude and peace of the slow-moving West Country rivers of England! What ineffable heart's-ease comes to a traveller who finds himself once more near their banks! Well he knows that every summer-time for the last thousand years hay-makers have been busy in the rich pastures that lie between Ilchester and Longload, where the river Yeo laves the Saxon masonry of the old stone bridle-bridge that still stands some few miles of sweet meadow lands west of the Fosse way. How many generations of chub have been spawned here, and grown into great lubberly fish, how many generations of Kingfishers have been hatched here, and flashed under the alders, disturbed all their life long by no other sound than the whetting of a scythe or the purling of milk into a pail.

If there be anyone who has a mind to savour the homely old civilization of England, let him sit on the banks of the Yeo on a fair Easter morning when the forget-me-nots about him are bluer than the sky, and when, across the cowslip fields where the children laugh together in their Sunday frocks, comes the sound of bells 'knolling to church.' Even winter cannot make savage these happy acres. In January when the wild duck and snipe come down to the flooded fields and a certain melancholy seems to descend upon the bare hedges, the ribbed gates, and forsaken haystacks, one has but to catch a glimpse of a single, far, twinkling light in cottage or farm-house and the sadness has gone. Even to this day how mellow is the life lived by these simple people, as harmless and slow-moving as their own cider-coloured rivers. They go to market on Fridays, they mind their hedges and ditches, they feed their cattle as they stand in placid rows with shining chains round their necks; they have not so much as heard of Charing Cross, or Notre Dame, or the Woolworth Building.

But it is not only these delectable rivers of the old world that possess a romance associated with the life of the human race. Take the small boat that plies between Dobbs Ferry and Sneyden's Landing on some late autumn afternoon when the air is clear and crisp with frost, and then if you are long-sighted enough you will, perchance, looking downstream, beyond the ruddy sun-tanned features of the captain of the craft, be able to see some twenty miles away, on a silver horizon, rising tier upon tier like some fabulous Ilium, the 'topless towers' of New York. The whole city is so small that it could be hidden by the white wing of a passing seagull, but it is there none the less, rising in all its familiar grace by the side of the Hudson, as that majestic river sweeps on, past the docks and the Battery, to meet the salt waves of the Atlantic.

Previously unpublished in book form.

AN ALPINE WEDDING

THE marriage ceremonies of every country provoke interest. Next to birth and death the consummation of love between a man and a woman is the most important event of human life. It fascinated me in Africa to observe the various customs that took place in the forest on the night of a Wakikuyu wedding, when a girl, fleet of foot as a wild deer, her body shining with a preparation of red clay and eucalyptus oil, was finally given over to the eager bridegroom in exchange for I know not how many lop-eared goats and fat-tailed native sheep. How rashly the young warriors would race with their spears under the light of the honey-coloured moon, the enormous tropical leaves rustling above their heads, and groups of patriarchal natives—black as Satan—standing about in the patched moonshine.

In a remote mountain village in Switzerland I recently had an opportunity of observing the same ceremony, and I do not believe that the dominating emotions of the principal actors on this occasion were very different from those experienced by the African savages. At both gatherings the father was sad at parting with his daughter, the bridegroom eager for the full possession of his beloved one, and the bride under a glamour of romance, and yet tremulous too before the approach of so great a change in her life. In my conversations with the peasants where I am now living I had continually heard rumours that a marriage was in preparation between this girl of the valley and a young farmer of a neighbouring village. The maiden was one of four sisters who lived on the mountainside. There were reasons why the prospective wedding had aroused more than usual interest. It represented the happy fulfilment of a long attachment. The two young people had fallen in love with each other when the girl was a child of only fourteen years. They had seen but little of each other, when she fell sick; and no less than nine years had gone by without their being able to win the consent of their parents to the match. The sensitive solicitude the boy had shown for his sweetheart during this difficult decade of probation had caused everybody to marvel. And yet as soon as I met the girl I understood at once how deeply devoted any man might become to her:

> *The stars of midnight shall be dear*
> *To her, and she shall lean her ear*
> *In many a secret place*
> *Where rivulets dance their wayward round,*
> *And beauty born of murmuring sound*
> *Shall pass into her face.*

The moulding of her body was more delicate than is usual with Swiss peasant girls. In Welsh mythology there is the story of a bride who was formed out of flowers. This maid from the Gaschurna, for so her home is called, might have been formed from the foam spray of the mountain stream that goes tossing past her home towards the valley river. Her skin was of the softest texture, and her cheeks when she flushed had the rose hue of the flower called snake-weed which grows so plentifully in her father's fields. She was a woman light as air, and yet there was a firmness about her brown eyes that suggested great constancy of spirit.

To those unacquainted with Switzerland it would be difficult to describe the absolute isolation of the life spent in the more lonely houses of the mountains. In many of these homesteads the clothes are still hand-woven, the farm wool being spun by the old women during the long snow-bound months of the winter. The interiors of these homesteads differ very little. In one corner is, as a rule, a stove against which stands a couch reserved for the use of the father when he comes in tired from milking in the nearby stable where his cows remain for so many months munching mountain hay, their tails, as is the odd custom, tied to the ceiling for the sake of cleanliness. Against one of the walls, decorated with a solidly framed marriage certificate set within the circle of the carefully preserved wedding wreath, stands a cupboard full of the family crockery. This cupboard is made of the wood of the arven tree. The dinner plates are often very old and carry on their centres such suitable mottoes of earthly felicity as '*Mein ganzes Leben sei dir ergeben*' ('My whole life is consecrated to you'): *Zwei treue Herzen ein Leben*' ('Two true hearts for life'); '*Himmlisch lächelt mir die Au, denk ich dich als meine Frau'* ('The meadows appear to me like the fields of heaven when I think that you may be my wife'). There is one large table at which the family meals are taken, and the chairs about it are of plain wood resembling what we call in England kitchen chairs, but of a medieval design. On a small shelf is invariably to be seen a huge eighteenth-century Bible fitted with bronze clasps. On the fly-leaf of this book, the pages of which are brown with use and age, have been formally recorded from generation to generation the births, marriages, and deaths that have taken place in the family.

It was in one of these rooms that I first saw the bride, Ursula Ambhül. It was in the month of May and she and her three sisters were hard at work embroidering the sheets for her new home. The Swiss peasants still regard household linen as an important part of the dowry, and I was shown a pile of table-cloths, napkins, towels, and counterpanes high enough, so it seemed, to last a lifetime. The laughing sisters were that morning busily employed embroidering with nimble needles emblems of love upon the wedding sheet's 'enchanted web.' Seeing so many preparations going forward I wanted also to offer the girl some little gift. I had in my pocket a worked flint that I had picked up on the Dorset downs, and remembering how in the Middle Ages these 'elf shot' were valued as lucky stones I offered it to her explaining that it would ensure her a large family. 'But I do not wish for too many children,' she prettily protested to the merriment of her sisters.

It had not been my first visit to this house. In the dead of winter I had found my way there along a sleigh track with walls of marble-white snow rising high on both sides. The bride had been away that day, and the mother, while she prepared the mid-day meal for the family, had left me in the same room where the old grandmother was sitting at the spinning-wheel, with her spectacled head as close up to the small window as she could get it for the sake of the light, for her eyes were weak and inflamed. It was a half-hour I shall never forget—the old woman, with hair as white as her own carded wool, manipulating the thread with deft fingers until it was ready for her spinning jenny, which she kept revolving by a scarcely discernible movement of one of her feet beneath her black skirt. I remember that morning appreciating to the full the simple poetical lives of these people, who for so many days of the year have nothing to look out at but the monotonous shape of the same timber-grown mountain opposite, or at snow falling, falling, falling past small square windows. Those waiting minutes in the old workaday parlour were to me almost religious in the intensity of their quality, with nothing but the regular sound of the old woman's ancient wooden machinery to disturb the stillness of the bare-floored room.

Now all was different. I had approached the house through meadows that were opulent with the sweetest meadow grass in all the world—the flowery meadow grass of the high mountains! This bride, whose carnal beauty might have been compared to snow 'before the soil hath smutch'd it,' was well fitted to appear treading across such a carpet of fair flowers.

True to the superstition of the old rhyming proverb,

> *To a wedding in May*
> *Always say nay*

the marriage ceremony was fixed for a date in the middle of June a little before the hay-making weeks began. Very early on the morning of the appointed day I was awaked by the sound of a horse's trot, and coming out on to my balcony in the sunshine was in time to see the bride and bridegroom driving away to his village, the whip decorated with white silk ribbons. It is the custom that the bridegroom should fetch the bride himself on the marriage morning, and truly this faithful young man must have harnessed his horse before ever the first splash of yellow light had touched the Kühalp-horn glacier at sunrise.

The wedding was to be at Glaris at eleven o'clock, and this gave me time to take up a position at the little church before the procession appeared, led forward by the Zwingli clergyman of the district. The bride and bridegroom followed close upon the clerygman's heels, and after them the bride's sisters, and after them the women walking two by two up the narrow path, with the men behind. The church of Glaris is at the foot of a mountain; a little white building very solidly built, with a low spire below which is to be seen the round face of a huge clock with one long black hand to mark in sun, rain, and snow the unpausing flight of the happy Alpine hours. As the solemn troop came up the steep path to the church I remarked as closely as I could the wedding garments of the pair. After the custom of the mountains the bride was dressed in black with a simple veil covering her hair, a veil just long enough for the end to be held by a child. Across her forehead was a delicate fillet embroidered with myrtle flowers. The groom, Simon Wehrli, a dark reserved peasant strikingly handsome, was also dressed in black with a white stock and a white favour pinned to the lappet of his coat. The silent passionate man and the gentle constant girl had their eyes upon the ground as they walked, and they were pressed very close together. I was told that it is the custom for a bridal pair to look down during their advance to the church lest they should be led to entertain even a momentary desire for another, and that it is also necessary to walk as if they were one lest an evil spirit should take advantage of a chance to slide its malignant shadow between them.

> *Not two but one*
> *Till life be gone.*

Over the door of the church a garland had been hung. It was made out of sprigs of the red fir entwined with Alpine roses. The pews in the chancel of the church were also decorated with garlands of Alpine roses and these garlands had been made bright in their turn with small bunches of blue gentians.

The service was a sober one. The men sat together on the right side of the little aisle and the women on the left. I made my way to the last pew, from where I could observe all that took place. Each man as he came in stood with his Sunday black hat held before his face, praying. He then sat down in a resigned way, curious to take in all that was going on. The clergyman himself played the organ when an accompaniment was required for the hymns, and after he had delivered an exhortation to the two young people he beckoned them to come forward to the chancel step. I was uncertain whether it was the clergyman or the bridegroom who placed the wedding ring on the bride's finger. A ring from the earliest time has played a very important part in the marriage ceremony. It is the symbol of eternity, and hence has been selected to represent the steadfastness of human affection. In all countries it is worn by the girl on the third finger, the finger dedicated to Apollo, and quaintly named in old days in England the Betty Bedlam finger, the tradition being that it possesses a nerve connected directly with the heart, a belief that explains the meaning of the posy to be seen sometimes on the inner side of wedding rings:

> *My heart and I*
> *Until I die.*

The service over, the marriage party went to the village inn for the wedding breakfast. I did not attend the breakfast, but was present when the dancing began in the late afternoon.

It is a very ancient custom that for the first three dances the bride and bridegroom alone should be allowed on the floor, a ceremonious regulation designed, it is said, to allow the gossips an occasion for judging whether or not lovemaking has been over-hasty. The dancing at these marriage feasts is a striking spectacle. On this occasion the music was supplied by three men seated on chairs placed upon a kitchen table—one with a flute, one with a concertina, and one with a violoncello. It did the heart good to see how these hay-brown countrymen made merry with their jigging instruments. By each of their chairs there was a bottle of red wine, of Veltliner, and this perhaps contributed to their excessive jollity. Round and round the couples spun, old men and young men, old women and young girls, cheeks red as September apples side by side with chops wagging with square cow-straw-smelling beards. I do not think this mountain folk can be matched for their passion for dancing; they often begin in the middle of the afternoon and do not stop till the sun is high above the mountains the following morning.

In the valley the next day I met a young man whom I had noticed at the dance. I asked him what time he had got back to his hut. 'In time for the milking,' he answered self-consciously. Milking I knew took place at five o'clock, for at six-thirty the cattle are driven out upon the mountains and for half an hour every valley echoes with the sound of cattle-bells and with the voices of the herders as they call to the heavy beasts, urging them forward into the dewy upland lawns in the huge landscape of the mountains.

From *Swiss Essays* (1947).

FLOWERS OF THE MOUNTAINS

EVEN though in the vegetable world there commonly exist thorns, prickles, poisons, and strangle-clutches, no other kind of life would seem to be as innocent as that of flowers, and nowhere, I think, the whole world round, do these herbs of grace flourish to more perfection than upon the upland meadows of Switzerland:

> *All the flowers of the spring*
> *Meet to perfume our burying.*

In Africa I used often to marvel at the excellent freshness of the land after the heavy rains—the green floor of the open veldt backed by escarpment forests that trailed their wild jasmine above fretted mats of maidenhair fern. In the Rocky Mountains the many-coloured lupins would fill the air with an Olympian fragrance as they bowed their spires beneath the bellies of our ponies; but never to my mind did the flora of either of these remote places, no, nor yet that of the paradise pastures of Palestine—fertile, rock-encircled—come near to rivalling the prodigal beauty of the mountain meadows of Switzerland as they are in the month of July before the first mowing has begun.

When I came to Clavadel as a young man it was in the late autumn, and for several months I looked out upon nothing but snow and sunshine, so much so indeed, that for a while I was possessed by a restless nostalgia for the winter greenness of England, for the soft opulence of its island summers, with the small birds merrily singing in every thicket and hedgerow. In my exile I used to go walking with another invalid, a middle-aged German, and on one occasion I remember attempting to convey to the imagination of this solid Teutonic citizen something of the mid-summer wonder of England's landscape, with rain-drenched sorrel-tossing meadows put up for hay, mowing-meadows juxtaposed to fields, broad and wide, across which cattle would be moving in serene detachment, like quadruped Gods, licking up with unhurried intention large vernal mouthfuls of buttercups and dairy grass. My companion let me talk on for a while, and then, prodding impatiently at a nearby snow-bank with his Alpine stock, suddenly said, 'But isn't it the same everywhere?'

When the snow began at last to vanish, and week after week I witnessed the dramatic transformation that comes to the mountains with the softer winds of spring, I recalled his words, and have since often smiled to think how I had been caught indulging in the old folly, a folly of believing that one's own beloved home-paddock surpasses all the paddocks the world over. It is perhaps the sensational contrast afforded by the winter and summer seasons in the high Alps that is able, in so special a way, to startle the spirit out of its customary sloth, startle it till, with the thousand eyes and the thousand ears of the God Mithra, it apprehends, as never before, the created world?

> Lord over Nature, Lord of the visible earth
> Lord of the senses five.

On my coming down from Cambridge in the year nineteen hundred and seven I got work as a schoolmaster at Bromsgrove. It was not a happy period of my life and if anything redeems it in retrospect it is the interest that I learned to take in wild flowers. I discovered that the finding of these sely weeds, and the learning of their names, offered me a sure escape from my spiritual imprisonments. Issuing one afternoon from 'the Steps'—a fine old eighteenth-century house where I dwelt in dolorous unease with my colleagues—I happened to notice in a damp ditch a little yellow flower that was obviously neither a hawkweed nor dandelion. I enclosed it in my Sunday letter to my mother and soon received an answer: 'Your dear father says that the flower you have found is a very common one and that its name is coltsfoot.' The ancients used to call coltsfoot *Filius ante Patrem* and in after years a chance sight of this flower never failed to bring back the discomfiture I experienced over my father's casual comment.

It so happened that for five years I lived in the centre of a garden preserve of these very flowers. This was when we rented one of the coastguard cottages on the top of White Nose in Dorset. Here in a neglected glistening sea-salt parterre—square as a barrack plot

—they grew in great profusion as early as February, lifting up their narrow faces of good cheer, and in the late spring covering the ground with their broad sheltering leaves, under the cool shadows of which I have known more than one meadow-pipit to rear its brood in safety. It is the appearance of this same gallant flower that encourages the Swiss to believe, when all is still crisp and hard, that the snows of the long winter will presently really and truly take their departure. Indeed the flower is sometimes called Lauene, on account of its being seen on the edges of the earth-avalanches that are so often laved and loosened in the universal thaw. The plant takes its name, of course, from the shape of its leaf rather than from that of the flower, the leaf being supposed to resemble a hoof, the hoof of a donkey or filly—*fulli fuess*. Swiss children are fond of making toy sunshades and looking-glasses out of these singular leaves. The looking-glasses are contrived by removing the furry white gossamer-like veil that is spread over the leaf's underside, a procedure that exposes to the view, beyond all expectation, a miraculous surface of shining satin-like green, a ready enough mirror to a child's fancy for the reflection of the pert, privy face of a darling doll.

The coltsfoot is quickly followed by the spring crocus, which before the dung has even been spread, populates the meadows in unnumbered hosts, offering to goat and sheep a dainty diet, but one villainously ungrateful to man and cattle. Then follow the gentian and the spring anemone, the latter featly furnished with mantles of fur to clout it from the cold. Dr. Martha Egli, in an excellent little book, tells of an old play that children have with gentians, with this matchless mountain flower that borrows its hue from the sea, from the sapphire, from the sky, *Herrgottsblumen*, God's flower, as it is called. Holding the gentian between finger and thumb the little girls boldly chant the words, 'Dead, dead, come out,' and at the same time squeeze and twist at the flower until its pistil—a little pale corpse—is propelled from the bell. By this ritual they actually think to surprise and exorcise death himself, curiously couched for the nonce in the orifice of these triumphant trumpets.

The gentians are in their glory when the goat-boys first begin to bring down from the high mountains bunches of Alpine roses, still only in bud. The fragrance of these tough immature nosegays is as dear to a true Swiss as is the first sight of an edelweiss.

The odour that these wild rough bunches emit is feral beyond all conception. They smell of mountain winds, of mountain rains, of moss, of bark, of lichens cold to the touch, of the fells of chamois, and of the breath of eagles. This wild rhododendron gives a glow to the high slopes, a glow like the dawn, the colour of its flower strikingly contrasting with the dark green of its lancet-shaped leaves. Another name for this low bushy plant is mountain-hen-flower, *Hühnerbluest*, a reference to the impenetrable shelter it offers to these shy game birds.

The Alpine roses are still in full blossom when the dandelions begin to gladden the valleys on every side with their fairy gold. Not a footpath way, not a lane, not a grey fence or swart stable but is fringed with the gaudy discs of these life-affirming flowers. I have often met children carrying them home by the basket-full, the little girls, as much as the flowers at their elbows, savouring of the first hot sunshine of the year; bland and blameless and sun-saturated as window-sill kittens. These same children are fond of using the milk-filled stems of this gypsy salad for the making of shepherd's pipes so that they may play to toads and snails and dutiful lady-birds the plaintive nursery ditties of long ago.

> *O evil day! if I were sullen*
> *While Earth herself is adorning*
> *This sweet May-morning,*
> *And the children are culling*
> *On every side*
> *In a thousand valleys far and wide,*
> *Fresh flowers; while the sun shines warm*
> *And the babe leaps up on his mother's arm.*

When the dandelion clocks are all 'telling the time,' and the Alpine roses are past their blossoming, the valley meadows lie ready for the first swath to be cut. Often it happens that the butterflies and faltering moths which, hour after hour, wander and waver above the clustering flowerheads, hold their frivolous surveillance over fields of separate colour-patches, certain flowers dominating certain acres, or creating in wide patterns mono-chrome carpets of gold, of pink, of violet, of Chinese white, according to the wealth of the ranunculi, of the pink campions, of the hearts'-ease, of the Queen Anne's-Lace, that occupy this or that portion of the sloping grounds. I once visited the tents of two little sisters, Marteli and Anneli, tents pitched at the edge of the wide green seas of these quilted plots; honey-plots that would have outdone in their light loveliness even the floors of Botticelli's imagination. And when I looked at these broad prospects of jostling flowers, I could not but believe that life in itself is its own justification, and that however transitory its passage, and however charged it may be with execrable savagery, it can indeed be rightly carried upon wings of trust without despair.

It would serve us little to make an over-scrupulous list of the flowers that decorate the hay-fields of the valley, those valleys where 'azure pillars of the hearth arise' from the houses of the peasants. Rampions, snake-weeds, wild pink, and man's troth are perhaps the most conspicuous. Man's troth, or *Nigritella*, is a heavily scented dark-headed little orchis that has gathered about it in the passing of the centuries much romantic lore. The peasants regard it with suspicion, not only because it flourishes best on poor soil and is rumoured to give a bluish colour to the milk of the cows that eat it, but also on account of other less ponderable properties. Women, it is rumoured, know how to brew love-potions out of it. It is likely enough the very plant that the wife of Lucretius put to such ill use, for a single one of its flowers slipped beneath the pillow of a too light-hearted boy will make him utterly besotted, just as a mountain girl, before, free as the wind, can be made complaisant by the lodging of the head of one of these worts in the pocket of her apron.

The second mowing sees the valley sadly scanted of its flowers. The grass is luxuriant enough, but the scythes are sharpened before ungarnished slopes. As at the earlier time, the implements glitter and glance like swords at the hour before dawn, but the honour of the fields has departed. It is an emerald aftermath. This is not yet the case on the mountain tops, with the hay made upon those heights that brush against the ceilings of the sky:

> *Mountains on whose barren breast*
> *The labouring clouds do often rest.*

On the very crest of the Jacob's Horn above Clavadel there grows a pasture patch of the yellow flower called Villous hawk-weed (*Pervière Villeuse*). It is a favourite food of the chamois, a golden food that dances and nods against those lofty spaces.

In the house of the moon where I was born
They fed a silver unicorn
On golden flowers of the sun.

Gone now and forgotten in the dales is the soldanella with its fringed edges, gone the water-avens, gone the grass of Parnassus, the white dryas, and the heaven-keys (*Primula auricula*). A few white clovers only remain—God's flesh, or heaven's bread, as they are called. Then follows the idle season of Martinmas when every hour the rowan tree berries ripen and redden, and the days grow shorter and the nights grow longer, and the spirits of men and women are troubled by vague misgivings. It is a time of recollections; and there is suddenly to be seen everywhere the last lonely flower of the year. This flower is the autumn crocus, the saffron crocus. In all directions they open their frail petals with solicitude, decorating the lifeless faded fields before the winter whiteness envelops all. This colchicum autumnale, or *Herbstzeitlose,* as the Germans have named it, is a flower wistful as a solitary street-cry heard at Michaelmas by a weeping child.

Its appearance is a sure sign of the nearness of the dark solstice. In the old days it was the custom of women to pick the first autumn crocus that they saw and to cover their hands with its juice, hoping that some occult virtue in it would preserve the suppleness of their fingers through the long 'spinning evenings.'

To a poet's eye the smockless nakedness of these flowers is a delight, and yet the mere look of them has provoked cruelty. If a girl's chastity is suspected it is an ancient usage to strew the path that leads from her father's house to the family washing-well with handfuls of these flowers. A happier association may be found in the name *Chilte-blumen,* meaning the flower that shows itself at that time of the year when young men, after the evening milking is over, are drawn to the houses of their sweethearts; the windows, because of the thickening autumn twilight, being already lamplit.

Then at the end of November, or at the beginning of December, the snow falls in real earnest, and all the bulbs and seeds and tiny twisting roots of the fugitive summer flowers hide and huddle for months together under massy snows, not under snow that easily melts away as in England, but under weighty loads that day after day press down ever more ponderously upon the wintry grass. In the high mountains the only living thing that thrives is the lichen known as Icelandic moss. Legend declares that this moss was at one time a succulent grass-green herb, a herb that provided the cows with so much milk that the men of the mountains grew careless and made, out of their plenary surplus, cheese-balls for their children to sport with, and, worse still, washed their women in the white fluid.

> *Up he has taken his fair lady,*
> *Gar'd was her wi' the milk!*

The legend relates that one day, out from a grove of arven-trees, Jesus appeared in the form of a beggar. He accosted those luxurious dairy-men, and on being refused the alms he craved of them, the gentle God who had always prized highly the grass of the fields, punished these come-day-go-day rogues by changing their valuable milk-producing weed, nish as water-cress, into Icelandic moss, into 'the misery that grows under the snow.' He made it a sapless dead dry lichen that never again would have anything to do with the spring-time meadow-valleys, where fieldmice, blunt of nose and as large as water-rats, frolic at the breaking of their hibernating fast; and where 'the myriads of rivulets hurrying thro' the lawn' mingle their tinkling with the tinkling of cattle-bells and with the haunting sounds of children's voices intermittently heard shouting through the happy hollow air of an April afternoon.

From *Swiss Essays* (1947).

LITERATURE

STYLE

IT IS difficult to analyse the airy substance we call style. At its
best it seems to escape all definitions. It is as evasive as life.
It would be as hard to predict the dancing flight of a flock of
finches, or the subterranean movements of a single mole, as to
explain a great writer's peculiar gift. The reason for this seems to
lie in the fact that style is the ultimate expression of the author's
unique spiritual consciousness. This spiritual consciousness has
been arrived at through various influences. Ancestry has bequeathed to it a certain fundamental disposition, environment has
thickened this congenital inclination, and the chance temperament
of each individual has flashed it into life out of nowhere.

It has been suggested that style consists in saying what has to be
said as exactly as possible. This, however, is a different matter
altogether. True style has nothing to do with imparting information lucidly. It is not this. It is the scent of the herb, the mist
over the blackberry hedge, the soul of the man. It is begotten of
the senses, it is the quintessential feeling, the quintessential thought,
of those fleet messengers finding unity at last in the person of the
being they serve. All the nights that a man has experienced,
clouding in so mysteriously over the native earth; all the dawns
that he has witnessed with wakeful eyes, have engendered it. The
taste of wheaten bread, the taste of milk and wine, has caused it
to grow. The sound of church bells heard in a wild place far from
village or town has impelled words to dance like children in a
May-day procession. The contact of sea-waves against the skin,
or the grateful warmth of fire against human nakedness can, and
should, have an influence on every sentence. The smell of snow,
the smell of a hay cock in the sun, nay, the smell that rises from
the intestines of a rabbit when a man is paunching it with his
pocket knife, should prove its periods.

A perfect style is the perfect expression of a man's secret identity. It makes arrogant claims. It demands that the ordinary everyday world should give attention to the wandering goat-cry of a

supreme egoism as sensitive as it is tough. It is for this reason that great writers are seldom recognized in their lifetime. Commonplace readers invariably appreciate commonplace writers. They prefer books that reflect ideas and methods of thought with which they are already familiar. At all costs the pamphlets they peruse must be partial and platitudinous. They shrink from that terrible spiritual sincerity that burns like fire and prompts a writer to leave his own seal, his own thumb-mark, upon every page he writes.

If I were to be asked by any young person the best way to acquire a style I would tell him to live intensely. The style of a man is the direct result of his passion for life. Learning and scholarship are of small value here. Style is the affirmation of a man's heightened awareness of existence and always grows up from within, from out of the marrow of his bones.

If it were my task to treat of this matter with under-graduates I should draw their attention to certain notable passages of English prose and show them clearly by specific paragraphs, sentences, or even idiosyncratic words, how these men have succeeded in preserving their spirits on parchment for all time. This particular and singular use of the country's language is beyond the scope of the vulgar. It would seem that the innate complexion of a man's mind finds for itself fitting expression. Powerful and original characters write in a powerful and original way, shallow and commonplace characters write in a shallow and commonplace way. Style has to do with the grace, health, and vigour of a man's soul. It is a secret thing dependent upon a natural depth of feeling and no amount of playing the sedulous ape can pass off as authentic what is in truth counterfeit. Just as in the love between a man and a woman true emotion will find convincing expression so it is with writing. Sham feeling makes sham prose and it is easily recognized as such.

My own method is to give no thought whatever to the form of what I am writing. I put down my ideas as they present themselves pell mell to my mind, fanciful, extravagant, sentimental, bawdy, irreverent, irrelevant, they are all equally welcome. In going over my work, however, I am prepared to spend a great deal of care in endeavouring to find an adequate balance for any particular paragraph. I have noticed that when I am writing at my best I experience a peculiar physical sensation. I first became aware of this peculiarity at school as a boy of twelve when we were given an essay to write on the Pied Piper. I have never been able to think a subject through before writing. I daresay I should do much better if it were my nature to adopt such a method. I consider the greatest difficulty to be overcome by immature, untrained writers is lack of confidence. They are too self-conscious. When once the pen is in the hand it is important to forget about the opinions of others and to write away after our own fashion with careless, proud indifference.

From *Types and Times in the Essay*, an anthology compiled by Warner Taylor (1932).

Chydyok, Chaldon Herring, Dorset, looking north. This was the home of Llewelyn Powys from 1931 until 1936, when he went to Switzerland.

Bats Head, which lies almost due south of Chydyok, a few minutes' walk over the downs. Weymouth lies along the distant coastline, with the Isle of Portland rising at the left.

THOMAS SHOEL

D URING the last quarter of the eighteenth and the first quarter
of the nineteenth centuries there was living and writing
in the village of Montacute a most uncommon poet. The
work of Thomas Shoel has been unduly neglected. In its lively
apprecation of the passing of the seasons it represents a strong and
valuable tradition in English poetry. From one century to another
the imaginations of English people have responded to the changes
that take place in the open fields, and there have never been
lacking native poets capable of expressing such reciprocities:

> *Sumer is icumen in,*
> *Lhude sing cuccu!*
> *Groweth sed, and bloweth med,*
> *And springth the wude nu*
> *Sing Cuccu!*

With little education Thoman Shoel not only became a
composer of sacred music but also an inspired poet. Copies
of the various editions of his slim, unpretentious collections
of poems are now extremely difficult to come by. The single
one in my possession was bought for a few pennies in a second-
hand book-shop at Bristol, but it is unlikely that so lucky a
find will be repeated.

Shoel was susceptible to literary influence, and it is possible that
the critics of the time, observing from the manner of his best-
known poem, 'Miles Hill,' that he had read Goldsmith's *Deserted
Village*, passed a somewhat too hasty judgment upon his work.
However, the memory of this remarkable man has tenaciously
lingered in his native village, so that more than a century after
his death I have been able to patch together much interesting
information concerning him.

Thomas Shoel was born in the year 1759. His father and mother
died when he was still young. He first attempted to earn his

living as a weaver, but his health giving way in that employment, he eventually became a farm-labourer and village carrier. He married a woman named Phyllis Bool when he was twenty-three years old. They appeared to have been passionately attached to each other and to the children of their marriage, but hopeless poverty wore them down and brought death to all but Shoel himself and one boy, who was afterwards drowned at sea. Shoel's mind never recovered from the shock of these pitiful years, and much of his poetry is made up of reiterated lamentations.

In 1797 he was married a second time by the Vicar of Montacute, William Langdon, to a woman named Mary Taunton. By her he had three daughters—Mara, Miriam, and Julia. He died in 1823, but even then disaster continued to pursue his family. His daughter Mara inherited his exceptional sensitiveness of nature and after his death became obsessed by religious emotions. As late as her fiftieth year she gave birth to twins, and this exceptional occurrence may have accentuated her weak nervous condition. In any case, she took her own life. Shoel's second daughter, Miriam, died young, living as an invalid for the last few years of her life at Norton-sub-Hamdon, from which village her corpse was borne through sandy bye-lanes to the Nonconformist burial-plot at Five Ashes. It is in this same Puritan graveyard that Thomas Shoel himself lies. The acre is romantically situated in the middle of an arable field on the top of the long windswept ridge that lies between Odcombe and Ham Hill, far from any human habitation. The cemetery is surrounded by a high stone wall as a precaution against possible body-snatching, and has for an entrance a single narrow aperture fitted with an iron gate, the rusty bars of which only reluctantly clank admittance to a traveller. The place is said to have been first used for burying some of Cromwell's soldiers killed in a local engagement at the time of the Civil War. Shoel's youngest daughter Julia alone of his children lived to a great age, and was still alive in the year 1886 when my father became Vicar of Montacute. Indeed, one old woman remembers seeing my father hurry along after Julia Burt in order to carry for her a bucket of water that she was bringing to her cottage from the fountain at the Cross. There are still living in Montacute two of Julia Burt's grandchildren. Mrs. Ellen Greenham, one of these great-grandchildren of the poet, has allowed me to see a family Bible given by Thomas

Shoel to Mara and the old book still contains the poet's careful calligraphy and the date 1819.

Thomas Shoel published three books of sacred music: *Ode for Christmas Day, The Chearful Psalmodist,* and *Peace*; also innumerable Psalm tunes, hymn tunes, and 'Easy Anthems.' The best known of all his religious tunes is perhaps his *Joy to the World* which when I was a boy was regularly sung by the carol singers at Christmas. There used at that time to live at Montacute an old man named Samuel Geard, a lusty member of the church choir. The family of Geard had seen better days. Samuel Geard's own father had been a prosperous sailcloth manufacturer. He, however, had been content to earn his bread without cark or care as an under-gardener at Montacute House. On a certain Christmas midnight when the Borough, as the village square at Montacute is called, was white with a fine nativity snow, and a bitter wintry wind was huffling against the sloping roofs from the north-east, Geard heard the carol singers begin to strike up with the 'old tunes.' In a moment he was out of bed, and opening wide the casement window, stood in his nightgown exposed to the shrewd 'draughts,' joining with his magnificent bass voice in the 'Shepherd's music' as heartily as the best of the carol singers. His friends called up to him not to risk his life in such a foolish manner. 'I can't bide in bed when you be out singing Wold Tom Shayell,' came back the obstinate answer. (The local pronunciation of the name Shoel was Shayell and not Shoel.) In those days they used to make a great deal of carol singing, the orchestra that accompanied consisting of clarinet, flute, fiddles, and bass viol, and I have been told it was the custom of the cellist to go to the churchyard and tune his strings to the tone of one of the six bells—perhaps to the one which has 'He that heareth me to sound, Let me alwaies praies the Lord,' engraved about its wide rim.

Montacute is encircled by sloping woods and protected towards the west by Ham Hill. St. Michael's Mount, or Miles Hill, or Montacute Hill, dominates the village. It is conical-shaped and surrounded by a look-out tower built by one of the squires, Robert Phelips, in the year of the poet's birth. It was on the summit of this hill that Shoel wrote many of his poems. 'Great Granfer used to bide and sit on the top of Miles Hill where he could look down upon Middlestreet.' His eccentricities and fastidious habits evidently made a deep impression on the imaginations of the in-habitants of the village and I have been able to recover interesting scraps of hearsay. He is said not to have allowed his children 'to kill flies,' and himself would never eat flesh; especially did he recoil from all that had to do with 'swine's wine,' or the favourite poor man's dish called 'black pudding' made out of groats and the 'flick' or blood of a hog freshly killed. He lived in a small yard to the east of the Montacute Borough. In the old days this yard was called Hallet's Yard, and it was within its precincts during the reign of Queen Victoria that Ellen Mitchel, the mother of the 'Man from the Plough,' brought up her family. In following his employment of pedestrian carrier Shoel was often observed 'to sink down under the weight of his burdens.' His wages as a farm-hand were only six shillings week, but he was in certain seasons able to supplement this by undertaking 'piece-work' after hours, 'tutt work,' as it was then called. One morning on seeing his cup-board bare and hearing his children crying for bread he is reported to have sat down and offhand to have composed some sacred music, walking with it across the fields to the hamlet of Lufton and successfully selling it there to the clergyman.

Once at Montacute Feast Day, or Club Walking, which for time-out-of-mind has taken place in the village on the first Monday after Trinity Sunday, the brass band arrived without their music, and Shoel was commandeered to compose a tune for them to play, as in holiday mood they headed the procession marching to the outlying farms for cider tasting, banners waving bright between the fresh green overhanging hedges. Seated on a barrel of beer in the yard of the Phelips Arms, he wrote out the score for each of the instruments, and his tune, which had for its title "Rejoice, O Daughters of Jerusalem" was regularly played for many years afterwards. He was paid sixpence for it.

Thomas Shoel, however, was not without his patrons. On one occasion he walked from Montacute to Calne in Wiltshire to call upon the poet Bowles, who happened unfortunately to be away. It was a great disappointment to Shoel when he was compelled to retrace his steps without even having seen the famous garden at Bremhill. Bowles, this extraordinarily good-natured and extra-ordinarily uninspired clergyman poet, was himself an eccentric character and had special gaiters made so that he might feel him-self to be secure against the possible bites from mad dogs; and when, towards the end of his life, he was appointed a Prebendary of Salisbury and took up his residence in the Cathedral Close, he is said to have carefully measured the distance between the Cathedral and his Queen Anne house in order to be assured that in the case of the famous spire being blown down it would not crush him in his stately domicile. A musician himself he seems to have been interested in Thomas Shoel's welfare. There also exist verses in which the Montacute poet laments the death of a Lady Ilchester who had evidently been kind to him, possibly the first Countess. His poem to Glastonbury Tor is dedicated to one of the Grenvilles of Butleigh, while members of the Phelips family are more than once mentioned in a spirit of gratitude. There appears also among the subscribers to *Miles Hill* the name of William Bridle, the notorious Governor of Ilchester Gaol.

Shoel would travel considerable distances in the hope of selling his poems. He would sometimes go as far as Bristol, using for this journey Joel Hockey's stage waggon that left Montacute on Monday and was back on Thursday. He sold his tunes for threepence. Mrs. Greenham remembers her grandmother telling her that at the age of ten years she had walked with her father to Bridport with this purpose in view. More than twenty miles separate Montacute from this Dorset market town. He would often write his poetry or compose his music in a field or wood.

> *Here sit retir'd beneath this jess'mine shade*
> *Those branches from the heat shall screen your head*
> *And with th' informing page employ your time.*

He would give his tunes titles to remind him of the places where they were composed, such as Abbey Farm, Windmill, Woodhouse, Combe Fountain, and Norton Field. He was a man of wide interests, but history, astronomy, and religion seem especially to have appealed to him.

One of the present inhabitants of Montacute recalls hearing his grandfather tell of meeting Thomas Shoel 'down by the Mill.' The celebrated comet of 1812 had just appeared in the sky, and the poet had walked back to the village talking of the wonders of the heavens. Shoel composed his poem to the comet that same evening.

Spelling was always difficult for him and errors remain even in his printed works. There are touching indications to show how sensitive he was to the deficiencies in his education. In one of his poems he refers to the sun moving across the sky, but nervously adds a note to explain that he, the author, is not unaware that it is the earth that is revolving about the sun and not the sun about the earth. In his reference to a poet's gravestone which occurs in his elegy on a country churchyard, his mind may have been occupied with his old anxiety.

> *Who yonder lies, where stands the rugged stone,*
> *With ill-formed letters, and with words spelt wrong?*

Actually his handwriting was a remarkable one—each letter meticulously formed and of a clerkly legibility, and his vocabulary was a wide one, though he was inclined to repeat certain favourite expressions. He always, for example, referred to his children as his 'train,' and the word 'charming' too easily filled the place of more precise epithets. His most ambitious poem, 'Miles Hill,' was written in 1800, in the year that the poet Cowper died. It is of considerable local interest, but is too much affected by the modes of versification then prevailing to be of any general importance.

> *Sweet Michael's loveliest of the hills around,*
> *With beauty clad with constant verdure crowned*
> *Beneath thy shade (with name from thee derived)*
> *Sweet Montacute, through numerous years has thrived;*
> *Laid out with beauty, open, spacious air;*
> *Blest with a fruitful soil and healthy air;*
> *Water'd abundant with the purest rills;*
> *And screen'd from tempest by the surrounding hills.*

From his favourite position on the crest of the hill the poet first contemplates the village where

> *The leather dresser at his perch too stands,*
> *And the keen knife employs his busy hands.*
> *While the neat glover, seated at the door,*
> *Or in the porch, employs the busy hour;*

He scans the far-seen horizons.

> *Now Dorset's mountains interrupt the view*

Here Langport seated midst the fattening moors
With ample Parrett visiting her doors——

And then in an unstable frenzy his imagination flies free

To loftier scenes, and treads the sacred road,
That leads from nature to the throne of God;
Views power Almighty, in th' amazing whole
The thron'd archangel and the grov'ling mole.

His poems are most often addressed to the forlorn and unfortunate:

ON HEARING A DERANGED YOUNG WOMAN UTTERING SOME DREADFULLY MELANCHOLY LANGUAGE:

Yet how can I thy woes behold,
Nor feel a pang of sorrow rise;
Thy shiver'd frame expos'd, and cold,
Thy poor wet feet, thy clouded eyes?
And when at last, the hand of death
Shall stop the throbbings of thy heart,
May angels watch thy dying breath;
Mayst thou in heavenly peace depart.

And again,

ON A BEGGAR

Cold was the air, the wind blew strong
And darkling grew the evening sky,
When pass'd a beggar-man along
And wished a friendly shelter nigh.

His coat was rent, his feet were bare,
And slow he crippled o'er the stones;
Through his torn hat high stared his hair,
His shrivell'd skin disclos'd his bones.

Now to the stall behold him hie,
Glad with the ox a bed to share;
But poorly cover'd from the sky
And shiver'd by the piercing air.

Good natur'd hind! O don't deny
A shelter in your master's shed;
O grant some straw that he may lie
A little warm for such a bed.

Come gentle sleep, and let thy hand
Find out the beggar where he lies;
O let thy care-deceiving wand,
Seal for a while the sufferer's eyes.

And how delicate in conception are these slight but touching verses addressed to a dead canary:

Farewell, my lovely warbler, O Farewell!
But my fond heart reluctant bids adieu
No longer shall I hear thy song's loud swell,
Nor with delight they beauteous plumage view
Methinks I see thy pretty feet alight,
With gentle movement perching on my hand
Thy little form appearing all delight,
While taking there thy oft accustomed stand.

Ah! then no more wilt thou my walk attend
Sweet seated on my hand and chirp thy joy;
To other songsters mute attention lend,
Or else to rival them thy pipe employ.

But thou art dead, alas! for ever dead
No more thy pipe shall charm, thy form delight,
Thy little life alas! alas! is fled
No more to please and entertain my sight.
Sweet bird adieu! to thee I bid farewell,
No more thy song shall warble in my ear,
But let this artless verse to others tell,
That thou wast lovely, that I loved thee dear.

Some of the most pathetic of his verses give us glimpses into his cottage interior. His poem addressed to "Poverty" displays in all its cruelty the life of a farm-hand towards the end of the eighteenth century when the labouring classes of England, cheated of their

independence by the arbitrary Enclosure Acts, were entering
upon a long period of degradation.

> Thou pale companion of my state forlorn,
> My constant inmate every night and morn
> Come prompt my numbers, and inspire my verse,
> While I attempt thy sorrows to rehearse.
> To naked walls and cobweb's dwelling lead,
> Where hapless children cry for want of bread.

> .   .   .   .   .

> Begin with him who with such constant toil
> Ploughs up the field and cultivates the soil.

> Then homeward see him labour on his way,
> And close the toil of long and tedious day;
> His poor coarse meal then soon behold him take
> Potatoes salted, or a barley cake;
> Cold water serves his painful thirst to slake,
> Or Indian leaves a half strained beverage make:
> His lisping prattlers hang on either knee,
> Well pleas'd again their father's face to see;

> His dear lov'd partner eyes him with delight,
> So well beloved, so pleasing in her sight
> And both perhaps let fall the trickling tear,
> While they behold in rags their children dear.
> Whose scanty meal soon finished see him hie
> On clotted flocks or beds of dust to lie,
> Whose scanty head and foot can scarce contain
> Himself, his partner, and his hapless train.

Of these poems of his home life the one "On Seeing My Child
Smile in Her Sleep" is possibly the most lovely. What a clear
picture is here given of the life of this working man of so humble
and civil a spirit, with his face 'transported' to see his little girl, and
yet so nervously overwrought with ill-feeding, work, and worry,
that his trembling knees could scarcely support a baby's weight.
The poem tells of evenings when he tried to comfort his child by
his singing, though with a heart too sad for such a task.

O, who unmoved can view that lovely face,
That image sweet of innocence and grace,
That smile that does thy bounteous lips adorn,
That cheek more charming than the blushing morn?
O say, sweet babe, what kind benignant power
Regales thy spirit in thy slumbering hour?
In what illusion does thy fancy roll,
What blissful vision claims thy ravish'd soul?
And at the luscious banquet bid to feast;
Upon her bosom does her darling lie,
And meet the fondness of a parent's eye?
While thy sweet mien with smiles of pleasure glows
And thanks her for the boon her love bestows?
Or dost thou view thy hapless father's arms,
Extended wide to clasp thy infant charms,
His face with transport does my darling see,
Or is she dandled on his trembling knee?
Then oft my babe has sank to pleasing rest;
While to my throbbing bosom fondly prest;
And oft tho' wrung by grief, and rack'd by pain,
I've sooth'd my charmer with a pleasing strain,
Or does he bear thee to the verdant fields,
To view the various scenes that nature yields
To pluck the flowers and see the lambkins play,
And hear each feather'd warbler tune its lay
While pleasure sparkles in my infant's eyes
And all her soul is wonder and surprise?

At the time of the restoration of St. Catherine's, the parish church of Montacute, there was found a remarkably carved stone. It showed a figure of a man playing upon a harp, and archaeologists identify this figure with the Psalmist, King David. This stone today may be seen amongst others supporting the organ loft, where that structure projects from the 'Priest's chamber' into the nave of the church. The odd block, although so uncouth in appearance, seems *alive with melody*. Thomas Shoel was a musician whose origin was as simple, rude, and mysterious as that of this royal oaf struck out of a mute block of Ham Hill stone.

The luckless 'tutt-worker' was as responsive to the opening of the spring as a beech tree leaf expanding its tender green in the new sunshine. And in no village in England can those first spring days be more limpid than in the neighbourhood of Montacute. What an incense-laden murmur can arise on an April morning from a thick-clustering mass of snow-white arabis, with tiny petals hot to the touch easily scattering. Large anemones, red and blue, are open wide on the terrace border—struck out of the garden mould, as it were, by a miracle! These are the magical, swift-passing weeks when the plovers are nesting on the flat plough lands beyond Windmill; when rooks, with their careless droppings, have smutched and blotched the garlic under their swaying attics. Now have come the Sunday afternoons when in Horse's Covert, smelling of moss, children are out picking primroses, their shrill ephemeral voices sounding between the tree trunks, while a yaffle, like a tropical parrot, flashes by them in a succession of strong undulating flights along the woodland path. On the first day of the week men are out on the grounds rolling the grass of the old Abbey meads into parallel shadowy patterns, and Sam Hodder's bull is blaring near Marsh lane, where the moor-hen, under the alders, sits faithful to the last upon her mottled clutch. From the male stickleback who far below the shining surface of the stream constructs with flickering art the nursery of his predestined race, to the 'dappled' lark against the sky's serene blue, all is delight, all is worship!

In the West Country they have a poetical expression to denote that first grey hour of a spring morning when birds for an interval celebrate with ecstatic throats the opening of a new day of shower, and sunshine, and clouds, and green leaves. They call it 'the charm of the morning.' Thomas Shoel's nature was of so fine a texture that, with notes as spontaneous as a blackcap's on a bramble, he could fly through the material bars that cabin our drab minds. Many poets more sophisticated and better-known have not his power for creating the feeling of a spring morning, swift as the flight of the first swallow, clear as the note of the first cuckoo, apparent as the smell of the red flowering currant, apparent as a pheasant's eye narcissus in a garden bed, or a spray of forsythia on a garden wall! He knew the primrose banks under the lofty white ash-tree columns on the way to Ham Hill with 'their faintly tragic scent.' He knew what the stitchwort looked like and the golden faces of the dandelions brushed over with the first pecks of road-side dust, where the stone stands marking nine miles to

Ilminster! He knew where linnets, with rosy feathers and hearts of elfin levity, were to be seen balancing on prickly sprays of gorse above Witcombe, above the place where the short-stalked wild daffodils grow, and hellebore friendly to melancholy. His lyrics fell from his lips as carelessly as the chittering of the swallows that prompted Hezekiah to plead to God for the residue of his life. 'The living, the living, he shall praise thee as I do this day.' Lightly this humble man cast nets over the transient moments of those distant summers, nets of as fine a mesh of gold as ever entangled the elbows and knees of laughing Aphrodite, nets intangible as the heat motes seen at the end of the road when shepherd Dove drives his flock towards Odcombe, and for the first time in the year feels the sun 'pricking' upon his back.

The following poems should ensure for Thomas Shoel a modest but honourable place in English literature:

ON HEARING A SMALL BIRD SING IN THE WINTER

Pretty little sprightly thing,
That so charming canst sing:
Tho' the rough wind keenly blow,
Bringing rain, or hail, or snow.

Lovely songster! sing again,
Whistle loud thy thrilling strain;
Winter soon will pass away,
With his short and gloomy day.

Earnest of the genial year,
Soon the snowdrops shall appear;
Soon the primrose too shall shew
To the eye its lovely hue.

Then the furrows shall display
Beauty clad in green array;
Pointing to the eye of hope
Autumn's rich abundant crop.

While along the orchard-rows
Wide the varied blossom blows;
Humming bees and insects round,
Buzzing with delightful sound.

Then the feather'd minstrelsy
Loud shall pour their melody;
While the forest, dell and grove,
Echo to the song of love.

TO THE LARK

Hark! while morn's gay herald sings,
Mounting high on dappl'd wings,
While his song with thrilling notes,
Through the liquid ether floats.

See his lofty height he gains,
O! how charming are his strains:
While the brilliant beams of morn,
Far and wide the skies adorn.

Songster hast thou gain'd thy height,
Art thou tir'd with such a flight?
Yes! his airy journey ends,
Now how rapid he descends.

VERSES ON HEARING THE BIRDS SING BEAUTIFULLY
EARLY IN THE MORNING OF APRIL 10TH, 1819

How pleasing to the list'ning ear,
A song so charming thus to hear!
While num'rous different voices join,
And all in harmony combine.

Here is no disagreeing note
From any harsh discordant throat,
In perfect chord they all unite,
And feast the sense with rich delight.

The Blackbirds' sequence full and strong,
The Thrush's sweetly varied song,
The Robin's liquid thrilling sound,
The little Wren's melodious round.

WELCOME TO RETURNING SPRING

Welcome spring's returning day,
Welcome sun, thy clearing ray,
Welcome to the fruitful showers,
Welcome blooms, birds and flowers

Welcome to the thrush's notes
Welcome songs from various throats;
Welcome larks at morning light
Welcome nightingales at night.

Welcome April's springing scene,
Welcome May's delightful green;
Welcome cowslip's yellow hue,
Welcome to the violets' blue.

Welcome to the fragrant rose,
Welcome ev'ry flower that blows,
Welcome verdure on the trees,
Welcome to the fanning breeze.

Welcome to the shepherd's lay,
Welcome to the lambkin's play;
Welcome richly cultur'd soil
Welcome future plenty's smile.

Welcome to the orchard's bloom,
Welcome bees, your charming hum,
Welcome insects, buzzing round
Welcome purling rills, your sound.

Welcome milk-maids, to your strains
Welcome rest to you ye swains;
Welcome stars so bright that show
Welcome planets milder glow.

Welcome hours of soft repose,
Welcome sleep, respite from woes
Welcome rest to bless the night
Welcome to the morning's light.

From *Somerset Essays* (1937).

ANTHONY À WOOD

THE Oxford Antiquary, Anthony à Wood, was a perfect example of his kind, a perfect example of those easily recognizable individuals who advance through life with their heads turned backwards. These people cannot abide that any scrap of the material world should go unregarded. They are precious over each single bone and shard. Their purpose is to mark, to record, to register, and their work, sneered at by the heedless of their day, is often of the greatest value to posterity.

The autobiography and journal-notes of Anthony à Wood, so admirably assorted by the Rev. Andrew Clark forty years ago, recreate for us in a most lively manner the life of Oxford as it was in the latter half of the seventeenth century, so rude, so nice, and so extravagant. For what a picture is evoked of the old university by this limited and tetchy archaeologist! How far removed from the city of our imagination, from the city of Arnold and Peter, from the city whose dreaming spires were seen by Jude the Obscure shining bright, far away over dreary stubble fields!

Oxford was Oxford with a difference. In these pages we look in vain for that atmosphere of grace associated with sweet scholarship. Often Mr. Wood's pages do not make very pleasant or very refined reading, but like all plain-spoken 'back-stair talk,' they have upon them the stamp of authenticity. If any student of the great century wishes to get a first-hand report, unadorned, unpolished, of the college chit-chat of those days here he may find it. Anthony à Wood had nothing of the lovable personal aplomb of Pepys, nothing of the sober well-bred dignity of Evelyn. He was, however, *a character*, a splenetic character, who went about his dedicated business with tireless intention. It may well be that the narrowness of his mind, his signal lack of imagination, his signal lack of literary artifice, actually adds to the value of these miscellaneous and indiscreet jottings he left behind him. They are blunt, unaffected annotations upon events and upon persons, intimately revealed by the details of their daily lives.

He was born on December 17th, 1632, at about four o'clock in the morning in an ancient stone house 'opposite the forefront of Merton College,' and he died in the same building on November 29th, 1695. One of his earliest memories was that of seeing King Charles I with his Queen ride down the High, into the great quadrangle of Christ Church. His next adventure was to be knocked over and kicked on the head by a carrier's horse that was being taken to water. This untoward event left him, so he tells us, with 'a slowness in apprehending with Quickness things,' but it evidently did not deprive him of his love of strict history, for he is careful to put on record that the name of the horse was 'Mutton,' and that it belonged to Thomas Edgerley, the university carrier. His education was sadly disrupted by the civil war. Alarums and excursions distracted the academic life of Oxford. Undergraduates became 'besotted with the training and activities.' His own brother 'left his Gowne at the Town's end, ran to Edghill, and did his Magestie good service.'

Anthony Wood entered Merton College at the age of nineteen and after several years took his degree. When his father, Thomas Wood, died 'to the very great Grief and Reluctancy of his wife and children,' Anthony was left, under his will, with a very small independent income. He now began to interest himself in music. He played the violin, but especially did he take a 'ravishing delight' in the sound of church bells, 'the music nighest bordering upon heaven.' He records hearing the eight 'statelie bells' of Merton College ring out one summer 'at his approach to Oxon, in the evening, after he had taken his Rambles all the Day about the country to collect Monuments.' For, already, as a very young man his passion for ancient buildings and for the ancient times was showing itself. He was allowed free access to the Bodleian Library 'which he took to be the happiness of his life . . . and into which he never entered without great Veneration.' Dr. John Wallis, the keeper of the university registers, allowed him the key of the room where these were kept 'to the end that he might advance his ensurient Genie in Antiquities.' Except for certain excursions to London and to Bath, and to places in the immediate locality, he remained at Oxford all his life immersed in his 'vertuous studies.'

He was extremely peevish, and an eccentric. He quarrelled with the great Doctor Fell, who helped him to get his *Antiquities of Oxford* published; he detested his sister-in-law, his brother Robert's wife; and he made himself a parlous nuisance to the Warden and Fellows of Merton, and to innumerable other University dignitaries. He could not bear to see how college men pushed for preferment at the time of the Restoration, and his intent, cantankerous presence must have been extremely disturbing to an ambitious gownsman of those days. 'Nothing became more ridiculous to a wary observer than to see these widgeons over-do a thing and that uncouthly too, without the least suspicion that any person took notice of them.' Anthony à Wood took notice of all. He missed nothing.

Just as naturally as a cuttle fish ejects poisonous ink so did Mr. Wood eject spite, and towards the end of his life his malice fairly 'got on the nerves' of the Doctors in their 'scarlett formalities.' Of John Haselwood, Fellow of Merton, he says, 'A proud, starch'd formal and sycophantizing clisterpipe who was the apothecary to Clayton when he practised physick.' Of the wife of Sir Thomas Clayton (the warden of Merton) he records, 'She put the College to unnecessary charges, and very frivolous expenses, among which were a very large looking-glass, for her to see her ugly face, and body to the middle, and perhaps lower, which was bought in Hillary terme 1670 and cost, as the bursar told me, about £10.' Often even on paper he cannot contain his venom. It seems to spit at us out of the pages. 'Mr. Roger Brent and I playing at cards, he fell out with me, called me all to naught and struck me. He looked like a rogue, like a whoring rascal, like a whoring rogue.' Indeed, his malignant misanthropy flies out in an ever-widening circumference. 'Sir Henry Benet, sometimes of Christ Church, was created "Lord Arlington of Arlington" and the reason why he would not be called "Lord Benet" was, as 'tis said, because the name did not sound well, and 2nd because there was an old bawd at Westminster called Lady Benet (a baker's widow).'

Anthony à Wood's real name was plain Anthony Wood. It was an arbitrary whim of his to add the 'à'. He preferred that his name should go down to posterity with this distinguishing letter attached to it, and with this purpose in view he destroyed his original book-plate, and went through all his papers, crossing out, blotting out, and pasting over.

For a considerable time after the death of his father he lived as a kind of boarder with his brother Robert and his wife in the family home, taking his meals downstairs. However, on June 26th, 1669, we read this entry, 'was dismist from his usual and constant diet by the rudeness and barbarity of a brutish woman ... It made him (Anthony) exceeding melancholy and more retir'd, was also at great charge in taking physick and slops, to drive noises out of his ears.'

From that date he confined himself more than ever to his two rooms in the attic. He had a chimney built, and, as the isolation incident to his deafness grew, he lived almost entirely by himself. There he would stay working, surrounded by his papers, his notes, and his letters. He seldom allowed his friends to enter his study. For example, Doctor Arthur Charlett, the Master of University College, never got himself inside the room till its occupant was on his death bed, and even then he noted that his intrusion caused the recluse to fall 'into a Fit of Trembling and disorder of mind, as great as possible.' We are given the names of certain privileged bedmakers, that is all. 'July 4th, 1679, Goodwife Freeman began to serve me upon Mary's breaking her arm (She served me 5 days at Midsomer when Mary made hay).' There he remained undisturbed with his 'blew shagg gowne' in his wardrobe, with his 'stack-faggots' at the bottom of his cupboard, refreshing himself now with 'a pye from Blackman's,' now with 'pruans to stew,' or 'cherrys and whay,' and paying Jone, on occasions, 'for mending my clothes 6d.' It mattered not whether the air was relaxed 'and the wayes slabby,' out he would go each afternoon, either to visit the booksellers (in order to pick up the ballads, broadsheets, and almanacks he liked so well) or to loiter on Magdalen Bridge, or to walk as far as the hazel-nut copse at the bottom of Shotover Hill. After supper he would again be abroad, either going into some 'bye alehouse in towne, or else to one in some village neare, and there by himself take his pipe and pot.'

And so the long years passed by. He remarks upon the peculiarities of each season. One winter it was so cold that his ink froze, though it was placed near unto his new chimney. It was so slippery out of doors that the old women tied rags about their feet for fear of falling. A famous huckster of fruit, 'old mother Slye,' died, and he himself, snug and safe in his attic, is at pains to give an immortality to the rude and simple epitaph made on her by 'the witty and waggish cook of St. Alban's Hall.'

Another year was so mild that 'spring flowers were sold in Oxon marcet as early as February 20th'; the summer so hot that 'the poultry in Abingdon market died with the heat,' while a certain July turned so cold that 'the king's foul at St. James could go over the river upon the ice.'

It becomes abundantly clear from reading his pages that these old-world university divines were strangely uninhibited. It is no wonder that the great Robert Burton found his own home pasture provided with sufficient scurvy-grass. We are told that when Dr. John Wall, D.D. and Canon of Christ Church, lay dying, Dr. Richard Gardiner offered his services to pray with him. Dr. John Wall had suffered much bantering from Dr. Gardiner at the High Table, and not unnaturally he refused to have his last hours disturbed by the presence of the academic bully. When this rebuff was communicated to 'old Gardiner' he railed at the dying man, and shouting out that he was nothing but 'a mudde wall, a tottered wall, a torn wall, nay! a towne wall!' he broke the canon's windows 'with his staff'.

Mortality! Nothing absorbed Anthony à Wood's attention as much. From his garret he would hear the various great bells of Oxford 'ring out' to toll the departure of this or that celebrated figure. 'Henry Marten,' he writes, 'died suddenly with meat in his mouth'; also Thomas Trappan who 'sewed on the old King's head when he was beheaded and always said he had sewn on the goose's head.' If a vault was to be opened Anthony à Wood was there studying in the charnel house shadows, candle in hand, to give a name to dry bones. 'I think they are the bones of Dr. Henry de Abendon . . . a hart inclosed in lead . . . perhaps Dr. Fitsjame's hart.'

He visits Godstow nunnery and in St. Leonard's chapel is shown by 'one Jeffryes' the place where the dust of fair Rosamund lay. The well-known tragedy of this young girl, poisoned by the jealousy of the proud Queen, was exactly calculated to arouse the interest of the old bachelor, and he collects copious notes about it. He is as much concerned with the fate of her body in death as in life.

'Sweet chucks, beat not the bones of the buried; when he breathed, he was a man.' Wood had the greatest reverence for the remains of mortal man, for that other strange life that our bones enter upon when the living ghost that animates them has vanished and dissolved. On April 2nd, 1669, we read, 'My father's bones were removed to my mother's grave by old Robin Church.' It was natural enough that this man with his 'inclinations towards venerable antiquity' felt himself out of touch with the frivolity that possessed Oxford, that ran through the shires of England at the time of Charles II. 'Temperate, abstemious and plain and grave in the apparell,' he despised the riotous, vulgar monarchy men almost as much as the 'Fanaticks' who were 'so brisk in Oxford.' 'Divers things are desired by most sober men to be reformed . . . disrespect to seniors, sawciness. . . . An age given over to all vice—whores and harlots, pimps and panders, bauds and buffoones, lechery and treachery, atheists and papists, rogues and rascalls, reason and treason, playmakers and stage-players, officers debauched and corrupters (proctor Thomas infected with the pox while proctor) . . . .'

The interest he felt in older times caused him to fall under the suspicion of being a papist. The same fate had overtaken John Stow in the days of Elizabeth. 'A man that is studious and reserved is popishly affected.' Though Wood had royalist sympathies they did not require that he should be taken in by the fine manners of the courtiers who were in the train of the King when he resided at Oxford. How Anthony à Wood hits them off! 'The greater sort of the courtiers were high, proud, insolent, and looked upon scolars noe more than pedants and pedagogical persons. . . . To give a further character of the court, they, though they were neat and gay in their apparell, yet they were very nasty, and beastly, leaving at their departure their excrement in every corner, in chimneys, studies, cole houses, cellars. Rude, rough whore mongers; vaine, empty, carelesse!'

As the years passed little improvement was found in his temper. More and more he became like a spiteful spider in a cobweb loft. And Oxford reciprocated the enmity of this man who 'pretended to be deaf more than he was.' His *Athenae Oxonienses* received savage criticism and was officially burnt. Wood became more and more unpopular. He suffered endless insults. As he was crossing Magdalen Bridge a man, Barksdale, 'came out of the hole between it and the new herb-house' and followed him, muttering. 'I was feigne to hold up my cudgell at him.' He was also abused in the public street by Mr. Davies who was riding on horseback and 'looked red and jolly as if he had been at a fish dinner at C.C.C. and afterwards drinking as he had been.' Dr. Bathurst, President of Trinity, criticized the spelling in the *Athenae Oxonienses*, 'like a poore spirit and snivelling fellow, he fell foul upon me.' William Richards, Arch-deacon of Berkshire, when he was asked to subscribe to it, answered 'He would rather subscribe to have it burnt'; Wood observes 'Words as ugly as his face.'

At the age of sixty-three he was overtaken by a 'total suppression of urine.' The illness began in November, 1695, a few days after the University had entertained King William and Queen Mary, and when the proper old chronicler had been annoyed at seeing 'some rabble and townsmen,' who had got in by the connivance of the men at the doors of the hall, 'rudely scamble away all the banquet and sweetmeates, all sorts of souse fish (lobsters, crayfish), fruit etc. . . . in the face of the whole Universitie.'

With his disorder heavy upon him he went out as usual, and accidentally meeting Dr. Robert South, the Oxford Don whom he particularly disliked, he was unwise enough to confide to him his trouble. It seems that South's celebrated 'graphic humour' was provoked by the unusual predicament. 'Anthony Wood, if thou canst not make water thou hadst better make earth' was all the comfort he got. After more than a week closeted in his rooms he still apprehended no danger, but was 'very froward.' His relations thereupon (perhaps his two young nieces who were to inherit his property) begged Dr. Arthur Charlett to come and explain the situation to him. This hearty friend lost no time in being 'plain with him,' and under his reasoning, that fell only too pat, Wood was persuaded to make a will and put his papers in order, those papers of such inestimable value 'to any of his own temper.' 'Two bushells-full he ordered for ye fire . . . expressing both his knowledge and approbation of what was done by throwing out his Hands.' Absolutely convinced at last as to the correctness of Dr. Charlett's prognostication the old man would not be satisfied until he had superintended in person the digging of his own grave in the exact spot he wished his bones to lie 'in Merton College Church, deeper than ordinary, under, and as close to the wall (just as you enter in at the north on the left side) as the place will permit.'

It can hardly be doubted that the contemporary rhyme made while he yet lived will receive fulfilment:

Merton Wood, with his Antiquitie
Will live to all Eternitie.

Introduction to *The Life and Times of Anthony à Wood* (1932).

MERTON WOOD'S LUNCHEON

W HEN the Librarian of Merton College wrote to Mr.
Wishart[1] on the eve of the publication of my abridgment
of Andrew Clark's *Life and Times of Anthony à Wood*,
congratulating him on producing a tercentenary edition, nobody
was more surprised than myself. Suffering as I always have from
'a slowness in apprehending with quickness things,' I had entirely
missed the fact that my own very personal presentation of the
antiquarian's work was destined to appear so opportunely. After
such a manner will Providence upon occasions cast down crumbs
to wild birds when there is a scarcity of hedgerow berries.

This letter from the Librarian was followed by an official
invitation to me from the Domestic Bursar of Merton to attend
a luncheon to be given in honour of Anthony à Wood's tercentenary. I felt flattered by the compliment and, in respect for
the memory of the dead writer I so much admired, decided to be
present at this University celebration.

On my arrival at the College I sent up my card to the Librarian's rooms, and I was received by a scholarly-looking English
gentleman. He began to introduce me to a number of dons who
stood gossiping by the fire. In Dorset I had felt a slight disquiet
about my proposed excursion. I had confessed this misgiving to
my brother. 'They will have only two thoughts in their heads,'
he had answered, 'their viands and their wine.' I was reminded
now of his comfortable prediction.

'What kind of a luncheon are they going to give us? It is a day
for a good hot stew,' said one of the group. It might be supposed
that such honest talk would have put me immediately at my ease,
as, in truth, I think it was intended to do; and so I believe it would
have done had not my confidence, still tender, been suddenly
destroyed by having it explained that the invitation of which I
had been so proud had in reality been intended, perhaps, for my

---

[1] The Publisher of Llewelyn Powys's edition of Anthony à Wood. I have included
this essay as an informal footnote to the preceding essay.

architect brother. A younger don, aware of my discomfiture, detached himself from his companions and came across the room, saying to reassure me that he was quite certain that I had received my invitation 'on my own merits.' He was an extremely courteous man and my relations with him, then and later, did much to soften a certain resentment that I came to feel towards this ancient house of learning.

The ante-chamber, to which we all presently adjourned, was filled with other dons, and somebody suggested that I should go straight up to the dining hall. I came through its door and down the steps to the daïs, where, finding myself standing a little awkwardly among a group of gowned strangers, I thought it best to look for my place at the table, and this I discovered without difficulty and sat down upon a bench opposite to it. Here I drew myself in upon myself as I have observed hedgehogs to do when they find themselves in an unsympathetic environment. From my isolated position I was able to pass several moments in un- disturbed meditation upon the scene before me.

After lunch the Chancellor of the University addressed the company. I had never seen Lord Grey before and was impressed by the presence and personality of this distinguished statesman. As I looked at his proud sensitive head the word 'religious' came to my mind. There was an innate simplicity about him which might have belonged to a shepherd, and yet something patrician also. He stood out in that hall as aloof and different as a monolith surrounded by a flock of sheep. He spoke with urbanity, but for the most part what he said had nothing to do with Anthony à Wood. He referred to the fact that he had for a long time paid tithes to the College, he recounted anecdotes about Bishop Creighton; and then confessed that he had never read Andrew Clark's volumes, and knew of Wood only through 'a recent article in *The Times Literary Supplement*,' from which he had gathered that his writings were not suitable for reading aloud.

And so it was with the subsequent speakers. Slowly it became apparent to me that not one of them really appreciated at its true worth the extraordinary originality of this son of their house who had been treated so abominably by their predecessors. They were willing and glad to have acknowledgement to his services as an antiquarian, but they seemed to wish to dissociate the College from the scandal of his outspoken personality. In Oxford, it appears, they have long, long memories. These dons have learned nothing and have forgotten nothing; and the Sub-warden of Merton did not hesitate to remind us, who had come together in order to do honour to Wood's memory, that he was *not a Fellow of the College*, and that, though he was a member of the Common Room, he was *turned out of it*. It was clear to me that they actually were half ashamed of this writer whom chance had so closely connected with their house. A reference was made to some Fellow recently deceased—'I never thought to associate *his* name with the name of Anthony à Wood'—the implication being that, in this parochial pocket of academic prejudice, the comparison was not in Wood's favour, though Anthony à Wood is an historic figure whose 'esurient genie' belongs not only to Merton or to Oxford, but to the commonwealth of the world's literature.

Certainly I was attending a very half-hearted and grudging tercentenary festival. Why had these dons not appeared in their 'scarlet formalities' instead of in their informal gowns? How Wood himself would have eyed this tepid gathering with all his old rancour! 'These people,' I thought, 'are the same that persecuted him when he was alive.' They hated him then as commonplace people always hate anyone who is out of the ordinary and who is more spiritually intense than themselves. The passionate zeal that Wood showed in his chosen way of life was beyond their capacity to understand. From the beginning to the end it was in the face of ridicule, carping criticism, and gross stupidity that he carried through his self-imposed, laborious purposes. In actual fact, there was a strange 'innocence' in Wood's nature which has never been properly appreciated, and this sensitive quality provoked from those who knew him nothing but derision, contempt, and animosity.

Quite apart from Wood's fearless honesty of thought, quite apart from his hatred of all hypocricies, he has won his lasting position in English literature because of his quaint idiosyncratic confederacy with antiquity. It was the high prerogative of this solitary and slighted recorder, working day after day in his attic retreat, to hear the wings of the centuries pass over England more clearly than did anybody of his own time and perhaps of any time. The fact that he was such an obstinate and eccentric character made him an object as desirable to bait as a blind bear.

To this day the mention of his name in Oxford provokes either frivolity or moral disapprobation. The truth is, these men of the world have never understood nor cared for his genius. The dons of Merton are still the same, the same, the same! Like one of God's spies, I observed them, watched them, these breathing phantoms sitting solid at their repast, at their refectory tables; some of them deep set in the illusion of the passing moment; others with pallid idealistic faces looking up to heaven; all of them utterly removed from any imaginative realisation of life. One thing only can be relied upon to awaken them,—the shadow of a menace to the security of their ancient foundation; then it is a wonder to see how these 'furred cats' and 'clerg-hawks' can scratch and clutch. It is not surprising that these Merton dons murmur out their self-interested motto, *Stet Fortuna Domus*, with an almost mystical fervour. Make no doubt of it, they have a brave time in their pleasant garths—a fine view over the flowering meadows, the most perfect miniature library in the world, victuals in plenty at each ting-tang-ting of the dinner bell; wine in the buttery, pipe upon pipe, bin upon bin, tun upon tun!

If the ghost of Anthony à Wood was present in that dining-hall hidden away somewhere in the rafters, like a tetchy winter bat too inquisitive to sleep—an assumption far less incredible than are many of the foibles these men teach to the youth of our land— how he, 'whose rhetoric served him to curse his bad fortune,' would have trounced them after his old unregenerate manner. *His* tercentenary fish dinner, *his* own tercentenary, the tercentenary celebration he had been waiting for for so many, many afternoons down there in the key-cold clay; and it had turned out to be a matter of nothing,—cautious, dull, heavy, stupid; but good enough for 'old man A.W. . . . . Joan of Hedington will not have him because full of issues; I used to carry lobsters and crabs there . . . all that is good in my book is not of my putting in. . . . I understood not Greek.'

When I could escape I went across the quadrangle to Anthony à Wood's burying-place, and there alone in the chapel knelt upon the cracked slab that marks his grave. Turning my ears from the voices of these latter day 'banterers' as they dispersed in the street outside, behind the closed door of this hollow church I tried to call up the old man's spirit, tried to call it up out of the deep grave, to tell it that I, a simple man from the country, with chalk on my shoe-leather; living in a cottage with a rent not worth so much as a thousand groats; an Epicurean from the open fields, too ignorant and too illiterate to grace a book with an index; a guest who had been invited by mistake to the feast, resented with all my being the attitude of these supercilious scholars, as easily fluttered by a few broad expressions as pullets by a handful of chaff, men who still, after the passing of three centuries, could not find it in their hearts to give to the name of Anthony à Wood the unqualified honour that is its due.

From *Earth Memories* (1934).

THOMAS DELONEY

IN ENGLISH literature no great writer has been more neglected than has Thomas Deloney, the Elizabethan novelist. His three prose works, *Jacke of Newberie*, *The Gentle Craft*, and *Thomas of Reading*, have often enough been made centres of discussion by academic critics concerned to trace the origin and development of English prose fiction, but among the authors of all this scholarly research, there has been found no one to do adequate justice to his astonishing genius.

Outside of Christopher Marlowe, Shakespeare, Ford, and Ben Jonson, he has no match in the Elizabethan era. It is impossible for Thomas Deloney to write in a dull manner. His zest for life, quick as a sprite in a buttery, displays itself in every sentence, in every word that he puts down. His realism has never been equalled. His power in this kind is as sure as ever was that of Boccaccio. The characters he invents are no book characters. They are actual shop-door, street-corner people who eat possets, drink sack or muskadine, and cry, and sneeze, and stand upon very shoe-leather.

His affirmation of the delight of being abroad in the ordinary common-sense world is very stout. To contemplate a dame 'carrying the keys of her cubberts gingling at her side' is for him reward enough. These three works might have been written by Sancho Panza, with such shrewd earth-aplomb do they present the impulses and the emotions of the indiscriminate crowd, of that section of the population which may be said to have their heads 'screwed on the right way.' Deloney's writing is never far removed from the dust of the King's High Road, from the egg-cobbles of the London streets, from actuality at its lowest level.

It has been a fanciful prejudice with me to remark a difference between flower-shop salesmen and ironmongers. The former, because it is their profession to make commercial profit out of beauty, grow, so it seems, shallow and artificial in their address, whereas ironmongers, because it is their business to supply people with utensils necessary for daily use, become sensible and honest citizens. Thomas Deloney may be said to represent the iron-mongers in literature; one who knows how essential colanders, kettles, frying-pans, and saucepans are to human beings. The unredeemed lives of ordinary people are his province. His sense of poetry is of that simple kind that can be understood by every-body—by the coal-man, by the iceman, by the fruit-man at the curb; the poetry that has to do with the yellow sun shining bright upon field and market-place, the poetry that 'women are not angels, though they have angel faces'—the poetry, in fact, that is concerned with the whole torrential stream of life, parti-coloured, manifold with its sudden turns of fate, turns of fate that overtake and surprise each one of us with their irrelevant unexpectedness. And what an observation Deloney had for the twists and quirks to be found in human character! Carelessly he etches in for us brabbling dames, penny-father old men, and prodigal youths; and at once these phantom puppets of his imagination are walking between the street booths, standing at their cutting-stools, or sit-ting at their removable refectory tables gutting pudding pies; are actually there before us, at one moment out of temper, and at the next grinning, but always there firmly set in farting flesh.

No lover of the sun should be content to remain unacquainted with the prose works of this master. 'Yes, by Saint Anne, and ginger shall be hot i' the mouth too.' He is kin to Cervantes, sib to François Rabelais. He belongs to those who do not trouble themselves with the idealistic foibles that besot the minds of so many human beings, to those who are satisfied with the world as it is, with that unregenerate world that wags on irrespective of beliefs, in taverns where reckonings are 'set up in very fair chalk,' and under the big elm trees in the square where the butter-women's tongues 'like lambs' tails seldom stand still.'

Thomas Deloney is not concerned with improving manners or with inculcating moral precepts. His vitality is such that he is able to celebrate every phase of life. He is in love with the whole of life, and his prodigious animal spirits make every object he sees, every person he meets, interesting to him. He has no desire to correct. He seems to take for granted that his art could have no better purpose than to present the great Shrove-Tuesday Proces-sion of life as it is, without comment.

Little is known about him. Nash refers to him as 'the Balletting

Silke Weaver of Norwich,' and it has been assumed from his name that he belonged to some continental Protestant family which, because of religious persecution, had settled in England. It was natural enough that the 'university wits' should deride the work of 'T.D.,' for when they wrote of the underworld, it was from above downward. To them Deloney was little better than 'a base mechanical.' He had sold his own ballads in Cheapside and sung them outside countless alehouse doors. All his life long, apprentices, tradespeople, porters, serving-wenches, had been his companions. He could write of Jack of Newbury with enthusiasm because he himself had not seldom been pinched of his victuals. He had the poor man's romantic admiration for the rich man's liberality because he had learnt how hard it is to come honestly by a gammon of bacon. His literary material is ever where human life is natural, without pretensions. It never would enter the head of a labourer going through the streets of a city to worry whether his hands were dirty, or whether the knees of his trousers had been patched: on such points he is without care, and Deloney wrote with the enfranchisement of one of the lower classes too pressed by life's realities to trouble much about its niceties.

He is supposed to have been born in 1543, and he died around 1600. It was by his ballad-writing that he first won popularity amongst skylarking prentices, cockrow ostlers, impecunious tradespeople, water-men, fairfield chafferers, and the unnumbered sweaty-caps of his time. Some disaster, a fire, a hanging, would be in everybody's mouth, and immediately up would start T.D., 'in his tawny coat,' to commemorate the event in jigging verse.

> *Like to the fatall ominous Raven which tolls*
> *The sicke man's dirge within his hollow beake.*[1]

Some popular discontent would be abroad in 'Merrie England,' and sure enough before long would find expression in one of Deloney's ballads. In the famine year of 1596 his 'Ballad on the Want of Corn' was written to such purpose that for some time the Mayor of London was 'in search for T.D.' The ballad represented Queen Elizabeth as speaking with her people. 'Dialoguewise in a very fond and undecent sort.' It may have been this particular happening that turned Deloney's attention to prose, for

[1] From a poem addressed to Deloney in Edward Guilphin's *Skialetheia* (1598).

we know that he had a son to provide for at his weaver's home somewhere in the parish of St. Giles, Cripplegate.

He wrote carelessly, 'composing as he goes i' the street,' giving the populace, to draw them from their dumps, imaginary stories of lives similar to their own. To do it was as easy as sop to Deloney, because he knew his subjects so well. We need not look for 'any matter of light value, curiously pen'd with pickt words or choice phrases, but a quaint and plain discourse best fitting matters of merriment.' The University wits, these masters of 'pick't words,' saw him doing better than they what they had been trying to do; and many were the flirts and frumps that used to float down to the groundling poet from the heights of their Euphues Parnassus. Greene, apologizing that he should demean himself by writing his *Defence of Conny Catching*, says, 'Such triviall trinkets and threadbare trash, had better seemed T.D. whose braines beaten to the yarking up of Ballades, might more lawfully have glaunst at the quaint conceites of conny-catching and crossebiting.' 'These fellows,' says another, ' are in every corner of cities and market Townes of the Realme singing and selling of ballads and pamphlets full of ribauldrie, and all scurrilous vanity, to the prophanation of God's name.'

'The Muse of Thomas Deloney,' wrote Nash, 'from the first peeping forth, hath stood at Livery at an Alehouse wispe, never exceeding a penny a quart, day or night, and this deare yeare, together with the silencing of his looms, scarce that; he being constrained to betake him to carded Ale.'

Kempe appended a note to his *Nine Daies Wonder* addressed 'to the impudent generation of Ballad-makers.' In this note he declares:

> I have made a privy search, what private Jigmonger of your jolly number hath been the Author of these abominable Ballets written of me. I was told it was the great Ballad-maker T.D., alias Thomas Deloney. . . . But I was given to understand, your late general, Thomas, died poorly (as you all must do) and was honestly buried, which is much to be doubted of some of you.'

How often in Shakespeare have we longed for more talk from the country people, from his God's idiots, and weasel-brained hedge rogues! The pages of Deloney are packed with such unstudied chatter, packed with kitchen wisdom. His is the wisdom of a coffin-bearer meditating upon a life that is over; the wisdom of old Gran Prat, the midwife, slapping a new-born baby to life, and meditating upon its future of lust and hunger and piety; the wisdom of a town crier; of an aged priest; the wisdom that belongs to men and women who have been so jostled by the years that they can be surprised by nothing, with minds sharp, shrewd, and disillusioned that hit the mark at the first jump. 'For cunning continueth when fortune fleeteth . . . it is gone, farewell it.' All those apt saws, broad expressions of speech that are to us so refreshing, like time-resistant, homespun patches from the cloak of human wisdom, abound in these little-read pages. It may be for their very outspokenness that they have received such scant recognition. Always Deloney is a 'groundling' writing for 'groundlings,' and his unintellectual simplicities and grossness may be an offence to the official appraisers of literature who pass through life removed from too close contact with the 'rabblement' who sweep their floors, make their fires, and roast their capons. Anybody who is directly concerned, day in and day out, with the mean employments indispensable to human living cannot be utterly foolish. To be entirely superficial, one must be safely removed from scouring pans. When a woman is hemming a nightgown or cooking a Christmas dinner, without conscious effort an awareness of the realities of existence presses in upon her, and the same thing happens to a man who strikes an ox to the floor in the shambles, or who spends the greater part of an April day digging a grave.

Deloney's world is a world of tradesmen, of fickle-headed tailors, of weavers who sit at their looms 'in a row'; of the people who, though not invited to the banquet, scrabble for the ortes behind pantry doors and then return home to sleep in truckle-beds; of the boys who play at push-pin in the streets; of the boys who go to carry water from the conduit; of the old women who pummel soiled linen at the bottom step of a stairway leading down to the Thames—indeed, of all poor people whom, as Deloney remarks with gentle irony, 'God lightly blesseth with most children.'

If ever he has occasion to refer to the gentry or nobility, it is as privileged, faery-land folk with gracious manners and 'lily-white hands,' with whom he and his fellows, fighting for 'bitten apples,' have little in common. The motive of his plots often enough is

The block of Portland stone carved by Miss Elizabeth Muntz which stands a little inland from the cliff edge near White Nose, marking the place where Llewelyn Powys's ashes are buried.

the same motive that is popular to-day in the cinematograph theatres—the industry of a simple and good character suddenly rewarded, out of all expectation, with riches, and whose generosity—Deloney's most highly esteemed virtue—remains still, under the changed circumstances, uncorrupted by the 'slyding wealth of the world.'

It is in the London of Queen Elizabeth that his whimsical, jocund, and matter-of-fact characters live and move and have their being; in that London whose houses were, for the most part, mediaeval, and where the Mermaid Tavern, with its two side-doors, the one opening into Friday and the other into Bread Street, was still present: at a time when half an hour's walk through any of the city gates, through Ludgate or Moorgate or Bishopsgate, would bring a man into the open country of reddle-bellied rams, of white-bonneted maids, of sweet-breathing, patient cows. To-day, not far from Westminster Abbey, there is a street called Tuttle Street. It marks the place of Tuttle fields where was a meadow, famous in Deloney's time for assignations, a meadow to which went, in the Gentle Craft, the two 'proper neat wenches' looking for heartsease and thrift. This is the London of Deloney's stories: the London of timbered house-fronts, of peeked gables, of steep-tilted roofs shining with snow over which one might expect to see witches flying astride upon broomsticks. It is the London of the train bands; the London of the prentice boys crying 'Clubs,' the London where 'souls' cakes' were baked for All-hallow-e'en; the London resonant with the hearty calls of night-watchmen, 'two of the clock and a cold and frosty morning'; the London where lighted lanterns were hung in the church steeples after dark for the help of belated travellers; the London of cobble streets and garbage litter; the London of enclosed tavern yards, encircled with balconies, where, as the night passed, the 'anon, Sir, anon, Sir' of the drawer would imperceptibly give place to the stillness of the dead hours, when the only sound was an occasional stamp from tired horses, as King Charles's Wain rose high and higher over the 'new chimney.'

As it is so often with great artists, this 'halfpenny chronicler' created within the circle of this actual Elizabethan London another London of his imagination, and this new London presently takes to itself its own reality, a fabulous Rabelaisian reality under old St. Paul's.

Afterwards they proceeded, and came to Paules Church, whose steeple was so hie, that it seemed to pierce the cloudes, on the top whereof, was a great and mightie wether-cocke, of cleane silver, the which notwithstanding seemed as small as a sparrow to men's eyes, it stood so exceeding high, and which goodly weather cocke was afterwards stolen away, by a cunning cripple who found means one night to clime up to the top of the steeple, and tooke it downe.

Which of us has not been teased out of mind by a desire to have free entrance into the London of 'Shakespeare's boys'? Ignorant we have of necessity remained. 'We may as well push against Powles as stir 'em.' It is all here for us in Deloney's work. To read these three novels is to be privy to the stir of those far-off, noisy alleys; it is to rub shoulders with these vigorous men and women, and to hear their exact speech, the very words of the formal burgomaster in his velvet cap, the very words of the man 'well whitled' staggering by a red-latticed sill, the very 'prittle prattle' of the drabs in the rain.

To read Thomas Deloney's novels for the first time is an unequalled experience. He himself boasted that they were 'very fit to passe away the tediousness of the long winter evenings,' and he never spoke a more true word. There is none who writes after his sort, so nimble, so solid, so honest. What a smack of ancient actuality has been hidden away in these incomparable paragraphs!

Thomas Deloney defeats Mortality. The prisoners that Death over three hundred years ago herded out of Cheapside and Pudding Lane no longer play at 'mum budget,' are no longer dumb. Their everyday canting talk comes to us pat across the centuries, as if they themselves were 'rounding us in the ear.' For Thomas Deloney knew them as a *gamin* knows his pennies.

> Twittle, twattle I know what I know. . . . Life, why, what is it but a floure, a bubble in the water, a spann long and full of misere: and trust me I doe detest life, worse than a goat doth hate basil. . . with hey trickse, tringoe tricksee. Under the greenwood tree.

From *Rats in the Sacristy* (1937).

MEMORIES OF THOMAS HARDY

In the spring of 1938 there was an auction sale at Max Gate
of all the possessions of Thomas Hardy that had not been
judged of sufficient interest to be included amongst the objects
bequeathed by Mrs. Hardy to the County Museum at Dorchester.
A report of the sale appeared in the local paper and to one who had
for many years known and honoured Mr. Hardy the account
given of the final dispersal of his goods could not fail to be moving.
The Three Marys, a small picture that had once been in the
possession of Thomas Hardy's neighbour, William Barnes, fetched
no more than four and a half guineas, and this in spite of the fact
that it bore the inscription in the novelist's handwriting 'bought
at sale of Wm. Barnes Dorset poet, by Tho. Hardy'. Came
Rectory, where William Barnes spent the evening of his life,
stands scarcely half a mile distant from Max Gate.

It was reported that a walking stick of Hardy's was knocked
down to a Dorset farmer for twelve shillings, and that the looking-
glass from his bedroom, for a sum no more considerable, fell to
the bidding of an unknown young lady. We can scarcely doubt
that the two last auction chances would have pleased the poet. In
what better hands could his staff have fallen than in those of a man
all the hours of whose life would be spent in the hayfields, harvest
fields, stables, cow-yards, and market places of Wessex? And how
could 'casualty' have indulged Hardy's fancy more than to have
placed his familiar dressing-table mirror in the possession of so
enterprising a bargainer? On how many mornings of neutral tone
had not this crystal plate reflected the countenance of 'a thinker of
crooked thoughts upon Life in the sere!' It would do so now no
longer. In its place the bright features of a young girl would shine
out in the bedroom light, with cool hands arranging her hair,
while planning perhaps for a summer tryst in a Frome valley
buttercup meadow, or in some well-selected bracken hollow of
Bockhampton heath.

This plain newspaper report of the sale at Max Gate set me

pondering on Hardy's long life and especially upon those occasions when I myself had been privileged to be in his presence.

The house of his birth still stands at the furthest end of Upper Bockhampton's blind lane and I do not think any great man ever had a nativity home more suited to his genius than is this small unobtrusive Dorset freehold cottage, with its thatched roof embowered among the apple trees of its own small garden, to that of Thomas Hardy. Over the hedge of the plot, on both sides of the lane, great forest trees tower high, huge-boughed leafy trees in which all day long rooks caw, wood-pigeons murmur, and small birds twitter and sing and flutter from one cool shadow to another. On the further side of the white gate which marks the end of this sequestered privet-hedge-way lies the great heath of *The Return of the Native* with its acres of fern and heather. It was here that Hardy played as a child and it was here that he experienced his first passionate love affair. In such a locality it would be strange indeed if the mind of a young man had not turned to thoughts of love. Nowhere in Dorset do primroses cluster more gently about the beech tree boles; nowhere in Dorset do the silver rains of a midsummer morning patter more softly down through the woodland foliage; nowhere in Dorset can there be found safer and more secret 'lovers' cabinets' than amongst the tall stiff-turreted bracken jungles of this wild, west country heath.

Mr. Middleton Murry told me once that Hardy's first memory was of looking at the shining belly of a kitchen kettle newly brought from Dorchester market by his mother, by that same mother who in the very heart of Victoria's spacious reign had fallen in love with Mr. Hardy's father, the black-bearded village builder, her maidenly heart being struck, in an instant, by the mere spectacle of an elbow wagging at an old viol up in the musicians' gallery of Stinsford Church. The kitchen utensil was truly an honourable and a fitting first memory for a great poet, a memory Homeric in its association with man's common needs on earth where receptacles of clay, of bronze, of copper, or of iron have for so many millenniums been used for convenience in eating and drinking.

It was in the nineties, I think, that I first heard the syllables of Thomas Hardy's name spoken. We had all been invited to the Abbey at Montacute for a picnic and there was present at the gathering the West Country novelist Walter Raymond. It was this man, with his fine head of white hair, who informed my

brother John in a spirit of modesty as charming as it was magnanimous that there was living in Dorset a writer far greater than himself. When a few years later my brother's first volume of youthful poems[1] was published it contained an Ode addressed to Hardy:

> Master of human smiles and human moan,
> Of strange soul-searchings, raptures, agonies,
> Passions that ask for bread and find a stone,
> Hopes hungered into madness like the seas,
> And pity dumb with pleading like the wind:
> Prophet art thou of that mysterious tongue
> Wherewith our ancient Mother deaf and blind,
> Her griefs immortal and her joys hath sung
> In the unheeding ears of human kind.
>
> .   .   .
>
> And there, in commune with thy mighty heart,
> I saw how life's light wreath of summer roses
> Remorseless Fate's inveterate frown discloses,
> And sullen Death's intolerable dart:
> Saw man's last hope beneath a soulless sky,
> To live for Love, and for Love's sake to die.

The novelist was evidently gratified and wrote an encouraging
letter, a courtesy which later resulted in my brother paying a visit
to Max Gate. Hardy did not fail to appreciate John Cowper's
temperament, with its romantic undisciplined imaginings. The
friendship between the two men, and Mr. Hardy's confidence in
my brother's remarkable gifts, lasted until the novelist's death.

I well remember my brother's return from his first visit to Max
Gate. It was during the summer holidays and the rest of us
children were crowded together in a wooden hut which my
youngest brother had built for himself in one of the shrubberies.
This brother had invited us all to tea and his saucepan was just
beginning to boil under the laurel bushes when John appeared full
of exciting talk about his expedition. I recollect how he drew for
us a caricature of Hardy on one of the white deal boards that
formed the walls of this 'Bushes' home,' a striking picture of the
novelist that the passagings of snail, ant, and wood-louse were
never able quite to obliterate. Especially did the sketch emphasize
the writer's hooked nose and goblin eyebrows. It was, I believe,

[1] *Odes and Other Poems* by John Cowper Powys (1896).

in these same holidays that Hardy and his first wife paid us a visit. They walked up from the station at Montacute arriving at the Vicarage in time for luncheon. Hardy, I remember, wore a pair of tight snuff-coloured trousers which oddly contrasted with the more sober colour of the upper part of his dress. My father had not read a word he had ever written, but he had heard rumours enough of the freedom of his thought to qualify his enthusiasm for this new hero that his eldest son had discovered. My mother's attitude was different. Her literary interests had always been so strong that any writer would have been honoured by her, and, as Mr. Hardy's place was at her right hand, all went well. Hardy at the time must have been about fifty years old. His lips were pale and his face did not give the impression of good health and I remember my mother rashly predicted that he would not live to a great age. The first Mrs. Hardy was a kindly woman whose forehead was adorned by two curls which appeared to my irreverent little boy's fancy like the feathers at the end of a drake's tail. In the afternoon my brother took Mr. Hardy over Montacute House and through the village, finally returning to the Vicarage in time for him to write in the visitor's book of the 'Mabelulu,' another garden play house that my brother Bertie and my sister May and I had built, the words—*Thomas Hardy. A Wayfarer.* After the old-fashioned family tea was at an end John and my sister Gertrude and I accompanied our guests to the country station. It was a lovely summer's evening and presently I found myself sitting alone with Hardy on the well-varnished yellow-painted bench that was on the platform outside the lamp-room. He remained silent with his legs crossed as though absorbed in contemplation of the quiet landscape. Suddenly it came into my head to begin to describe to him the dancing that each summer took place on the Club-Day and at the School-Treat under the village apple trees. I told him how these dances would continue late into the night, which was to say the least of it a gross exaggeration, for my father would soon grow uneasy if ever the Kingsbury band continued to play by the lee light of the moon; and in my eager eloquence I referred to the remarkable number of old-world dances that still were known in the district. I had intended that this second prevarication should arouse the poet's attention but I was not at all prepared for the extreme interest that he now showed, as, concentrating his whole mind upon me, he began asking for the names of these same dances, prosecuting his enquiries with a resolution not easy to be evaded even when my brother came to join us. The mortification I felt as I sat on that bench in my white flannel trousers, green at the knees from where I had recently fallen, has remained with me to this day, together with a clear memory of those suspended moments before the train's arrival, with voices of harvesters coming from a distant field and the look of the softness of the summer grass opposite, where cows moved at peace under a mackerel sky.

The next time I saw Hardy was after I had come down from Cambridge. I had been staying with my brother Theodore at East Chaldon. This little village is situated some ten miles from Max Gate, and I ventured on my way home as I had two hours to wait in Dorchester, to call. I was extremely nervous as I approached the front door by the short curving drive. The servant showed me into the drawing-room. I observed the room narrowly. There was a bust of Sir Walter Scott at the top of a tall book case and, on each side of the fire place, pictures of Shelley and of John Keats. I also noticed a small water-colour of Westminster Abbey painted by Hardy himself when he was a young man. Mrs. Hardy presently entered the room. She informed me that she had sent a servant up to Mr. Hardy's study but doubted whether he would be able to come down and see me. She was mistaken, however, for almost immediately the door opened and Mr. Hardy entered looking to me unchanged from what he had been on the occasion of his visit to Montacute. He asked me questions about Chaldon and also talked to me about my future plans. I remember he advised me to join the Dorset Society in London. My romantic hero worship could scarcely be concealed. He must have seen it shining out of my eyes. I did not dare to stay long and when I rose to leave he conducted me to the garden gate, truly a signal courtesy to offer so excitable and immature a youth. Before taking my leave I ventured to ask him what he was then writing, and well do I remember his answering with a kindly, self-depreciatory, quizzical glance that he was occupied with *The Dynasts*.

I walked away in an ecstasy at having once more seen him and I remember buying a picture postcard in Dorchester, which not only included a drawing of Hardy's head, but also a miniature sketch of the novelist's home. This postcard I had the temerity to send to H. R. King, my old school master at Sherborne, telling him that I had just returned from a visit to 'The greatest living English writer,' words that must have appeared grandiloquent enough to the sarcastic, lovable, old pedant to whom they were addressed, a man whose fad it was to believe that English literature had reached its glome with Wordsworth, Dickens, and Thackeray. *The Dynasts* is an epic I have always admired greatly, but apparently such appreciation has not been universal. Edward Clodd once told my friend Louis Wilkinson that on his stepping to his bookshelf on the occasion of a visit of Meredith to Aldeburgh the novelist's cold, cultivated, sarcastic voice had sounded across the lamp-lit summer room 'I hope you are not bringing us *The Dynasts*.' At the time of which I write George Meredith was still considered in the know-all contemporary literary world of far more consequence than Hardy and it has been a deep satisfaction to me that I lived long enough to see so shallow a judgment reversed and the native, homespun, Shakespearean genius of Hardy reverenced above the fashionable clever talent of the mannered stylist of whom Scawen Blunt remarked 'tailoring parentage was the great tragedy of Meredith's life.' An interesting contrast between the essential natures of the two men is afforded by the following odd happening. When Wilde was serving time in Reading Gaol a movement was started to petition the Home Secretary for the shortening of his sentence. Overtures were made to the leading men-of-letters to see how many of them would be willing to give support to such a project. Hardy volunteered at once to sign the paper, but Meredith, sensitive to the popular feeling which had been aroused, refused to have anything to do with it. And yet Oscar Wilde and his manners were extraordinarily remote from the simplicities of Hardy's upbringing and character. 'Is not Oscar Wilde rather a hard-hearted man?' he once said to my brother John.

At this period I spent a year or more at Davos Platz and on my return to England my brother Theodore invited me to stay with him at Chaldon. It was during the autumn of 1911 and this should have given me a good opportunity of other visits to Max Gate. Such a possibility however was upset by the following childish accident. One of my sisters was an enthusiastic collector of autographs and as she was passing Max Gate one day on her bicycle it occurred to her that Hardy's signature would make a notable addition to her book. She did not know that it was

Hardy's custom never to indulge such requests. Her discomfiture was only matched by my own consternation when she confided her unlucky adventure to me with the words 'Well, I don't think much of your great hero.' The embarrassment I underwent over the solecism tormented my foolish mind so much that I never ventured to make a single overture in the direction of Max Gate during the whole time I was staying with my brother. I did not, however, abandon the vain hope that either in the streets of Weymouth or of Dorchester I might one day meet Mr. Hardy by chance face to face.

One evening, when sheltering in the waiting-room of the little wayside station of Moreton before starting for my dark walk across the moor to Chaldon, I imagined for a few moments that my sanguine expectations had actually been fulfilled. Just as I was preparing to set out the London express came in. In a brightly lighted first-class carriage opposite where I stood I was sure that I recognized the familiar features of the novelist. The drenching rain that ceaselessly splashed down upon the roofless lamp-lit platform made it difficult for me to see clearly and for several minutes I remained motionless gazing and gazing through the carriage window dimmed to a mysterious opaqueness by the continual stream of rain drops. Presently the traveller who was, in actual fact, a perfect stranger noticed the exaggerated attention I was giving him and to my utter confusion I received in response to my stare of childish adoration the patronizing easy smile of an unpleasantly supercilious First Class passenger.

In the early spring of the following year I was again in Switzerland. It was on my return from this second convalescence in the Alps that I began to try to write. My first paper was entitled 'Death' and in later years it was included in an early collection of essays called *Ebony and Ivory*. I sent the article to the *New Age* and immediately received an answer in Mr. Orage's artistic, spider-like writing accepting it and assuring me that it was 'good enough for publication in any journal.' No eaglet who for the first time tries the strength of its wings could have been prouder than I was on reading his words, and, as soon as the piece was printed I ordered several copies of the weekly, one of which I ventured to post to Max Gate. An answer came back by return from Mr. Hardy thanking me for my kindness and saying he had enjoyed reading my article very much indeed, adding that he himself had but recently passed through just such an experience as I described. There is no doubt that Mr. Hardy had felt the death of his first wife—the heroine of a *A Pair of Blue Eyes*—deeply.

With the greatest pride I showed the letter to my brother John and I well remember his declaring that only a really great man would ever have been willing to write in so intimate and natural a way to a young writer who had nothing but enthusiasm to commend him.

In the year 1919, after an exile in Africa of five years, I was again back in England. My father by that time had resigned the living of Montacute and had retired to Weymouth so that once more I found myself in easy reach of Mr. Hardy. My sister Gertrude arranged that I should go to tea one afternoon at Max Gate. I reached Dorchester in plenty of time and crossing the railway bridge slowly approached the house. The young chestnuts that bordered the road were in fresh leaf and although I was now thirty-five years old, my heart seemed no less responsive, no less romantic than on the occasion of my former visit. And yet I was discouraged also. My African sojourn had interrupted my writing career and I could not catch the attention of a single editor. At the back of my mind I held to the hope that Hardy would be able to give me just the advice I wanted. All turned out different. He was no longer the grave-eyed man-of-letters I had remembered. My impression as he crossed the small hall to shake hands with me remains fixed in my mind. He was dressed in a tweed suit that might have belonged to any country squire, a suit that seemed to suggest partridge-shooting, with calls of 'mark over,' rather than the quiet of a writer's study. It was as if old age had not only lightened his marrow bones but gone a little to his head. I realized at once that the hope I had entertained of getting help from this talkative, dapper, little gentleman was an empty one, and sitting at tea I contented myself with listening respectfully to his anecdotal memories of old Dorchester. In my desire to make some kind of impression I would sometimes relate my own sensational experiences in Africa. The diffidence I felt in approaching the subject of my personal affairs was increased by the fact that I was not the only guest. When I was first shown into the drawing-room I had found myself in the company of a young woman occupied in playing with a white terrier. This terrier was the dog named Wessex who held an important place in the last years of

Hardy's life. The young lady diverted herself with the animal in a way that showed her as being a familiar and favoured visitor and I received the same impression when her husband arrived, a self-possessed young man who wrote reviews, so I was told afterward, for the *Times Literary Supplement*. I myself had only written for the *New Age*; yet this young scholar from London and Oxford, living at a nearby mill (which of the mills I never discovered) had already at twenty-five firmly established himself in contemporary literary circles. The two young people left after tea and while Mr. Hardy was conducting them to the garden gate I stood with Mrs. Hardy at the window. We looked out at the spring twilight in silence. It was the first time that I had met Mr. Hardy's second wife. She was a dark, nervous woman of an awkward carriage, but one who possessed an odd distinction of her own. As I stood by her side in that room emptied of its company I received a draught of romantic Brontë-like melancholy the strength of which I have never forgotten. In after years Mrs. Hardy, on more than one occasion, proved herself a good friend to me, but I never rid myself altogether of that first impression of a hopeless attitude of life-disavowal which seemed, indeed, to find ultimate justification in her lingering death from a malignant cancer in middle life. At tea I had ventured to speak of an essay I was writing on the engraver Bewick, and I remember Mr. Hardy referring to one of the famous tail-pieces that represented the old North Country-man's own coffin being carried away from his home, Cherryburn, a house of stone very bleak in appearance, so Hardy explained.

Six years passed before I saw Mr. Hardy again. I had been living during this time in New York City. Though I found it difficult to earn my living by writing these were happy years, and in due time under the wise and understanding guidance of Mr. Alfred Harcourt America gradually began to give me the recognition that I had failed to win in England. The necessity of paying the monthly rent of my hall-bedroom (into which the sun only shone by reflection from the factory opposite) often put me to my shifts and on the occasion of one of these crises the idea came to me of writing an article on Thomas Hardy for *The Dial*. In this article I was indiscreet enough to allude to a conversation I had had with him which seemed to be of general literary interest. He had con-fided to me, as we sat talking together after tea, that he remem-bered as a boy a family of saddlers living in the nearby village of

Broadmayne named Keats and, recalling that John Keats's fore-bears had been saddlers, he had often wondered whether this Dorset family could not have been related to the poet, a surmise that appeared to receive support from the fact that the features of some of the members of the Broadmayne saddlering family had, he had often thought, remarkable racial resemblance to those of the author of *Endymion*. Indeed, he told me that he had sometimes indulged his fancy that Keats might have actually walked over the downs to visit these West Country cousins during those days when, on his voyage to Rome, his ship, because of bad weather, was driven to take shelter in Lulworth Cove, where was composed the famous last sonnet, with thoughts of hills, stars, and the sea, un-mistakably reminiscent of this particular Dorset locality landscape.

As ill luck would have it my essay fell under the all-seeing eye of Amy Lowell who was just then collecting material for her biography of Keats—and what must she do but bustle off to Max Gate to harass Mr. Hardy with cross-questionings after the manner of one who wants facts rather than fiction and has a mind to sift all evidence to the bottom! It was not until I had returned once more to Dorset with my American wife, Miss Gregory, that the full repercussion of this awkward affair reached me. My brother John, as was his custom, had written to ask whether he could pay his summer visit to Max Gate and on this occasion bring with him my brother Theodore. Just before the two of them left East Chaldon a letter arrived from Mrs. Hardy com-plaining of my ill-conduct in having published in *The Dial* an intimate communication that had never been intended for literary use. My brother Theodore, though he had already put on his Sunday jacket, forthwith abandoned out of hand all idea of visit-ing Max Gate, and as those who know him will guess, much Frome water had to flow under Gray's Bridge before ever he crossed the great man's threshold. I felt humiliated on my own account, and indignant with Miss Lowell, recalling with renewed irritation the bluntness of her speech when, on our first being introduced, she had remarked in her autocratic manner 'In any case I am glad you are not your brother.'

The vexing business was not quickly forgotten. I was truly con-cerned that I had given Mr. Hardy this trouble and I wrote the most propitiatory letters to Mrs. Hardy. Eventually the notion came into my head to send Mr. Hardy a snake's skin for a book marker. The skin I had taken from an adder I myself had killed in the long cliff grass. I think it was this homely tribute from the White Nose that finally caused him to forget his annoyance. He even made an attempt to call on us in our coastguard cottage, but found the exertion of walking so far over the open downs too much for his octogenarian bones. It was at this time that I received a letter from Mr. Clarence Darrow, the American lawyer, who was on a visit to England asking whether I could arrange a meeting for him with Thomas Hardy. Under the circumstances it was not an easy piece of diplomacy, but when it had been arranged and the two famous men did meet, all went well.

Not long after Mrs. Hardy invited Miss Gregory and me to tea at Max Gate. The visit remains one of my happiest memories. In his great old age Mr. Hardy had recovered the simplicity and dignity so native to his genius. When I left his presence I felt as I might have done had I been sheltering behind an old hedgerow holly, or under the wall of an ancient grange, or with back against a grey-wether on Salisbury plain. He appeared to have forgiven and forgotten all about the Amy Lowell worry. We talked together freely on many matters. He insisted that the correct name for the cliff on which we lived was White Nose and not White Nore or White Nothe, all of which names are to be read upon maps. 'The name of the cliff is White Nose and if you stand and look at it from Weymouth esplanade the reason for its being so named becomes clear. It is like a human nose, like Wellington's nose.' He was particularly anxious to learn, and it was so characteristic of his mind, deep sinking always to the simplest facts of life, how we managed to get on for water in so remote a place. I explained that the Government had built large cisterns for the storing of the rain-water from the roofs. The idea pleased him and he declared that rain-water was more wholesome for drinking purposes than spring water. Horses, he said, will always choose the water of the foulest pond that has had sun and air upon it rather than that of the purest fountains that jet up from the earth .'Water that has stood a while is good for the "bots",' the old man concluded. We mentioned, I remember, Frank Harris. I told him that I had been reading his *The Man Shakespeare* and found the book penetrating in certain ways though I was repelled by its lack of style. How could he, for example, use the objectionable word 'smutty' in connection with Ophelia? Hardy sympathized

with this resentment. He concluded the subject by remarking that
Frank Harris had the gruffest voice of any man he had ever heard
speak, an observation with which I could acquiesce, well remembering how Harris, after having driven me back to my Waverly
Place lodgings, had boomed out at the top of his voice so that
the whole street might have heard him: 'It will all come out in the
wash'—a remark that referred to the approaching publication of his
My Life and Loves. Hardy spoke also of the degrading influence of
blood-sports and told me that he believed that the feeling of the
general public towards animals was far more sensitive than it had
been in his childhood. Even on the farm the labourers were now
not so brutal. He recalled as a young man remonstrating with a
carter for flogging his mare and receiving the answer 'But she
bain't no Christian', a remark that suggested to my mind an odd
expression of the Alpine graziers—the utterance *unzanimegezellt*
that must invariably accompany every reference to the cattle that
these hardy stockmen spend their lives in tending, and which,
literally, means 'not to be confused with men'—an utterance
coming without doubt into use as a cabala to emphasize this same
sense of the 'pathos of difference' which the religious have always
believed to exist between man and the beast who has no soul.

I remember telling him that a pair of ravens was still to be seen
frequenting the precipitous walls of our great sea promontory. In
his boyhood he said these birds were much more common and he
had often observed cottage people bless themselves on seeing one
of the dolorous fowls fly over their 'tuns' (chimneys) in the village
of Bockhampton.

When we rose to leave he walked with us to his white garden
gate and it was here that I said good-bye to him for the last time.
News of his death reached me when I was in New York as visiting
literary critic for the *Herald Tribune* in the winter of 1928.

When I returned to England Mrs. Hardy invited us to stay
at Max Gate and I slept in Mr. Hardy's dressing-room. There hung
over my bed an old oil painting of a shepherd. I could scarcely
imagine a portrait more in harmony with Hardy's own much-
enduring genius than was this weathered countenance of the herds-
man under a felt hat. Here was a man who must have hurdled many
a flock of ewes, a man whose thumbs must often have been greasy
from handling of fells. The picture pleased me extremely and Mrs.
Hardy told me it was one of which Mr. Hardy himself was

particularly fond. He had bought it in Salisbury. It was necessary for me to leave England for Switzerland soon afterwards and I never saw Mrs. Hardy again. On receiving, in my exile, the local paper with the account of the Max Gate sale I wrote to the auctioneer asking whether this picture of the shepherd had been sold. He remembered it well, and it had been sold, but he promised if possible to trace it for me. Homer is fond of using the words 'Shepherd of the people' for the Heroes he sings of. Such a shepherd Hardy surely was. No one since Shakespeare has understood so well the troubled hearts of human beings and especially of women. But his comprehensive compassion reached to the dumb beasts—to the cattle penned for butchering, to the pheasants preserved for slaughtering, even to the humble hedgehogs that crossed the dewy lawns of Max Gate on summer nights. How fitting, how full of his own simple inspirations was the poem he wrote anticipating his death!

When the Present has latched its postern behind my tremulous stay
And the May month flaps its glad green leaves like wings,
Delicate-filmed as new-spun silk, will the neighbours say,
'He was a man who used to notice such things?'

If I pass during some nocturnal blackness mothy and warm
When the hedgehog travels furtively over the lawn,
One may say, 'He strove that such innocent creatures should come to
        no harm,
But he could do little for them; and now he is gone.'

If when hearing that I have been stilled at last, they stand,
Watching the full-starred heavens that winter sees,
Will this thought rise on those who will meet my face no more,
'He was one who had an eye for such mysteries?'

     Here first published in book form;
     originally published in *The Virginia*
        Quarterly

TRAVEL

Two chapters from

HENRY HUDSON

I

The Wintering

IT WAS during the very month that William Shakespeare's *Winter's Tale* was being put on the stage for the first time that this other winter's tale began. It would be hard to conceive a more desolate landscape than that which now surrounded the marooned company. The brackish water of James Bay was frozen over and disfigured with hummocks of snow-covered ice. The shore to the westward was very low, with wide mud-flats, out of which projected an endless series of snow-hooded rocks. On the edge of this white waste grew small Arctic willows, so stunted by cold that only a few inches of their twigs were visible above the snow; and behind this dwarfed vegetation, on each bank of the river now known as the Nottaway, grew spruce, and pine, and juniper, their branches mossy on the south side, and all of them contorted and bowed as though in paralysed flight from the cruel winds that swept down upon them from the north.

The ship still contained a good supply of victuals, but not enough to get them through the winter and bring them back to England. For this latter purpose they already relied upon the number of birds that they had seen nesting on the cliffs at Cape Digges and at Cape Wolstenholme. Hudson began regulating the distribution of the provisions, 'for it behoved us to have a care of what we had; for that we were sure of, but what we had not was uncertain': also, to increase the supply of food, he offered rewards for any bird or beast brought back to the ship; at the same time giving instructions that no sailor should go hunting by himself, but always two together, the one carrying a gun, the other a pike. Some time before this, John Williams, the gunner, died. Now, it was the custom amongst sailors, in those days, that if any of their number died on a voyage, his clothes were forthwith sold before the mast to the highest bidder. The unlucky gunner had possessed a mariner's gaberdine of grey homespun; but instead of following the usual practice Hudson promised to sell this garment to Greene, who, as we know, was without clothes other than the ones supplied to him by Master Venson. This arbitrary disposal of the prized clout formed a fruitful subject for discussion amongst the rest of the crew. However, as it was in the province of the captain to arrange as he thought best, the matter rested there.

Hudson now decided to build a house on shore, in spite of the fact that when this very step had been suggested at the end of October, he had refused to consider it. Philip Staffe, realizing the difficulties of putting up even the roughest shelter in the dead of winter, when every plank would freeze to the ground, and the nails, when he held them in his mouth, would take the very skin off his lips, sent back word to the master 'that he neither would nor could goe in hand with such worke.' When these words of the carpenter were reported to Hudson, he lost his temper and went down to Staffe 'and ferreted him out of his cabbin to strike him, calling him by many foule names, and threatening to hang him,' thereby once more revealing a fatal weakness in the management of his crew. Men, like animals, respond best to reasoned firmness. A policy of 'frightfulness' is dangerous, but nothing is so dangerous as conduct that vacillates between propitiation and a show of false force. This psychological axiom may be put to the proof with any group to-day, with Russian moujiks, with American or British strikers, with the Riffians, or with a band of naked spear-bearing Masai in Africa. Men will recognize monsters as their masters and saints as their saviours, but in an emergency they will invariably cut the throats of those leaders who are neither the one nor the other. In this case the carpenter delivered himself of a considerable amount of 'back chat,' declaring that he knew 'what belonged to his place' better than Hudson did, 'and that he was no house carpenter.'

The next day, while still out of favour, Staffe, who was one of the best hunters in the ship, took his fowling-piece and went on land. Henry Greene went with him; and this so displeased Hudson, that to punish Greene, he allowed Robert Bylot, who at this time seems to have been in high favour, to have the gunner's gown. It was a method of retaliation unworthy of the great explorer, and one calculated to excite bad feeling. As soon as Greene heard about it, he went to Hudson and challenged his former promise, at which Hudson began railing against his favourite, telling him that he was a rascal whom no one would trust with twenty shillings, and that unless his manners improved he would not receive from him a penny in wages.

It seems that after this, a reconciliation took place between Hudson and Staffe; for the latter went to work and, like the skilful ship's carpenter that he was, soon put together some kind of shelter.

So the dark hours of the winter slowly passed over the heads of the stricken and dejected men. Scurvy, that unrelenting bane of sailors, broke out. The blackened gums of their jaw-bones rotted round their teeth, and their limbs swelled; and Prickett grew lame and the nails were frozen off the feet of Francis Clemens. And ever about the isolated men was the same dismal landscape, the same dismal and monotonous sea. Nothing but miles and miles of snow, cusping the ridged and rocky strand, and drifting higher and higher against the juniper trees, which, like mute and despondent sentinels of misery, stood about on the upper slopes. And behind this immediate prospect lay the limitless northern continent, stretching from Labrador to the ice-bound swamps of the Mackenzie River, from the Mackenzie River to the northern coasts of Alaska, and beneath the burdened branches of the frost-resisting evergreen timber of this single vast forest moved the hardy animals, the prices of whose pelts were presently to fill the purses of London merchants. Enormous moose, too heavy for travelling over the frozen crust, stabled themselves in, keeping pathways open by their treading, so that they could nuzzle at the twigs of the jack-pines powdered over with snow. In snug hollows, huge pregnant sow-bears dreamed away the winter, undisturbed by any noise save the nature-drugged respiration of their curled-up mates. While to the north and to the south, over the crisp surface of the forest floor dibbled with fallen twigs and tiny dry-dead fir-cones, moved packs of timber-wolves, like grey shadows, between the perpendicular never-ending shafts of motionless, snow-drooping, perfectly silent Christmas trees.

Was there nothing to awaken these uncircumscribed regions out of their accustomed prehistoric torpor, no sign by which their furry denizens could be made cognizant of the abomination of desolation that was approaching, that was indeed heralded by this band of white men cooped up on the shore of this great dead sea of the New World? A few more decades passed, and the Hudson's Bay Company was shipping beaver skins to London in cargoes of fifty thousand. Bears, martens, foxes, and, indeed, every breathing creature whose backbone was covered with warm fur, were now ruthlessly flayed. Not for nothing did the great Company select for its motto *Pro pelle Cutem*, Skin for Skin, not for nothing has it selected for its telegraphic address today the single significant word 'Beaver'.

As the days drew on towards Christmas, Hudson and his crew came to subsist more and more upon ptarmigans, birds provided by God for these, His chosen people, after the same manner that He had sent down quail to satisfy the hunger of the Children of Israel long ago among the sandhills of Mount Sinai. But no token of divine dispensation was capable of softening the hearts of Juet, Greene, and Wilson, hearts harder than ever was the heart of the obdurate Pharaoh of old. However, as long as Bylot stood by Hudson, all was well. The hour of darkness was nigh, but had not yet struck. In the secret crevices of their minds they fed their black thoughts and watched them grow.

We cannot refrain from contrasting the malignant atmosphere of this splenetic winter's camp with the air of good-fellowship that had prevailed in the hut of William Barents, fourteen years before, when he had wintered in Novaya Zemlya. This, for example, was the Dutch entry for Christmas night, 1596: 'It was foul weather on Christmasse day, and yet though it was foule weather, we heard the foxes runne over our House, wherewith some of our men sayd, it was an ill signe; and while we sat disputing why it should be an ill signe, some of our men made answer, that it was an ill signe because wee could not take them to put into the Pot or roast them, for that had been a very good signe for us.' Imagine Juet giving expression to any such merry speeches! Imagine it! Robert Juet, who from the first had predicted that the action would 'prove bloody to some.' At the first indications of the approach of spring, the willow-ptarmigan, 'white as milk,' became scarce, its place being taken by migratory water-fowl such as the swan, the goose, and the duck, flying towards their incredibly remote breeding haunts far in the North. These birds came down only for a few hours before continuing their audible, undeviating flight across the frozen bay, and were exceedingly hard to approach. 'Never did I see such wild-fowl,' wrote Captain James, who wintered in this same locality twenty years later; 'they could not endure to see anything move.' As the season advanced, even those migratory birds were no longer present. Then it was that the thoughts of these men, twenty-one men and two boys, were troubled with the most primitive of all lusts, the lust for food! Time and again it has been proved that the clamour raised by the belly will more than anything else drive men to extremities. A hungry human being is dangerous. This it is, and nothing else, that causes revolutions. When guts are empty, kings quake. The most omnivorous of all mammals cannot easily brook being without food, and it is an exigency that he scents afar off. As soon as ever he begins to suspect that there is likely to be a shortage of the viands that support life, then, civilized or uncivilized, he looks about him with a ferocity primordial and unscrupulous. Hungry baboons! Who with the utmost civility can persuade them to remain in barren fig-trees? When the roped intestines grow dry the heart grows hard. How should it be otherwise? Does not some deep instinct, some imperative foreknowledge out of the long past, instruct us?

In the reign of Henry VIII the expedition of Master Hore in search of the North-West Passage caused many a gentleman of the Inns of Court and of the Chancery to find palatable the well-basted buttocks of their companions. Lieutenant Greely, in his unfortunate adventure, had Private Henry shot, for no better reason than that the other men of the party feared him because he was stronger than they and stole bacon! Already Juet and Greene and Wilson realized that there was danger of starvation; and we may be sure that not one of these three men would be content to die whistling through his fingers. Eat they must, but eat what? The animals were fleet of foot and the brant geese swift of wing.

They wandered into the woods, up over the hills, and down into the valleys, searching like knavish foxes for 'all things that had any show of substance in them, how vile soever.' They ate moss, ' than the which,' writes Prickett, 'the powder of a post be much better.' They ate frogs, those grotesque bladder-bellied caricatures of humanity, to the taste, 'in the time of their engendering, as loathsome as a toad,' who, as the snow and ice melted

215

under the soft influence of the spring's grace, had emerged from their wintry quiescence to satisfy their uncouth love-longings by the edge of pools and swamps. For already, through the obscure vegetable arteries of every tree and bush, the magical life-sap was moving; already in every direction 'the ice was being exhaled by the sun and suckt full of holes, like honey comb.'

One day the mathematician brought back from the woods the buds of a certain tree—of the tamarack, perhaps—'full of a turpentine substance'; and these, being boiled by the Portsmouth surgeon, 'yielded an oily substance,' which was used not only as a salve, but also to make up a decoction for drinking which proved an excellent remedy for the men, 'whereby they were cured of the scorbute, sciaticas, crampes, convulsions, and other deseases, which the coldness of the climate bred in them.'

Then, when the ice was beginning to melt in good earnest, their sense of absolute and unrelieved solitude was suddenly broken by the appearance of a native, 'coming to the ship as it were to see and be seen.' This unexpected event, in the time of their utmost destitution, filled Hudson with hope. He made a great deal of the savage, and tried to get from the crew certain knives and hatchets for him to carry back as gifts to the place from which he had come. John King and Prickett responded to Hudson's appeal, and the savage went away with a knife, some buttons, and a looking-glass, making signs to the effect that after he had slept he would come again. There is something curiously provocative in the picture of this wild man of the woods, with his matted and coarse-fibred hair, like the mane of a horse, retreating into the wilderness with a mirror in his hand that had reflected with detailed accuracy so many times the countenance of Sir Dudley Digges' serving-man, and was now to enable this Indian, this wandering Cree, to contemplate, far more clearly than he had ever done in forest pool, his own extraordinary features.

When he returned, which he did shortly, he came drawing behind him a sled, on which were two deer-skins, two beaver-skins, and some meat. He was also carrying a script under his arm, from out of which he presently drew the things that Hudson had given him, gravely laying the knife upon the beaver pelts and the mirror and buttons on the deer-skins, as though he did not realize them to be presents, taking them rather to be tokens of future benefits.

This simple honesty, and the fact that he had returned as he had promised, so reassured Hudson, that he now felt himself—his communications with the Indians being assured—in a position to drive a good bargain. He had limed the branch and the bird had come to settle. When, therefore, the Indian offered to barter one of the deer-skins for a hatchet, Hudson insisted that the implement was worth both the skins. The native consented to the explorer's exaction at the time, but evidently formed a secret resolution never to come near him again. One authority asserts that he was 'badly treated' by Hudson; and although this is improbable, there can be small doubt that he detected in the overbearing attitude of the Englishman that latent avarice presently to have so great an influence on the fortunes of his race, the same avarice which caused that bold adventurer, Radisson, to fix the price of beaver-skins once and for all by declaring to the Indian spokesman that if he would not agree, he, Radisson, would travel to his country and 'eat sagamite out of his grandmother's skull,' the very same spirit that showed itself in the directions given by the Governors of Hudson's Bay Company to their factors in the early days, when they found their huge profits were being reduced by inter-tribal warfare. 'Tell them,' they wrote, 'that it doth nothing advantage them to kill and destroy one another, that thereby they may so weaken themselves that the wild, ravenous beasts may grow too numerous for them and destroy them that survive,' directions that were soon replaced by others, instructing the agents to refuse to supply the nation beginning the next fight with powder and shot, 'which will expose them to their enemies which will have the master of them, and quite destroy them from the earth, them and their wives and children.'

As the native never returned, Hudson and his men were once more thrown upon their own resources. James Bay was now almost free of ice, and Hudson sent Greene, Wilson, Perse, Thomas, Motter, Mathues, and Lodlo out in the shallop to fish. Here were some brave fishermen to go casting nets in this Sea of Galilee! The first day their draught of fishes numbered five hundred, made up of trout and some other kind 'as big as herring.' Immediately they assumed that their anxiety on the score of food was at an end. It was said afterwards that Hudson, had he shown prudence, would have begun salting down fish for the return voyage. Every one was profoundly relieved. 'They were in some hope to have our wants supplied and our commens mended.'

Alack! Their confidence was premature. Try as they might after that day, their efforts were never rewarded with the same plenty. Food once more became scarce, and some of these fishermen began to contemplate leaving the ship, as rats leave a granary when they see the corn sifting out of the last sack. For you may be certain that the heads of Henry Greene and William Wilson were not occupied with any nice theological disputations, as they stood to let down their nets. The plan devised by Wilson was 'to steal awaye' the shallop, which had recently been got ready by Staffe, and to escape to some place where hungry mouths were less plentiful. This they undoubtedly would have done, had not Hudson, before their plan could be put into execution, suddenly announced that he himself intended to use the small boat in an excursion of his own, towards the south-west, where, because of the smoke that he saw, he knew there must be natives.

Hudson, giving instructions to the men left behind in the ship to occupy themselves by taking in water, wood and ballast, set out, carrying with him the fishing net and a supply of victuals to last him eight or nine days. He named no definite day for his return. He seems to have rowed away with the conviction that he would be able to get in touch with the Indians, who, living comparatively settled lives under their moose-hide tents, would be in a position to supply him with flesh, and 'that a great store.' We cannot but think that he acted unwisely in removing himself from the *Discovery*, and so many of his men at so critical a juncture. It gave the starved sailors the opportunity they wanted for meditating evil.

Hudson's expedition proved a complete failure. He found it impossible to come up with the savages, who evaded him at every turn, actually setting the woods on fire in his very sight. After several days he returned to the ship, utterly discouraged. For little or no reason, save his own ill-humour, he seems at this time to have committed the grave error of deposing Bylot from his position as mate and placing John King, the quarter-master, in his place. We can hardly doubt that in doing this he was playing into the hands of the malcontents. With Bylot dis-affected, those in favour of mutiny were in a stronger position than ever. Certain words they uttered as they got the ship ready for leaving its winter haven have been preserved for us, words muttered by ragged sailors holding to the lanyards or standing by the capstan bars. John King was an ignorant man, who could neither read nor write, and yet it was he who was now in Hudson's confidence. With scant provisions on board, they weighed anchor on June 12th, the men with many an oath declaring 'that the master and his ignorant mate would carry the ship whither the master pleased.'

II

The Mutiny

Before sailing Hudson had taken stock of the provisions that were left. He collected what bread remained, and divided it amongst the men with his own hands; and the share of each man came to one pound, 'and hee wept when hee gave it unto them.' He also sent the boat out once more to see what could be caught in the net; but it came back, after having been gone two days, with only four-score small fish, 'a poore reliefe for so many hungry bellies.'

As soon as they sailed, the demand for food again became pressing; and this time, 'to stop a gap,' he brought out what cheese remained, and divided it into equal portions, which came to three and a half pounds for seven days. The crew believed that there were more cheeses in the storeroom than had been divided. Hudson apportioned the cheeses all at one time, because he found they were not of one goodness, and in this way he thought to insure to each man an equal share of the good and the bad. The plan did not prove a success, because when the food was once in the men's possession, nothing could restrain some of them from eating up their fortnight's ration in one or two days. Greene, for example, gave his ration to one of his mates, to keep for him, but presently demanded it of him again and devoured it. William Wilson ate the whole of his allowance in a single day, and 'laid in bed two or three days for his labour.'

It seems that Hudson, during this critical time, still cherished his purpose of continuing the search for the North-West

Passage. They fell in with a wide sea, 'agitated by mighty tides from the north west,' and immediately he became obsessed by his old passion. 'This circumstance,' writes one chronicler, 'inspired Hudson with great hope of finding a passage, and his officers were quite ready to undertake a further search; but the crew, weary of the long voyage, and unwilling to continue it, bethought themselves of the want of victuals.' And, in truth, the suspicion that extra supplies were being held back was poisoning the men's minds.

Hudson also seems to have believed that the men had certain stores of food concealed in their cabins, and to prove this suspicion he sent the ship's boy, Nicholas Syms, to search their sea-chests, and there were brought to him as many as thirty cakes. With the temper of the sailors so uncertain, it was extremely impolitic of Hudson to take such a drastic step. We know how Juet had acted when his pillow was stolen by the Red Indian, and we can guess how little he relished having his private locker looked over by a cabin boy.

The mutual distrust that now pervaded the ship was not improved by the fact that Hudson had in the boat certain favourites, amongst them the young surgeon, whom he used to ask into his cabin, to enjoy, so the hungry men imagined, ampler fare. Indeed, it seems almost certain that Hudson did not act with complete honesty over the distribution of the remaining stores. Afterwards, in their evidence, the mutineers affirmed that he had 'a scuttle' between his cabin and the hold, through which he could receive separate supplies 'to serve his own turn.' The matter came to a head through the simplicity of Philip Staffe, who, being approached by Wilson to explain 'why the master should so favour to give meate to some of the companie, and not to the rest,' answered in justification of Hudson's action that 'It was necessary that some of them should be kepte upp.' We can guess the effect that those innocent words had upon the consciousness of Wilson. 'It was necessary that some should be kepte upp!' So that was the idea, was it! But if some were to be 'kepte upp,' what was to happen to Robert Juet, Greene, and the rest of them? That was the question that offered itself for consideration in out-of-the-way corners of the deck, in the darkened gangways, and in ill-ventilated bunks.

On Saturday night, June 23rd, while the *Discovery* was moored in ice, Wilson and Greene entered Prickett's cabin. There, in the confined space of that dim cubicle, with choked water of the great bay murmuring and lapping on the other side of a few inches of sound English oak, was conveyed to the intelligence of the serving-man one of the foulest plots that has ever defiled the records of exploration. In hushed voices the conspirators told how they and their associates were determined to put Hudson and the impotent men out of the ship into the shallop, 'and let them shift for themselves.' The two declared that they had not eaten for three days, and at best there was not left more than a fortnight's victuals for all the company; and as for themselves, 'they would go through with it, or dye.'

Though Abacuk Prickett was weak in the legs, his mind was as clear as ever. He expressed his astonishment at what had been communicated to him and appealed to the two men, for the sake of their wives and children, 'not to commit so foule a thing in the sight of God and man as that would bee.' Bachelor Greene, after listening to this pious 'chat' for a few minutes, told him to hold his peace; for that 'as the master was resolved to overthrow all,' he knew it to be a matter of starving or hanging, and of the two he preferred to risk the gallows.

They then imparted to Prickett the comfortable news that it had been decided by the ring-leaders that he would be allowed to remain on the ship, at which Prickett began to mutter something about not having come into the ship for the purpose of mutiny. They countered him by saying that if he felt like that about the matter, perhaps it would be best for him after all to try his luck in the shallop. To which the worthy Prickett answered, 'The will of God be done.' Greene, at that pietistical utterance, lost his temper and flung out of the cabin, swearing that he would cut the throat of any man who double-crossed them. The boatswain remained, telling Prickett 'that he intended to goe on with the action whilst it was hot,' and explaining that it was too late now to change their plans, seeing that if what they plotted came to Hudson's ears, they themselves might be served with the same mischief they were devising for the others.

In a little while, back came Greene, to enquire whether Prickett had been won over. To whom Wilson answered, 'He is in his old song, still patient.' Prickett again attempted to reason with them, pleading with them to delay the execution of their plan for three days, for two days, for twelve hours, adding that if they would only wait till the following Monday, he would then join with them in insisting upon having the provisions of the ship equally divided. He told them that he suspected that 'it was some worse matter that they had in mind,' seeing that they were impatient to carry through their deed at such a time of night. Whereupon Henry Greene, the professed freethinker, to prove that it was not 'bloud and revenge hee sought,' took up the Bible that Prickett ever kept near his bedside, and swore on his oath that 'hee would doe no man harme, and what he did was for the good of the voyage, and for nothing else.'

The other mutineers now came in and did likewise, each swearing to keep a promise which itself was nothing but a sanctimonious prevarication. There they stood together, those secretive and bloody-minded mariners, each vying with the other in assurances that there was no evil in the murder they planned. The old man Juet, whose skill and judgement they relied upon for their return voyage, went so far as to assert that he, when he reached England, would justify the deed. John Thomas and Michael Perse took the false oath, and after them Bennett Mathues and Adrian Motter. When these last two appeared, Prickett asked them 'if they were well advised what they had taken in hand,' and they answered him that they were, 'and therefore came to take the oath.' After all this, we can hardly be blamed for sharing the opinion of that hearty cheerful Yorkshire captain, Luke Foxe, or North-West Foxe, as he liked to call himself, who had met Prickett face to face, and who ends his observations with regard to him by saying, 'Well, Prickett, I am in great doubt of thy fidelity to Master Hudson!'

Prickett was now curious to know what other members of the crew would presently appear in his cabin to take his famous oath. But no one else came. The exact words that Prickett had invented for the men to say were: 'You shall sweare truth to God, your prince and countrie: you shall doe nothing, but to the glory of God and the good of the action in hand, and harme to no man.'

Remembered long afterwards, in retrospect those whispering midnight hours, so critical, nay, so fateful, were able to impart even to Prickett's graphic style a new glamour. 'It was darke,' he writes, 'and they in readinesse to put this deed of darknesse in execution. . . . Now every man would go to his rest, but wickednesse sleepeth not.'

They at first feared that John King, the new mate, was with Hudson, but were reassured to learn that he was talking with Staffe, who was sleeping 'on the poope,' and immediately Bylot was sent to meet him, as if by chance, so as to get him if possible into his cabin. Henry Greene, meanwhile, kept company with Hudson, watching over him like a death-house jailor, lest he, growing suspicious, should take steps to prevent the villainy they had in hand. Only once did he leave him, and then to bring to the mutineers a piece of bread that the cabin boy had given him. Well can we see him haunting the sleeping man, this dangerous and depraved youth whose black lawless spirit knew naught of pity.

And the dreamer, what dreamed he? Did his mind escape out of the coffined bunk? Did his spirit, under the dispensation of sleep, see before its unawakened eyes the Golden Gates of the East, which had for so many years haunted his imagination? Did the disembodied sprite of this slumbering seaman tread once more the wooden wharfs of Amsterdam, or emerge from Peahen Alley into Bishopsgate, or sail again in happy fancy up the great river he had discovered, with the cool autumn smells of the unmeasured hillside forests fresh in his nostrils?

The cabin arrangements of the *Discovery* were as follows: In the ship's kitchen lay the cook, Bennett Mathues, with Silvanus Bond, the cooper, who was crippled. Next to them were Wydoese and Syracke Fanner, the one sick and the other lame; next to them, the surgeon and John Hudson; next to them, Wilson and Arnold Lodlo. In the gun-room lay Robert Juet and John Thomas. On the larboard-side lay Michael Butt and Adam Moore, and near to them Michael Perse and Adrian Motter. Outside the gun-room lay John King and Robert Bylot, and Prickett and Francis Clemens. Amidships, between 'the capstone and the pumpes,' slept Nicholas Syms, with the empty berth of Henry Greene at his side.

And while the small tunnelled ship rocked to and fro at anchor, on the perfect balance of her keel, the whisperers with restless impatience awaited the coming of the dawn, awaited the hour when their vigil would be over, and they would be free to perpetrate their crime without further fear of surprise. The death-watch beetle was silent; no scratch was heard from the tiny feet of the bugs, as, led by an obscure instinct, with the utmost deliberation they moved from one dark beam to another. No sound was made by the deep-swimming fish, as they touched with their blunt noses the slippery keelson far under the ice-bearing water. All was stillness. Treachery and slumber lying together had brought forth silence.

And then, as the first indications of sunrise appeared over Charlton Island and over the cold stretches of water that lay between the ship and the eastern shores of the great bay, there was audible in each wan chamber the cheerful familiar sound of Mathues, the cook, going out, kettle in hand, to fetch water from the butts. This was the signal. John King was beguiled into entering the hold, and the bolt of its door slipped fast upon him. Greene and another went on deck, to divert the attention of Philip Staffe 'with a talk'; for although they had no intention of putting him out of the ship, they did not feel at all certain as to how he might act in the face of open rebellion.

Henry Hudson now came out of his cabin. Immediately the sound of a scuffle was heard. John Thomas and the cook had leapt upon him, and before he had time to resist, Wilson, from behind, had pinioned him with a rope. The Portsmouth surgeon, hearing a noise, looked out of his door. He shouted to Hudson, to ask what was happening, and Hudson answered that they had bound him. Immediately the mutineers turned upon Wilson, and enquired of him if he was well; and when he answered that he was well, then they said to him, with the sinister reticence of dangerous men, that 'yf he were well he should keepe himself soe.' Hudson now asked the men what they intended, and they answered him that he would know 'when he was in the shallop.'

The moment for swift action had come. The shallop was hauled alongside the ship, and Hudson was put into it, under the care of Bennett Mathues and John Thomas. Many of the men were ignorant as to what had been arranged. Bylot, who kept himself below deck, afterwards declared that he was under the impression that they intended to hold Hudson in the shallop only for as long a while as they would take to search the vessel for food.

To the majority it was 'utterlye unknowen who should goe or who should tarrye,' Greene, Wilson, and Juet acting as 'affection or rage did guide them in that furye.' Greene, for example, now that Mathues and Thomas were in the shallop, had

The Vicarage, Montacute, Somerset, the home of Llewelyn Powys from 1885 until 1914.

a mind that they should stay there; and he would have carried this double treachery through, had not Silvanus Bond and Francis Clemens, realizing what he was up to, had them back 'with much adoe,' and forced Arnold Lodlo and Michael Butt to take their places, men who, only a few moments before, had themselves been railing against Hudson.

'The authors and executors' of the plot now seized upon Wydowse, who had sufficient imagination to envisage what was in store for him, and went to his doom 'in the greatest distress,' calling out that they could have his keys and share his goods, if only they would allow him to remain on board. He was followed by Adame Moore and Syracke Fanner, mariners too sick to make trouble, and also by John Hudson.

While Greene, with oaths and curses, was superintending matters on deck, Robert Juet had gone down to the hold to bring up John King, but the old man had undertaken more than he could manage, for no sooner had he slipped the bolt back than he was attacked by the former quartermaster, who had his sword with him, and held Juet at bay, and would have killed him had not other mutineers come to his rescue and helped him to get King on deck and out into the shallop.

Meanwhile, Prickett had crawled from his cabin and put his head above the hatch which, when the mutineers saw, they told him 'to keep *himself* well' and get back again to where he came from, neither suffering him to speak to Hudson nor giving heed to his ejaculations that besought them, 'for the love of God, to remember themselves, and to doe as they would be done unto.' Prickett retreated, consoling his uneasy conscience by repeating to himself a favourite text, 'There are many devices in the heart of man, but the counsell of the Lord shall stand.' From the familiar security of his bunk, however, he did manage to call to Hudson in the shallop, using the horne (window) which gave light into my 'cabbin', to tell him that it was the villain Greene, and not Juet, who was at the bottom of the business, and 'I spake it,' he records with no little complacence, 'not softly.'

The shallop had now been manned to the satisfaction of the mutineers. But it was destined to hold yet one other. Philip Staffe, the Ipswich carpenter, who seems at first hardly to have understood, now delivered himself of his simple commentary upon the proceedings that were taking place. This honest man,

from the banks of the River Gipping, had not heard the bells
of St. Mary-at-Key 'knoll to church' for nothing. He knew what
was right, and what was wrong—no one better; and he was not
a man who could be easily budged from the narrow path.
Rough and illiterate as he was, he became gradually aware that
his own personal pride was in some way involved by what was
happening. It is true that he was at liberty—at liberty, and yet
at the same time bound by a stouter and more inextricable
sailor's knot than could ever have been contrived by the quick
fingers of young Master Greene. To his unsophisticated intelligence there seemed no doubt as to his present duty. Suddenly,
deep down in the heart of this rude man, born and bred in
Suffolk clay, the celebrated categorical imperative of Immanuel
Kant became audible; and he turned upon the mutineers, and
in the curious dialect of East Anglia, told them plainly what was
in his mind. 'As for himselfe, hee said, hee would not stay in
the ship unlesse they would force him.' Let him have his chest
of carpenter's tools and be damned to them, for he chose rather
to commit himself to God's mercy and 'for the love of the
Master go down into the shallop, than with such villaines to
accept of likelier hopes.' The mutineers could not dissuade him
from his purpose, and down he went into the doomed boat, with
his chest, his musket, some meal, and an iron pot.

And now, the shallop still being in tow, they stood out of the
ice; and when they were nearly out of it, 'they cut her head fast
from the stern of the ship,' and with top-sails up, steered away
into an open sea, leaving their captain and his son, with seven
poor sailors, abandoned and exposed, 'without food, drink, fire,
clothing, or other necessaries,' in the great unexplored bay.
There he sat in the tiny boat, dressed 'in a motley gown,' the
possessed sea-captain who had sailed to the West in his endeavour
to find a passage through the ice-bound ramparts of the planet
itself. There he sat, this dreamer, in his coat of many colours,
until to the eyes of the mutineers, who watched the shallop grow
smaller and smaller in the wake of their stolen vessel, he became
a mote, a speck, a nothing, lost to sight on the unresting waves of
the wharfless wilderness that had been by him so resolutely, so
desperately discovered.

From *Henry Hudson* (1927).

DROUGHT

THE LAST year of my stay in Africa was terrible. Famine stalked through the land with Pestilence galling his kibe. Week after week the country lay prostrate under the blank stare of a soulless sun. Month after month the waters of the lake sank lower and lower. Its lagoons and shallows dried up, and each night a gusty burning wind carried across the veldt the poisoned sulphuric exhalations of its wide muddy reaches. It was as though the earth itself was undergoing some appalling process of putrefaction. The air was tainted, the flaked dusty mould stank. The buck no longer frolicked on the plains, but either trekked in long lines from horizon to horizon or congregated about the few streams where water still ran. Everywhere one came across the carcasses of animals dead from exhaustion, carcasses with long muddy tongues protruding, as though the wretched beasts up till the very last moment had hoped to suck in moisture. The vultures grew plump as Michaelmas geese. And still no cloud, no veil of mist ever appeared in the sky. The sun rose and sank in a blinding heaven, and under its hideous presence all sensitive life trembled and shrank. The lions and leopards lay up near the few befouled water-holes and, because the haunches of their victims were lean, killed the more often. As I rode through the forest I came upon gazelles from the plains searching nervously in an alien environment for cool retreats. Enormous coiling serpents battened upon their thirsty frightened bodies. Monkeys came down from the tree-tops and in wavering processions went looking for new watering-places. The crops never came up. The Government imported large quantities of grain from the South, but even so, a great many natives died of starvation. I used to see troops of them moving along the old caravan road, supported by the pathetic illusion that they would at length come to some fat land where there would be enough food for all. It was useless to tell them that their quest was hopeless. They would not listen, but continued to journey on, day after day, in trailing ant-like lines—tall men, women with milkless breasts, and little dazed, wrinkled children. My work, of course, became much harder throughout this time. I had often considerable difficulty in getting enough meal for the actual requirements of the farm. The authorities kept postponing their consignments, and although I never actually ran out, yet I often experienced periods of considerable anxiety. Stealing of every kind increased. Sheep camps were raided by native robbers, one night five ewes being taken out of the home yards, under my very nose. In this case I suspected the herder of being in league with the thief and made what investigations I could. My suspicions eventually rested on a native called Kapingy, who was a squatter in the forest with six children to support. I was particularly exasperated, because I had done all that I could to help him, giving him every week an allowance of meal sufficient in quantity to keep him and his family alive till the evil time should come to an end.

I had felt sorry for the fellow. I knew him to be as hard-working as natives ever are, and I had noticed on his face that harassed, preoccupied look which comes to men, black, yellow and white, when they have children dependent upon them and cannot find enough food to keep them alive.

This feeling now turned to indignation. 'What a sly devil!' I thought. 'Just like all the rest of these people who have black hides: every time you are generous to them you are certain to be overreached.'

I made up my mind to catch him out by making a raid upon his hut. I let the affair slide for three days so that he should consider himself safe, and then one afternoon rode up to his forest home. As I came near the place I smelled very distinctly the odour of roasting flesh. Dismounting, I crawled through the low door into his darkened kraal. A huge cauldron was on the fire and round it sat Kapingy and his six starving children. I was certainly shocked to see how thin they all were. The flickering light illumined their bodies, bringing out into horrible relief first a rib bone, then a collar bone, then a hip bone. 'Jambo Bwana!' said Kapingy, as though he was glad to see me. ('Ah,' I thought, 'he is pulling wool over my eyes. He thinks to fool me like this, hoping that I won't look into his pot.') 'Jambo Kapingy!' I answered, and seizing two sticks I lifted out of the steaming saucepan the skinny body of a starved wood-rat!

With only one small permanent stream on the farm the stock became terribly congested. The tracks down to the various watering-places had for weeks been reduced to bare dusty wastes, upon which not a blade of grass was to be seen. When the famished panting flocks came to these arid places they would know they were near water, and animated once more would emit strange treble baas and scamper pell-mell down the last decline. Some of the flocks came from camps several miles distant, and one could follow the course of their return journey by the clouds of grey dust which rose above their backs into the palpitating air. It was wonderful to me how they kept alive at all, subsisting apparently upon nothing but water and dry grass stalks.

As the weeks passed the great lake itself fermented. The hippopotami grew fastidious, and, leaving their bubbling fetid resting-places, would come floundering up the river-bed to slake their thirst with purer water. One old bull actually left the river and took to drinking from a farm trough. This trough was made of tin sheets. I would not have objected in the least to his drinking from it, if only he had done so with care and decency. As it was, he must put his great hoofs in the trough and bend and crush it to pieces in an endeavour to get a greater flow of water. I sat up for him one night, but although I had a shot at his bulging body he got back to the lake, plunging into the black expanse with an enormous splash. I could see the gap where it was his custom to come through the fence which surrounded the trough; so I constructed a framework of tall poles and set a gun-trap over it. I found it tiresome, however, having to unset and reset this contrivance every morning and eveving, though it was a labour I could not neglect with so much stock about; but I had no sooner decided to remove it, when a native came flying in to say that a hippopotamus of a stupendous size had been shot and was lying at the lake's edge. I mounted my pony and rode to the place. The hippopotamus was indeed of extraordinary proportions, like a whale, like two elephants in one. I had often noticed colossal hippo tracks in the sand of the lake's margin, which I now concluded must have belonged to this animal, to this father of all hippopotami.

I cantered towards it. As I came nearer, its size seemed to increase rather than diminish. Its bulk was beyond anything I had conceived possible in the animal world—beyond anything I had ever read about. It was not until I was within a few yards of it that I became suspicious. The wind was not my way, but even so the air was foul. The explanation flashed upon me. This was none other than the hippopotamus I had shot at a fortnight ago. I had evidently mortally wounded it, and now, swollen like a balloon from decomposition, it had floated in here. I told a Kikuyu, a boy named Korogo, to get the ivory. I gave him an axe and instructed him somehow or another to chop it out of the beast's head. He brought it to me in the evening, declaring that he wanted the heaviest recompense for his labour. I gave him what he asked. I had not forgotten the glimpse I had of that mass of corrupting matter, with its huge four feet turned white. One day an old Masai told me that long before the coming of the white men he remembered his father telling him that there was water at the end of a certain cave in a distant valley. He told me it had never been used because everybody feared going in to the place, seeing that at the end of it there lived *an evil thing*. I pricked my ears at once. It would be wonderful to have a water supply in that arid portion of the farm. I knew the cave to which he referred. I had come upon it once when out shooting guinea-fowl. I also was sufficiently acquainted with geology to realise that it must have been formed by water at one time or other. I determined to investigate; and the next day, taking with me a large blizzard-lantern, I rode up to the spot. The cave lay at the bottom of a deep pit, the sides of which were overgrown with fig-trees and other bushes. I tied up my pony and with some difficulty clambered down to its mouth. This was about four feet high. I lit my lantern and entered. Once within, I found myself in a large cavernous room, a room paved with vast boulders which had evidently fallen from the roof. Some of the boulders were so large that it was difficult to get round them. The breath of the place was as the breath of a tomb. I did not like the look of things at all, and as I made my way forward I kept turning my head in the direction of the doorway, through which I could still see a glimmering ray of light. I was not afraid of meeting a wild animal in the place. It seemed to me unlikely that any beast would select so cold a lair; but I was apprehensive lest the rocks from the roof should either come down upon me or, what seemed even worse, obstruct in their collapse my passage out. It was no wish of mine to be entombed for ever in the bowels of Africa.

It was certainly an astounding tunnel, and it apparently went on for ever. I was reminded of the legendary entrances into hell. Presently, on looking back, I no longer saw light from the cave's mouth. I still went forward, however, picking my way amongst the rocks and stones as best I could. The light from my lantern irradiated vast slabs above my head, slabs of stone so smooth and flat that one could hardly believe that they had not been polished by human hands. From some of them I saw bats hanging, bats large as blackbirds, with leathery wings closed tight round their bodies. Suddenly I heard a noise and realised that something was beating up in my direction. I held my pistol ready, but I was extremely reluctant to shoot, for I feared that the concussion might cause some of the rocks to fall. A second later and I was reassured as a large white owl flapped its way past me.

Again I advanced, holding my lantern high and peering into the darkness ahead. Its light fell upon something leaning against one of the walls, something that quite obviously was neither rock nor stone. A chill dread held me in suspense. What in God's name was this muffled shadow standing so silently there? Was I, after all, not by myself in the cave? Was there someone else with me, someone at that very moment standing mute at my elbow? I put out my hand and touched it. I examined it closely. It was the skeleton of a large buck. The horns, though discoloured, were in good condition and the bones were still encased in a hide which was stretched over them like tight parchment. Behind the buck lay the dust-covered form of another animal. I cannot tell why, but there was something horrible to me about finding these remains in this silent geological chasm. I turned and with all possible expedition got myself out. How had they come there, I wondered—how and when? What terror had driven that sun-loving animal to take refuge in so strange a place, and when the hyena followed, what dread subterranean miasma had stricken them both dead? Had they been there for a hundred, for a thousand years? Doubtless to this hour they are there, sepulchred in the silent belly of Africa. The cave is situated under the crater with the steam jet, the crater which I used to call 'High,' not far from the group of trees beneath which in the rainy season the eland and grant like to assemble.

From *Black Laughter* (1925).

A VOYAGE TO THE WEST INDIES

WHEN I was a boy in England we used to long for hard winters, yet it seems to me now that the Christmases of my childhood were always green. How different it was last winter[1] in the Berkshire Mountains! The snow began to fly in October and afterwards there was no stint to the frost.

In New York State one realizes at once that the north wind blows directly down from the arctic regions. It has that feeling in it. It comes from remote northern valleys where the moose herd themselves in under jack-pines, their enormous horns clicking together as they reach up for needles feathered with snow. It comes over desolate wastes of loon-haunted marshlands. It comes from snow-fields where the musk ox congregate, and from the flat frozen acres of the north pole.

I would not deny that a winter passed in New York City has its attractions. It is pleasant enough on a gusty night to enter one of the city's 'speak-easies' where thoughtless, smartly-dressed girls stand taking off their furs in the hall, and where there is the sound of laughter and talk all about one, and wine on the glittering, well-appointed tables. I would not deny that there are rewards to be gained from such sophisticated gatherings —and yet can such rewards even when most fortunate be compared with the solid gain that comes from wintering in the country? Surely in retrospect the long, slow hours of a rural winter count for more in one's life-pilgrimage than ever could the febrile frivolities of late urban nights.

As I look back now upon the months I spent in the mountains above the small village of Austerlitz I know that I was given many chances of touching in time the flying wings of eternity. In the dead of winter on moonlit nights I used often to visit a ruined farm-house. I would feel my way up the creaking narrow stairs, cross the floor of the upper room, avoiding as best I might the holes in the sagging boarding, and, kneeling down at the

[1] The winter of 1930-1.

frameless window, send my spirit out into the night, out over the white valleys where foxes with bellies empty as purses were treading and sniffing, out over the mountain tops where ridges of trees were visible, fretsawed against the naked air. Alone in this forlorn, unvisited chamber where draught-driven snow lay in precise heaps, my identity could often win to a liberation beyond the yearning outcries of the blood and bones of my fleshly body.

The immediate contacts of my everyday life had also happy advantages. What delight to stumble along the narrow snow path to Edna St. Vincent Millay's house, and to enter her hall, and to see her there so gay, so grave, so peerless in the firelight! Or on some fine January morning, under a cloudless sky, how jocund to be drawn along the crisp road on a sledge with Eugen Boissevain perched behind his black geldings in his red coat as dazzling as a scarlet tanager. Our evenings were happy also. We would come back from the post to sit down to our tea of brown bread and buckwheat honey, and, after we had washed up, solace ourselves with the tales of Malory, so natural and reviving.

In America the winter sleep of the earth is very deep and the approach of the spring tardy. With the first tentative melting of the snow the skunk cabbages shove out of the ground their curled pagan ears, but even then many weeks have to pass before the hepaticas and Dutchman's-breeches are to be seen. To those accustomed to the way of the English countryside there is a burden in so long a waiting. When at home the hedgerows would be starred with celandines, icicles are still hanging from the penthouse eaves in America. It was because of this very impatience that we decided in the beginning of February to go to the West Indies.

Our boat sailed from Brooklyn. Once out on the open sea we went to the prow of the steamer to watch the sun go down. There were level lines of black clouds lying along the horizon and between them we could see the sun as though an imprisoned Cyclops were staring at us through bars. Then darkness gathered about us, the ancient darkness of night that so punctually each evening enfolds in its palpable presence all troubled life. A young girl sat at the table next to ours in the lighted dining-saloon. I could see the perfect movement of her bones beneath the bright clay of her living flesh. She was gay, irresponsible. The youth of her body had been animated by the very same breath of nature that had given freedom to the seagulls we had been watching rising and falling over the winter waves of the landless ocean.

We waked the next morning to find that the sun was shining. Steadily our ship broke its way southward, now tumbling the sea apart like the water of a mill-race, now pressing silently through it with scarcely a ripple—and how naked was the rim of the blue hoop across which we were speeding! We noticed great quantities of yellow seaweed floating by. 'From the Sargasso Sea,' they told us. Days followed and always it was growing warmer, until presently flying fish were skimming over the waves, propelling themselves into the air by two short fins below their bellies.

One morning I went on deck when it was still dark and, sitting under a boat, waited for the dawn. First there was a flush of red above the clouds to the east. It remained like this for several minutes, then there was a greater glory of red and then, sudden as a shout, the sun was above the horizon. Once again a happy daytime light was over the waters and I was alive to see it, with graveyard bones outstretched upon a swabbed deck, with my lanthorn skull fitted with an uncertain flame of thought —a witty and wicked wick! Montaigne speaks somewhere of a certain river where there are animals that live only for one day. 'How can we,' he asks, 'with any show of reason attribute either weal or woe to their moments?' It is the same, he reflects, with us. Yet all time measurements are relative. Misery of a second's duration can have upon it the cast of an immortality and a fleeting mood of happiness be of a substance eternal.

We woke on the sixth day to find we had arrived at St. Thomas. When I looked out of our porthole I could see green hills and red-tiled houses. We were away early. We did not go in the direction of the town but followed along the docks till we could get to the natural bush where there were no houses. It was lovely to be free to walk again, and even though we trod at first over ground blackened with coal dust it was apparent that we were in a new land. There was a hot, damp smell in the air which reminded me of Africa, as if the wings of locusts, the petals of flowers, the backs of pond frogs, were all drying after rain.

We found a rough native path leading up the hill. It had been cut through dense scrub. It was slippery, and there were tracks of naked human feet in its red clay. There were cacti and aloes and innumerable forest creepers on both sides of us. I saw a humming bird and two unfamiliar butterflies, one of them a kind of fritillary, I think. We came to a negro who was cutting down the bush with a panga. He looked lusty enough and yet possessed a happy and docile disposition. We talked a little and smoked together. The path took a turn and we found ourselves by the sea in a very secluded bay. I noticed fragments of white fossilized coral on the beach, quaintly shaped like the bones of mouse-high dinosaurs. The sun was so hot and the water looked so clear and blue that I was tempted to bathe. Slipping off my clothes I went in. The water was very warm, warmer than it ever is on the hottest summer day in England. I was a little apprehensive of sharks, but this preoccupation did not last long. I immediately trod upon some devilish sharp object. The pain was extreme. I limped to the shore as best I could. When I examined my foot I realised I had stepped on a sea urchin. My foot was bleeding and from heel to toe was peppered with infinitesimal thorns. I found it impossible to remove any of them. I was like a lion with porcupine quills in its paw. All my old suspicion of the tropics returned, all my suspicion of these countries which in spite of their favoured appearance, invariably conceal some kind of malicious intent.

By a distant headland we saw a native fisherman and with the help of a whistle, we were able to attract his attention. He brought the boat up to a rock and, getting into it, we were conveyed over the water to the town and thence by car to the hospital, so that in an hour's time I found myself lying on an operating table while a young American doctor, with slow deliberation, cut out each individual prickle. I felt convinced that our excursion was ruined and that a month would have to pass before I would be able to move freely, though as a matter of fact in twenty-four hours I could get about without too great inconvenience.

After leaving the hospital we spent an hour on the docks. We talked to an old negro, asking him the names of the fish. A negress came loafing by with a broad smile upon her lips. She gave our friend a familiar nudge. 'How are you, my darling?' he said. His tone had such sweetness in it, such natural genial affection, that we were mightily taken by the scene. It is as if these liberated slaves are in possession of such a store of good-will that the ordinary standards of human relationships as we know them in our white commonwealths appear in contrast to their sunny manners very shallow and meagre.

The next day we disembarked at St. Kitts. We walked through a public garden all odorous with roses towards the native quarter. The houses of West Indian negroes are built on stilts, small square houses with their walls patched up with wooden shingles and the rusty sheets of old debby tins. We followed a cart track out of the town towards the plantations. The sun was hot. I noticed yellow thistles. We saw some native women in the fields and went over to them. They were hoeing wide furrows, as wide as asparagus beds, in preparation for sugar cane-planting. They earned, they told us, only three shillings a week. A little farther down the trackway there were gangs of men cutting the ripe cane. They were using curiously shaped billhooks. Far away over the rustling acres I could see what looked like a ruined castle on a hill. They told me it was called 'Golden Rock' and to reach it we would have to walk three miles round by the road. We left them and followed along the edge of the cane. I could still see the ruins over the tops of the swaying 'food' not more, as I judged, than a mile away. We eventually decided to push straight through the plantation. We had not gone far before we realized that it was no easy matter to retain one's sense of direction in such a dense growth. For a long time we seemed to be hopelessly lost. It was very hot and we became weary of moving aside these tall bamboo-like stalks. There was an undergrowth of weeds also that impeded us. On every side the sultry wind made a dry, crisp sound as it passed across the swaying reed-like vegetation. We felt the greatest relief when we did emerge at last and walked up the grassy hill on which the ruined house was built. It had evidently been an imposing place. There was something sinister about it even in its present broken state. Surely no 'innocent' country house would require to be fortified by a wall and by buttressed towers. We sat on a kind of terrace, the flagstones of which were all but covered over with grass. Even in the full blaze of noon the atmosphere about the fallen stones seemed memory-stained. I felt as if there were only the thinnest separation between our lives and *their* lives, as if by a turn of the screw those past years would become part of my own experience. It would all be as clear to me as day; I would remember it all—the proud, indolent lives that these white folk had lived, with their hospitable tables and well-filled cellars, and the unphilosophic acceptance of their privileges as though established by divine intention, and the unyielding economic principal that lay beneath their stately courtesies.

In the foreground we could see a group of tiny black children, like living nursery gollywogs, filling their straw hats with the windfalls from a large fruit tree with shining leaves. The harvesting of the sugar-cane was in full view with mules harnessed to wagons and with farm hands shouting to each other. Such scenes must have been familiar enough to the people who had lived here, to those people whose names even were now unknown, and yet whose dream life had once been as actual as my own, with feastings and buryings and love-makings and births.

We walked back to the town by another way. We passed the house of the overseer. He came out to us, a coloured gentleman in a white helmet; his garden, all hot in the sun, had an orchard of banana trees behind it looking cool and very green. He told me the names of the flowers I was carrying—'Love-letters' and 'Sweet Williams'—but all the time he was talking I could not turn my secret attention away from his green paddock: for under those broad leaves I saw a pool of sunshine on deep luxuriant grass. Adam might well have prepared such a glebe as a pleasaunce-place for himself and Eve. They might have spent there long, idle, enraptured hours, laughing, talking, and watching the new-created insects beginning the diligent activities of their kind amongst the sweet-smelling, tangled, new-created fodder. It was doubtless in just such a cultivated parterre that God walked in the cool of the evening preparing in his moral, grudging mind fresh confusions for the froward images of animated clay with whom he designed to populate the earth.

From St. Kitts we sailed to Antigua. Our ship was delayed for some time in order to pick up the Governor of these islands. We happened to be going up the dining-saloon stairway just as this gentleman was coming down. We could not but regret that we alone amongst all the casual holiday passengers were privy to this stage entrance. In his white clothes, with his eyeglass and walking stick, he presented a superb example of one of these English colonial bellwethers. When tea was being served I had an opportunity of saying a few words to him and I found that his mind was as hollow as his person—a kind of moving-picture governor, a mock strong man consumed with a pompous sense of his own importance. We disembarked at Antigua and, finding myself passing Government House, I stepped across the road to have a few words with the coloured sentinel. I wanted to know what he thought of his master. 'He is not much appreciated,' was his guarded comment.

We entered the cathedral which was an impressive building with two fine early eighteenth-century towers. The great west doors of the church were wide open and through them we caught a glimpse of the sea against palm trees plumed and waving. The churchyard had a derelict melancholy appearance. Many of the stones had been overturned in a late hurricane and had never been set upright again. The ground was grassless and this accentuated the dreary look of the yard. Truly the bodies of these merchant adventurers were buried here in actual dust and not in healthy worm-engendering mould. Darkness began to fall. It was a cloudy night with a restless wind stirring in the trees. We walked into the country. We came to a pond and rested on its bank. Opposite us was a planter's house with lights in the windows. There was the sound of something moving. It was a gorbellied goblin West Indian toad advancing with self-centred concentration through the grass. Human footsteps became audible and a negro passed along a field path behind us, ignorant of our presence. He was talking to himself about some girl who had been taken away from him. He was waving his arms excitedly. From somewhere in the distance came the insistent crying of a baby. The ancient misery of the slaves, the ancient misery of all the populations of abused human kind was upon the air. The night was oppressive. It was as if we were inhaling the throat-breath of some enormous serpent; the dusky branches above us seemed to hiss.

We came back to the town and after dinner visited the native quarter. We sat on a bench outside one of their wooden shanties and talked with an old man and an old woman. We asked them about their lives and they filled our ears with a fine store of complaints. If they stole but one sugar cane it was tied behind their backs and they were taken off to gaol. They told one long story of poverty and oppression. 'Why,' the old woman exclaimed, 'when we are let out of prison they won't even give us back what we have stolen!'

Above the angular roof lines opposite I could see the stars and always there came to our ears the wap and wan of the waves at the foot of the street. I asked them about the Governor, but they also were reticent. Continually in their conversation they reverted to someone whom they called Sir Eustace. I presently asked them to whom they were referring and they said 'Sir Eustace Fiennes'. It was evident that this ruler was in great favour with them. 'He was a good man; he was a blessed man. We pray for him night and day, may the Lord bless his name. He was a friend to us poor folk. He would never have us want for bread. He would give us money. He would let us out of prison.' Upon my soul, I had never in my life heard such an outpouring of enthusiastic talk. The name Fiennes was unfamiliar to me, but as we visited other islands we again and again heard him talked of and always with the same kind of devotion. We would discover some lovely secluded bay and presently be informed that it was where 'Sir Eustace used to bathe'. We would see a group of negresses with bright bandannas on their heads bargaining for the flesh of a shark in a market-place and would be told that it was Sir Eustace's favourite pastime to catch these fish and distribute portions of their flesh to the poor. 'Blessed be his name.' I got an impression of this man as being a kind of Grangousier, a Governor unlike all other Governors, free, generous, wise, with the wisdom of the ancient giants. Equally indifferent to racial or class prejudice he must have gone on his way with benevolent aplomb having the cares of the meanest of his subjects under his paternal eye. I was proud enough that England could still produce men of such independent temper.

Our next stopping place was Guadeloupe. We took a steep sandy path out of the town and soon found ourselves in undulating country with cultivated dells lying one behind the other. These dells were utterly tropical, no breath of wind disturbed the circumambient scent of each motionless flower. In one of these valleys undisturbed by man or beast I saw two humming birds making love. Nothing was in this cup of torrid vegetation except the breathless sunshine and the sound of these small birds' wings

fluttering like moths' wings against each others' bodies as light
as dandelion clocks. The hen bird was brown as a nightingale,
unpretentious, submissive, the cock eager and aggressive with
the brightest sheen of emerald upon his diminutive forehead. I
stood stock still in wonder to see the performance of so delicate
an appetite in this hidden plat. Rare it is to consider the perfect
processes of nature as they are manifested to the living eye, the
movements of mindful bumble bees through pennant downland
grass seen against the waters of the channel, the sudden dampness
on the clustered flower heads of the yarrow when the dew is
beginning to fall at twilight.

We came to a path where we saw some pigs rooting. There
is a particular breed of these animals in the West Indies. They
are very lean and have long snouts like tapirs. We were told
that they are used for clearing the bush of snakes. Apparently
there is an hereditary discord between swine and these 'pretty
worms' that is much to man's advantage, this gross mammal for
some obscure reason objecting to the very existence of the
cozening intellectual reptile.

On our return to the town we entered the catholic church,
built all of iron. We observed a negress at her devotions. It was
a scene full of grace. I suspect that we approach a period when
the sight of human beings on their knees will be rare enough and
the act of prayer be regarded as a practice reminiscent of the
humbler days of the human race. I looked at the pictures representing the stations of the cross. The walls of Jerusalem were
depicted in one of them and I could see the very place where we
had sat watching the water carriers filling their leather jacks. It
was from that city set upon a hill that the murmur of this most
uncommon *new* God was first bruited—a God of the under-side
of the leaf of life, a God of suffering and compassion, the mere
thought of whom sets the hearts of men and women fluttering
like the hearts of birds, so that in every clime white knees, yellow
knees, and black knees may be observed bent in passionate sub-
mission on flagstone and on dusty floor.

We arrived at Dominica late one afternoon. As we approached
the island we noticed a village set between two mountains. Its
name was Portsmouth. I marked it as a place of retreat if all my
affairs were to go kim kam. Living there was good and cheap,
I was told. As soon as we disembarked we walked along the

water's edge to the right. Above the beach was a long rambling street of native houses, called New Town. We crossed this and entered a lane leading up a narrow gorge between two mountain sides. We passed a farmhouse. We continued up the gorge till we came to a grove of palm trees, their trunks rising grey and clear in an enchanted circle. I counted them and their tally came to thirteen, my own lucky number. We sat down here. The last rays of the twilight sun were upon the bank of the ravine opposite. A thin, light rain was falling, though I could see no clouds from which it could come. The vanishing sunlight had a particular loveliness, light as a single fugitive leaf in a staunch forest. We followed the path still a little farther and found ourselves in a cool enclosure of limes, with the yellow fruit lying ungathered in the grass, like golden apples in a Somersetshire orchard. I picked one up and kept it in my pocket for days, pinching its peel all over so as to extract its cordial fresh smell. A stream ran through the orchard and we heard an owl call. We had an idea of trying to get supper at the farmhouse, but the owner was away. We went and sat on the beach while we took counsel as to what to do. The beach was fringed with palm trees. It was made up of very large pebbles, far larger than those of the Chesil beach. There was still a streak of light in the sky over the horizon. Tiny ripple-high waves lapped against the shore. From the summer road behind the coconut trees came the voices of natives. We were reminded of the evening when we had sat by the Lake of Galilee and watched the moon come up over the cliffs where the madman nicknamed Legion had woned.

We got up and went back to the street. We saw a black man on a white horse and accosted him. We asked his advice as to where to go for supper. He moved his horse towards a small shop and called 'Roberts! Roberts!' He was evidently a person of importance. He told us his name was Grell and that he was a planter. A negro answered. His wife was out, he said, but would be soon back. While he was speaking she approached us. She was a half-caste, almost white, fluttering and with a soft peculiar grace. She conducted us to an upstairs room where we sat down to supper. The room was a small one and there was a cottage loaf on the table. I took out of my waistcoat pocket my bag of jewels and gave her my best topaz. We listened to her stories and felt content as we sat before her simple fare. All the time we were aware of the West Indian darkness outside behind the waving Venetian blinds. When we left we wandered down the street. We noticed a church-like barn with four open doors. A tall figure in white was preaching. The preacher was standing within a pen made of wooden railings. We entered and sat upon one of the benches prepared for the congregation. There were several negroes present, old negroes in wide straw hats, farm hands from the cotton fields. There were women also and little black children. Whenever the preacher quoted from the scriptures he would pause before repeating the last words of the text and the congregation would then chant in unison as though by this means they were giving confirmation to the truth. The man's voice was violent and the building resounded with the dissonance he made. It is not only toad-stool faeries who preach of God, but sable monsters also. The subject of the sermon was of the second coming of Jesus, and each rhetorical utterance was punctuated by the words 'Glory be' and 'Hallelujah'. We might have been witnessing an ecstatic slave service taking place in the Roman catacombs two thousand years ago. Evidences of the near approach of the end of the world were on every side. There were 'wars and rumours of wars'. The recent earthquake that had shaken the island and 'the whole earth almost' was a sure proof, a sure sign. 'Death had come to men through Adam, but the women had bruised the serpent's heel and had given us an advocate in the Son of God who had become flesh. It was faith we must have. We must trust in God. There were infidels abroad, deceivers, and yet if we believed we would have eternal life.' At certain moments the afflatus would pass so strongly through the preacher's being that he would raise his arms far above his head, and I noticed that on these occasions his hands with their fingers outspread would quiver like two black bats.

It was extraordinary! I thought of the world as I knew it, as I had observed it in my crack of time. I thought of the apparent stolidity of London, of New York, of Paris. I thought of the hushed, unparticipating peace of village hay fields after the carts and men have left them, and I pondered upon the pathetic unreality of these religious dreams. How truly moving to think of these simple men under their wide straw hats waiting and waiting for a day of deliverance, waiting with a passionate

longing for Jesus to come again upon earth; for this man to return
who had himself sat upon stones dampened with well water, who
had himself looked upon the awn of barley white unto harvest,
who had himself ridden on countless donkeys, their backs marked
with a natural cross; their hairy hides sweet-smelling under his
fingers; waiting, waiting, waiting in confident expectation for
the return of this unlikely deity in a latter-day dispensation!
Suddenly he would appear, suddenly he would be present on
these islands, bringing to an end the laborious days of these
exploited field-hands, bringing to an end the tormenting sorrows
of their secret souls amid cries of universal, of ineffable joy. I
could see it—the hot prickling sunshine lying over the plantations and the round heads of these black boobies thrown back in
unsurprised adoration as they looked up at the opening heavens,
their dutiful Ethiopic eyes wet with tears.

It was some time before I realized that the preacher was a
woman. She had the husky voice of a lion. Suddenly there was
the sound of a scuffle in the street and without warning a man
rushed into the building through one of the wide-open doors.
He was evidently taking sanctuary. We all stood up in alarm,
but the preacher was equal to the occasion, 'Peace be still', she
cried, raising her hand as in an act of benediction. 'You cannot
strike your brother in here. This is the house of God. The
Devil is abroad in the streets. Iniquity is added to iniquity, but
the time cometh, is now at hand, when judgment shall fall upon
all and the enemy of man the old black goat will be cast into
outer darkness.' Her words had effect and the service was concluded in good order with the singing of a hymn. Immediately
the spell of the woman's cult was broken and the little children,
with clattering feet, made for the door. The religious gathering
was at an end and only the palm trees remained to supplicate the
night, themselves destined to share after no long interval the gift
of a death without remembrance and without an end.

We returned to the dock and waited for a boat to take us back
to our ship. We had to step over the prostrate forms of many
drunken English sailors belonging to a warship. The stars were
shining above the sea and the pavement along the water-front
was illumined with shafts of light from the lamplit interiors of
the houses.

At Martinique we persuaded a native to climb a coconut tree.

I wanted to hold a green coconut in my hand and to drink and eat of it. Its immature shell was smooth as the back of a tortoise. The milk was sickly sweet to the taste as also was the soft sap. The boy simply walked up the silver column of the trunk. Apparently in the West Indies they do not cut steps in the trees as I have seen done in Africa. The road we followed was made of coral and fossils and gravel. There were native houses on both sides, each one of which was surrounded by a garden with expansive banana leaves shining motionless in the sun. We left the road at last and followed a mud path down to the valley. We passed a native woman carrying a debby of water on her head. In the distance we saw a farmhouse and went to it. We sat in the porch behind the kitchen talking to an old negro of seventy-five. He was wearing sandals made out of the red rubber of the inside tube of a motor car tyre. His house was filled with cheap manufactured furniture and with cheap modern china and there was an alarum clock on the dresser. His grandson stood by him, a child of two with an enormous bulging naked abdomen beautifully rounded. It was wonderful to observe how well this piccaninny had acquired the trick of standing erect, utterly separated already from the beasts of the field, a prominent specimen of *homo sapiens* created in two years, aberrant beneath the green leaves of these gardens, arrogant amongst the gay tropical petals.

The next day we drove to St. Pierre. We passed through high mountains. From the distance the foliage of the forests looked feathery soft. This effect was produced by the innumerable tree-ferns. Indeed, every mountain had a soft mossy look like a massed greenhouse fernery just after it has been watered. I have never seen such jungles, with creepers overmantling creepers, and parasites growing out of parasites. There was something depressing, terrifying about them. There were few birds and no animals. It was as if the vegetable world, eyeless and without tooth or claw, were in mute insurrection, its dumb, octopus-like legionaries for ever advancing, for ever throttling and suffocating, and for ever unvanquished. In a flash one comprehended what the earth would have been like had the miracle of life stirred only in boughs and branches and leaves and fronds—a strangling, speechless kingdom!

St. Pierre was a melancholy place. The city has never been

rebuilt and only a few people venture to live amongst its ruins. It is a more impressive city than Pompeii, its streets broader and its crumbling walls higher. Walking down its grass-grown thoroughfares we admired the gay *insouciance* of the flowers drooping so languidly over those awful lintels. The clerestory windows of the great church were as shocking to look at as the eye sockets of a churchyard skull. I have been taught that the destruction of St. Pierre ranks as seventh amongst the catastrophes that have fallen upon the human race. Certainly as I stood looking up at those idle flowers I had the sensation of being a revenant to a doomsday scene, so insistently did I experience a strange sinking of the heart to see how pitiful we appear and how helpless before such evidence of God's blasting fist. Out of nearly forty thousand inhabitants only one survived, a rogue entombed in the deepest dungeon of the town gaol.

I kept glancing up at Mount Pelée eternally belching out smoke. The bare, riven sides of the volcano certainly gave it an evil appearance. It overlooks the unfortunate town like a vulture which with bald craw and lidless vision sleeps wide awake, for ever on the watch to strike at any sensitive life movement.

I found that Barbados in many ways resembled Portland. It stands further out to sea than any other of the Windward Islands. We took an omnibus and walked to Saint Lawrence through some cotton plantations. We came up to two men talking in an allotment. One was a farm hand and the other a minister of some kind. He was dressed in a frock coat green with age and wore a soiled clerical collar frayed at the edges. The broad features of his large countenance had a kind of Gladstonian dignity about them. We sat down on the warm mould, between cotton shrubs in yellow blossom, and talked with him. He told us the 'white folk' were 'not very sweet' and that wages were only a shilling a day. There was much 'sufferation' on the island, he said. He seemed a good man and put me in mind of my own father. I remembered the majestic craft of the catholic church and was glad that protestant sects existed. Yet life may very well be floating on a bed of matter as unconcerned as Mount Pelée. I doubt but all human creeds are equally true and equally false, mere explanations offered of a mystery that can never be revealed. We believe what we have been taught to believe of the reasoning that prevails in our own particular environment.

There were many sugar-cane plantations with oxen pulling carts and a fresh breeze always blowing and sunshine and flocks of birds about everywhere like blackbirds, with yellow eyes and beaks. In the evening after our return we drove round the town in a carriage and I asked the old man on the box what this particular bird was called. He did not know, but pronounced it to be a 'bad' bird. I asked him why, and he explained that it would not hesitate to fly at a man's face if its nest was disturbed. So I thought might a bear complain against honey bees or an elephant against warrior ants. To this yellow-eyed Barbados fowl the human race were merely regarded as mischievous animals without prerogative. We passed a cemetery. The old man drove up and we looked over the wall. 'There are thousands of bodies buried there,' he said proudly, 'thousands!' 'I am glad I am not,' I said, and he gave me a sly grin. It was a jest to be understood by every race in every climate. A common fruit huckster was standing by and held up an orange. 'If you buy this,' he cried, 'you will never die.' I was in two minds to pocket the varlet's fruit.

After dinner we wandered about the streets. A pander nudged my elbow and in an insinuating whisper said, 'You can have any-thing you want in that hotel—do anything you want.' From a lighted upper room came the jangling of native music. We entered. It was a dance hall. The old procuress was a Creole. Her father had come from Aberdeen. We sat talking to her. Her favourite dance tune she told us was one that went to the words, 'I am dancing with tears in my eyes.'

The next day we were at the Port of Spain in Trinidad. I was eager to see the monkeys and with this purpose in view we set out walking into the forests. The path we followed was wet with overhanging grasses and branches drenched with rain. An un-common purple pea was growing everywhere. The atmosphere was stifling and humid and our clothes and shoes became soaked. We passed cocoa trees with purple pods often growing straight out of their trunks. We followed the bed of a dry stream. Sud-denly, far up above us in the forest trees, I heard the reiterated barking of monkeys. On and on we went, but always they sounded a little farther in front of us. Press forward as we might we seemed never to be able to catch up with them. At last we sat down exhausted, refreshing ourselves with some tangerines which lay strewn about us on the ground.

We had come apparently to a small cultivated plantation hidden away here. A white man approached us. We saw him in the distance walking through a grove of fruit trees. He was dressed in khaki. He was obviously a poor white. He had a refined face and very gentle manners. We talked to him sitting under the shade of a grapefruit tree while butterflies as large as swallows flew backwards and forwards across the sun-splashed, leaf-shivering spaces. I found the old man not to be without a philosophy and I envied him his days here occupied so quietly with the budding of his trees. He informed me that his name was Baily. His family were really Baliols, he said, and 'had a right to a crest.' We soon found that it was impossible for him to make any communication without using the formula 'Well! it is just like everything else.' He seemed to derive reassurance from these covering words as if in some way the reiteration of them deprived the universe of half of its terrors. He carried a pruning hook in his hand and a note-book was protruding out of his hip pocket. His face was pale and he wore a drooping grey moustache. I commented upon the beauty of his oasis and the magical wonder of the tropical forest. 'God,' he said looking gravely at me, 'manifests his invisible operations to us by those that are visible.' From this I concluded that he was a religious hermit of some kind. I asked him if he was married. He told me that he had been married for twenty-five years, but that his wife had died. 'She was a good woman,' he said. 'I never hope to see a better, she was goodness itself. We were like love-birds, she and I, like God's children, and never a cross word passed between us.' I asked whether she was an English woman. 'No,' he answered, 'I never believed in skin. It is just like everything else, I believe in the spirit.' 'Did she have any children?' I asked. 'No,' he replied quite simply; 'it is just like everything else. I have four sons and she was good to each one of them as they came. It is just like everything else, she was what you might call a coloured woman, but under the moon you would not find a better girl.' As he spoke these words the old man's voice began to tremble. He took out of his pocket a red-coloured handkerchief. His note-book came out with it and fell to the ground. He stopped to pick it up and then began blowing his nose. We looked away. 'It is just like everything else,' he said, 'Nature will always be too strong for me. I tell you I loved my wife better than food, better than drink. She had a spirit as gentle as that insect,' he added, quaintly pointing to a blue moth that went sailing past with drowsy fluttering wings on some secret quest of its own.

We now continued on our way. After we had gone a mile or so we came to another open clearing. In the middle of this space grew a single giant tree. The girth of its trunk was so enormous that it reminded me of some of the redwoods I had seen in California. I put my hand against its bark. The trunk was pocked with thorns and one of these pricked through the skin of my palm. I felt as if the tree, so large, so isolated, might mark a trysting place for strange and terrifying lovers, for half-animal, half-jungle lovers. It had the look of a tree whose every wrinkle had once been familiar.

We went on, pushing our way through dense masses of boscage. Presently I stumbled and found that my foot had hit against a large sheet of corrugated iron hidden under the matted grass. I could not imagine how it could have got to such a place. We went on a little farther. A succession of ruined buildings now showed themselves—fragments of walls, steps grass-matted, and chimneys grown over with creepers. Apparently we were passing some village that had been destroyed by fire, by a bush fire perhaps. From some of the walls I could see charred beams projecting. We came to a high fence, fortified with twisted barbed wire. It was impossible to see over this and I thought at first that it presented an impenetrable obstacle. However, eventually we found a broken space through which we could squeeze. Once on the farther side of it we were confronted by a large barrack-like building. It seemed in good repair, though utterly deserted. No crooked smoke came out of its chimneys, no face looked out of its windows. There was something very terrifying about this silent citadel hidden away in the heart of this Trinidad forest. The building had many doors and I went up to one of them and tried the handle. The door opened, and opposite it was a flight of uncarpeted stairs. Up them we went and into a large bare room. We looked out through one of the many high sash windows. Across a lawn as wide as the Great Court of Trinity College, Cambridge, was another long building exactly like the one we were in. Immediately below I could see traces of a gravel drive overgrown now with grass. I could not imagine what kind of visitors were accustomed to get out of their carriage here. Except for kiskadees on the lawn (a bird that resembles a Golden Oriole) there was no sign of life, no stir to tell of the everyday world we knew. I could not imagine the purpose of this imposing sanctuary into which we had wandered.

We went out into the quadrangle and stood in the sunlight looking up at the high galleries. On each side of the building stood two chapels. Their doors had been left wide open and we went in and examined them. They contained Christian altars. We wandered across the silent turf to a dovecote-like building constructed entirely of blocks of stone like Saint Catherine's chapel at Abbotsbury. There was a grille at the top of the massive door and looking through the bars I realized at once it was a prison. It was indeed like certain medieval prisons I have seen with arrow-slit windows and a close-stool of stone in one of the corners. Suddenly the explanation flashed into my mind. We were in an abandoned leper colony!

My surmise was correct. When the seven hundred patients had been moved to their present prison, a small island out to sea, the several houses in the forest had been burned down as a sanitary precaution. The larger collegiate buildings had been left standing, their doors open, their floors well-scrubbed, for no marauders would willingly select such a dwelling for shelter. I later inquired about the discipline and manner of life of the place. The men and women were segregated, and yet what devices they had for coming to each other, leaving dummy lepers in sleeping cots and I know not what else. They told me that on several occasions lovers had escaped into the forest and had never been heard of again.

We went down to the sea shore. All was shining, glittering in the sun. The silver sands were fringed as always with palm trees. A woman was digging for cockles. Near a boat, covered with dry palm leaves to keep the sun from blistering it, was a group of men playing at cards, a jolly sun-tanned crew, with the implements of their trade about them: wide box-like traps for catching fish, looking like cages. As we walked along the path under the palms, ripe coco-nuts would be constantly falling to the ground. If any child heard the thud he or she would come running to pick the nut up. I was apprehensive lest I should have my skull cracked open, as happened to the sconce of Aeschylus when the eagle let fall its prize.

We were at Pierre de Point, the next day. I was up before dawn and watched the steamer come into the wharf. Across the glass-still waters of the harbour pelicans were flying in long, precise, rule-of-thumb lines, beak to legs, legs to beak. A man in khaki was on the pier, a man fast set in our modern objective life. A voice from the prow of our ship hailed him. 'How are things?' 'Lovely,' came back his surprising answer as he directed a gang of coloured workmen to get oil pipes into a position suitable for supplying our ship.

That night for the first time since I left Africa in 1919 I saw again the Southern Cross. It appeared in the sky like a kite lying on its side. The stars against the rigging shone everywhere with startling brilliance and the sea was smooth and there was a summer breeze.

We had attended a Quaker meeting in a tumbledown back street of the town. The minister, a gentle and refined-looking man, directed the service. At a given moment the whole congregation, both men and women, left their seats and rushed towards the daïs which seemed to serve the purpose of an altar. There they cast themselves down on the floor and began to cry to God. I never saw such an emotional orgy. Deep, deep through our very beings go the roots of religion. In gay agony the men cried and howled at God. Revolving within the circumference of the solar system cold and remote was the moon, older than memory, flooding down upon the earth her wan reflected light. Moonlight I knew was upon the sea, upon the forests, upon the rivers, and upon the headlands. It was illuminating the roof of this very place of worship where human beings, with spirits passionate and distraught, called out to the mystery. Why could not God hear? The very ass I had seen tethered in the coco-nut plantation that morning would have at least turned its head, in spite of the fact that its long, listening, trumpet ears had been three-quarters clipped away. One negro's head was thrown far back, the chin was up, the mouth wide open. It was as if this man were petitioning for the life of his very soul on the Judgment Day, raised to terror-stricken consciousness again after a dusty sojourn of a thousand years underground. Surely there is a morbidity in this universal human weakness. I am not convinced that there is anything particularly noble about religious feeling. Who knows but that we might not be better off without it—careless and swift as the fish, self-interested, grossly absorbed as the animals, feckless, debonair as the birds?

A young girl of fifteen years perhaps slipped into the lighted meeting-room out of the velvet darkness of the littered yard. She sat next to me and watched with detached interest what was going on. I think she came in merely to provoke her boy lover. I could see his shadow at the door, furtively urging her to him again. Young as she was she had learned that in these matters there is power in evasion.

On the return voyage we called once more at Dominica. We had a day to spend as we liked, our last day in the West Indies. As soon as we reached the quay we noticed a crowd that had collected on the beach. We went to see what the people were looking at. It was a fish as large as a seal, but shaped like a whale. It was black and its skin was slippery as seaweed. Its head was fitted with small dusky eyes which even in death retained something of their deep-sea knavery. On the top of its forehead was an opening for spouting water. This was contrived with a fleshy valve which I could push down with my finger. The beast's jaws showed regulated lines of ugly teeth shaped like the teeth of a land animal, as large as lion's teeth. Men with choppers were dividing up its body and by the time we reached the market its flesh was already for sale.

We spent the day in the forest. We walked to the very top of a high ravine where we came upon a small plot of maize. We went to the back of this and, climbing through some bushes, sat on the very edge of the precipice which divided us from the next mountain. The ground was slippery. Between the leaves we could look into the dizzy valley. The buoyant atmosphere before us was hot and empty. We followed the ravine down to the sea. The vegetation was tropical—palms, banana trees, and tangled creepers. We saw a snake basking on a rock, much longer than an adder, and with scales of crisp silver. Far up in the sky swallows were darting backwards and forwards. We had tea in the house of Mrs. Roberts, but she was not there. They told us she had gone to our ship to visit us early that morning, and sure enough, as we approached it in our hired boat, there she was leaning over the taffrail. We recognised her from far away, this slender half-cast woman, so full of shy charm, and so different from our noisy fellow passengers. She had brought us gifts—some jelly, some sugared fruit, and some shells. We sat on the deck talking with her. She was trembling. She told us she had been waiting the whole day long. She had hoped we would have come back to the ship for luncheon.

A bell rang. It was time for visitors to leave the ship. We walked down the gangway with her. She seated herself in one of the boats. I would have liked to have paid her boatmen, but did not dare to offer to do so. She was very proud. At this moment down upon us came an overdressed English-woman, pretentious, colonial, tingling to her finger-tips with snobbishness. She saw Mrs. Roberts in the boat and in a loud, rude, querulous voice called out, 'I want a clean boat. I don't want to get into that boat; that is dirty.' We saw Mrs. Roberts shrink. When we were back on deck we kept wondering what we could have said to correct the woman. On such occasions one's anger and dismay seem to paralyse one's wit.

We stood looking over the side of the steamer. A little way off was a boat packed to the gunwales with pretty West Indian merchandise. It was just such a boat cargo as would please old-world sailors, a boat cargo from which they could choose gay trophies for their sweet friends, keeping them in their ditty boxes till the morning when in warm sunshine they would present them in secret on some spring bank. The sea was bright blue and utterly transparent, and buoyant upon it was this cockleboat piled high with turtle backs, stuffed fish, fantastic shells, fans of coral! Suddenly beneath us I saw a school of flying fish swimming just under the surface of the water. I had some pennies in my pocket and threw them down to startle the fish into flight. As the coins touched the water the fish rose into the air like scattering gold-finches. They skimmed over the boats of the traders—a flight of silver darts. One of the fish struck the brown bare neck of the man who was standing in the bows of the cargo boat. The impact evidently stung him. I saw him bend down to pick up the flying fish which had fallen amongst his wares. He took it by its tail and, beating its head viciously against an oar, threw it back into the sea. It was a gesture as instinctive as the twitching lash of a horse's tail when bitten by a horsefly. It was the last view I got of the islands.

In scarcely more than a week we were again in Austerlitz. There was still no sign of the spring. The snow was banked as high as each side of the road. I had brought back a necklace for our hostess made out of the coloured scales of West Indian fishes. I took it out of my pocket to look at it the first morning after our

return. There had been a hard frost the night before and the surrounding landscape was crisp and shining. I held the trinket in the
palm of my hand and as I did so a blue jay in flashing plumage flew
out of the larch tree. What could be imagined more marvellous
than life upon earth in all its manifold display? It is a thing beyond
appreciation, beyond praise. It is what the ancients would call a
ferlie, a wonder. Every inch of our planet's matter is charged
with mystery. All through our days from childhood till old age
we sleep, we tread, upon faery ground.

From *The Pleasure Ground*, a miscellany
edited by Malcolm Elwin (1947).

MOUNT CARMEL

IT WAS dark when our steamer came to anchor in the harbour of Haifa. We had the address of an Austrian Hospice on Mount Carmel, and it was in this house that we hoped to stay. We hired a car at the harbour and were driven with terrifying rapidity round the bends of a steep mountain road. It was too dark to see anything beyond the lights of the town below. We were received at the hostel door by nuns and were shown into a fresh, clean room with a bed on each side of the window. We had our dinner at a long refectory-table in the dining-room. There were three English officials present and opposite us a young Syrian girl with very dark eyes. The Englishmen imparted to us information about the land with self-conscious, unimaginative energy. 'And where do you come from?' one of them asked the native maiden. 'From Cana in Galilee,' she said simply. 'Ah! Is that so?' exclaimed the healthy-faced doctor in surprise, showing by his tone that he was not entirely oblivious of the charm of the answer.

After dinner we went out. Dark as it was, I was determined if possible to get on to the mountain. There was no moon, but the starshine was bright. We passed down a road that had been planted on both sides with pines and then branched off on the open hillside. On we walked, stumbling against the rocks and scrub, until we reached a position where only the stars and the bare outlines of the mountain and the shadow of the sea were visible. We sat down with our backs to a rock. With my eight finger-bones and two thumb-bones pressing into the ground I strained my imagination against the years. With suppressed emotion I realized that I was actually present in the body on ground where the Prophet had trod. All the romance and violence, all the poetry of the ancient story, drifted into my consciousness as though I were in actual fact close upon the footsteps of the obsessed holy man, with his cloak and staff and his wallet of parched barley. I saw his lean hairy legs roped with sinew, his unnoticed, uncared-for feet with toes tipped with tough nails, his breathing chest, the withdrawn ferocity of his religious eye, wilful, void of tolerance, God-drunken. I was glad that we had reached Haifa after dark. There seemed to be a privilege in the chance that my first wandering upon the mountain should be at night. With the mystery of the obscured earth around us it was more easy to be rid of the human reckoning of time, and with a sequence of reality link with one's own hour this wild tribal rumour out of the past.

That night I omitted to draw the mosquito curtains about my bed and in consequence was presently aware of innumerable small irritations as though my flesh were being nipped by acorn-high fairies furnished with tweezers. Sand-flies were biting me, but I did not know it.

In the morning we set out for a walk. We followed a small path that ran eastward. We passed a number of Zionist bungalows with what looked like nursery gardens of little pine trees around them, all of which were withering and most of them dead. The view was magnificent. The mountain stretched itself into Palestine like a sleeping beast. Above it was a cloudless sky of bright blue, to the westward of it a waveless sea of bright blue. Along the coast to the northward I could make out the Ladders of Tyre, a white chalk-like cliff which always reminded me of Bats Head. On this side of it was Acre, and between Acre and Haifa a curving sickle bay along the beach of which General Gordon had walked on a certain early morning long ago. To the south I could see the white ridge of the Mediterranean breaking upon a low straight coast with the ancient crusading castle of Athlit clearly outlined. Looking eastward, I fancied I could detect the Lake of Galilee, but this, so I discovered afterward, was an illusion. Mount Hermon, snow-capped and impressive, was always visible.

After we had walked several miles we sat and rested under a carob tree. From our position we could look down upon a secluded valley where some Arabs were camping. We watched every movement of the little tribe with absorbed interest. Their tents were black, as were also the shadows under the bellies of three camels which stood patiently not far off. We saw a child run out across the dusty platform with its mother after it; the chickens, small as mites, scattered. A wind was blowing from

The Dorset coast looking east from White Nose. The large valley is Middle Bottom, with the promontory of Bats Head beyond. The beach here is virtually inaccessible except from the sea.

the northeast so that in spite of the sun we kept cool. The mountain was grown over with wild mint, wild sage, thistle, snapweed, and burnet thorn.

We were again out on the mountain at night. Jupiter was shining over Athlit, the North Star over the Ladders of Tyre, the Fishes to the eastward over Carmel.

The following morning we went to Haifa by a steep rocky path past fig trees and low crumbling walls. It was a short way and made me think of going down into Stoke from off the 'Frying-Pan' end of Ham Hill. In the town I was completely absorbed in watching the camels. These were more like Somali camels, far larger than those I had seen at Mersina. I was amazed by their lofty carriage as they paraded along the street, lifting their legs mechanically, their necks decorated with bead chains and coloured worsted, and their fantastical Pharaoh heads tufted with feathers. Their presumptuous manners compelled my constant heed. I continually examined them with admiration and wonder, their hairy cunning upper lips, their slit nostrils, their weak quivering lower lips, and their beautiful brown eyes. They are queer animals, but they are by no means devoid of a fantastic stateliness of their own. The testicles of the males protruded oddly behind their legs. It was difficult to imagine that the sophisticated temperament of these beasts was ever disturbed by the procreant urge. Yet in the market-place I saw a female who was resting with her callused breast-bone upon the ground suddenly raise her hind quarters and, because her shin-bones were shackled with ropes, stumble *on her knees* to the side of her friend some distance away. I watched her settle herself at his side and nuzzle at him, the dung-stained hocks of her back legs protruding from under her tail. For all that I could judge the spirit of her companion was far withdrawn from her.

This day I felt apprehensive about my consumption and when I got back I had a fever and a bad headache. Was Palestine a poisoned country? It seemed like that as I looked giddily out of the windows at twilight.

I was better the next morning and we walked to the Carmelite monastery that guards the traditional cave of Elijah. The cave itself, under the altar, was formed out of the primitive natural rock of the mountain, grey in colour. It was adorned with scraps of tawdry tinsel. A bearded Irishman showed us round. He had a clear eye, but had been a little spoilt by intercourse with so many tourists. He certainly had managed to put up some hideous buildings to the glory of his God.

In the afternoon of the next day we followed a dry rocky valley down to the sea. We found that the water's margin is only one hundred yards from the foot of Carmel. We passed many caves and tombs. I looked into several of them and eventually crawled into one which contained, so I found by lighting a match, four loculi for bodies. I sat resting there for a little. Through the tomb's opening I could see a perfect square of blue water. I wondered whether it had been used first as a habitation by a hermit and only afterward as a burying-place. Certainly the outlook from it was not uncheerful. There were no bones now, all was darkness and dust. My trousers were very dirty when I re-emerged, and while I was trying to brush them my eye fell upon the body of a crushed chameleon. Its skin was as dry and parched as a dead toad's skin that has been first squashed by the wheel of a wagon and then kicked about for a fortnight by the boots of schoolboys and yet still retains its original shape.

We now crossed the narrow strip of ground between the mountain and the sea. I thought of Napoleon marching his army along it only a little more than a hundred years ago. I felt hot and bathed my forehead in a rock pool. The rocks were very slippery and there was a quantity of white seaweeed on the shore, of a kind I had never seen. It resembled goat's hair. My companion found some delicate shells. Not very far out in the surf were two native fishermen busy with casting nets. These nets were weighted, and after they had left the men's hands they spread out so that they enclosed a wide area of water before they sank. The men walked slowly toward them until, feeling the mesh with their naked feet, they drew the nets up with their hands. The figure of one of the fishermen was large enough to hide a fourth part of the city of Acre, which was visible from here across the bay. To the left the sun was sinking red and round over the sea. The prospect had about it a primitive and lovely beauty. Yet to receive life purged of sentiment—what a tough acceptance one must have!

We had hardly walked a hundred yards along the beach before we passed the carcasses of two dead horses, the one a bay with distended belly, ears rigid, teeth exposed, and anus gnawed at by jackals, and the other dead for a longer time, a black horse with half its ribs in and its tattered hide hanging loose.

We now set out to walk round the headland and to return to Haifa along under Mount Carmel. By going this way I knew we would pass close to 'the cave of the prophets.' It was almost dark when we reached it, however. A filthy slum-like house was built this side of the opening of the cave. We had to cross over the most stinking middens covered with tins and sordid refuse. When we entered the enclosure it was still light enough to see the figure of an aged man with a long white beard standing with his forehead pressed against a rock. He was obviously praying and we waited, not liking to disturb him. I never discovered whether he was Mohammedan or Catholic or Jew. It was impossible to know what whimsy was entertained by the venerable head of this old pilgarlic who, dressed in a dirty robe, stood pressing his brow against a dead rock in that befouled pound. He eventually noticed us and conducted us to the cave. It was large. Its ceiling and walls were all of rough rock, but its floor was paved like a church. Perhaps it was where Obadiah hid the prophets from the wrath of Jezebel. Christian tradition has it that Joseph off-saddled here when he was bringing his wife and child back from Egypt.

It was almost dark when we came out and we experienced some difficulty in skirting along the under slopes in the direction of the lights of the city. It was half-cultivated country without houses. At one time we found we were stumbling over graves. I had only just realized what such a succession of low hillocks indicated when we heard the most extraordinary sound—a long low wailing that rose to a shriek and ended in a cackling laugh. Only once in my life had I heard any noise like it, and that was the howling of a hyena witch-doctor outside the shutters of a mud house in Africa. Whether it came from the throat of a man furious at us for trespassing, or actually from a hyena that we had disturbed, I never knew! It may well have been the howling of a hyena because I had recognised the yowl of one of these overbold animals the night before as I lay awake cursing at the invisible sand-flies.

From *A Pagan's Pilgrimage* (1931).

TWENTY LETTERS

To John Cowper Powys

Gilgil, Nov. 1st, 1914.

My dear Jack,

I have been here now exactly a fortnight and although up to now I notice no marked decrease in my expectoration yet I am certainly feeling well and have an excellent appetite at Willie's table which is very well appointed—fresh meat twice a day and as much cream and milk as I could possibly want. I have sold my dove-coloured flannel suit of Venice fame to a 'Boy' for 5 rupees, he wanted to delight the eyes of a certain 'Boeby' in Navasha, the maiden wife of a friend of his, of his best friend. It certainly was strange to see this 'darkie' strolling about outside the native huts so as to display this suit to his friends, this dove-coloured suit with a black band round its left arm. We came upon him as we were returning from an afternoon walk, and as we looked across at High Stoy in the hazy distance, we were curiously reminded of that overgrown bramble country around Middlemarsh. Yes, this other country often reminds me of Dorset, there are downlands exactly like those by the Three Mary's, but the sides of them are grown with the high wood-like African forests full of huge cedars which don't look quite like English cedars and yet are somewhat the same. All are bearded with lichen as it were ancient tree-men.

I have given Willie the Moorish belt Frances gave me as a recompense for not going on shore at Tangier—it looks very well on him, with his hunting knife swinging at his hip. Willie is very well and looks simply splendid. Today he has gone down to Gilgil to buy cattle from the Somali who drive herds down from their country taking nine months to do it. It is strange to think they were coming nearer and nearer when you were composing the letter to Marion in the corner of the kitchen garden when you were in Spain, when we were climbing the rocks under Seaton White Cliff, and lastly when we stood looking at Mother's dead head that morning in the spare room.

FRIDAY, OCT. 23rd. Sacked the cook and then walked down to the river, cold dark water running swiftly over black scoriac rocks. Picked an orange-coloured flower of the most velvet texture. In the afternoon walked as far as the two cedars in the hope of seeing Willie come back, the sky was darkened, I sat by the side of the track looking across the valley, then I stood watching two native cows fighting—all the time conscious of a curious uneasiness, this country is so strange, so alien with its rocky escarpments, its humped-back cattle, its wild skeleton cedars.

OCT. 24th. Walked down by the river, saw many strange flowers, turned up by the cedar tree and crossed over the stubble. Came upon a number of natives pulling flax as though in an American plantation, also watched men ploughing with a disc-like plough drawn by a dozen humped-back cattle.

OCT. 25th. In the afternoon walked as far as the one Mary, was rather depressed because my temperature was up a little. In the evening Willie and I read English mail. Heard a hyaena howl, a long low howl rising into a kind of whoop.

> ' Ay, but to die, and go we know not where; to lie in cold obstruction, and to rot; this sensible warm motion to become a kneaded clod ; and the delighted spirit to blow with restless violence round the pendent earth.'

OCT. 28th. In the afternoon I walked a long way past the Tinbetimber (?) until I made my right lung ache. Willie hurt his thumb. In the afternoon as soon as the rain had stopped we set out for a walk. Mac began barking in the forest and we crossed the stream and clambered up a game path. I saw monkeys climbing about the tops of the cedars like cats. In the evening was tired.

> ' Sirrah! thou art said to have a stubborn soul,
> That apprehends no further than this world
> And squarest thy life according.'

OCT. 29th. Walked with Willie as far as the flax field, watched a troop of black boys plucking up the slender green stems so fresh and cleanly grown, with here and there a periwinkle flower. Anderton arrived and took Willie away to buy cattle. I had dinner and went to bed on the verandah. Mac came whining at the wire barricade. I lifted him through the window out of the reach of leopards.

Oct. 30th. Walked down to the flax field and then to the river where the pigs drink. In the afternoon gave out 'posha' and then walked with all the dogs to the further barley, put up some quail and two Kafferonda cranes which went flapping away making their queer grating cry.

Sat. 31st. Walked with Willie down to the flax field and then read and wrote. Coming home with Willie we thought how like the country looked to Dorset. There was something certainly homely and pleasing about that return in the dusk—the red flame from the fires, the round native huts, the misty darkness.

Your brother,
Lulu.

To John Cowper Powys

Gilgil, January (?), 1916.

My dear Jack,

Of course it is ridiculous of you to talk of staying here only a fortnight. You must certainly stay 3 weeks or a month. If you get leave for ten days you can just as well get leave for 30, no one will really miss you. . . . You will be able to write here. I have a lovely little room which I already envisage littered with cigarettes sadistically crushed and bent. If you sail straight for Naples you would only use up a fortnight of your holidays in the journey here. You ought to be able to get back in three weeks. You must remember to buy at Naples or somewhere a double Terrai hat or a helmet. You must play no pranks with this tropical sun which is different from the sun we know although it often may not feel so hot.

Yesterday we were busy shearing rams, their fleeces are very very delicate soft things with a wonderful lustre. I get pleasure from seeing and handling them. Will is on a 10 days trek across the border. Christ! bring him back safe again. The advance is to be in February so all the world says.

Last night after dinner I sat on Cole's verandah, he went to the rears and I was super-conscious of the scene—the moonlight, the sound of galloping zebras, the sound of running water and the English sky. He heard a lion grunt. I asked him where 'Oh quite close and by your house.' As I walked back two hyaenas came howling by. I thought of that Bible passage which used to amuse me of the old Semitic who went for a walk and a lion met him and he returned with pressing business to his house and a bear met him.

I really enjoy very excellent breakfasts now, sitting on my verandah with Lake Elmenteia before me—porridge and *cream*, cold bacon of the very first quality, fresh eggs and excellent tea and cigarettes. I long to receive your book 'Wood and Stone', an excellent title.

Your loving
Lulu.

To John Cowper Powys

Gilgil, March 26th, 1916.

My dear Jack,

It pleased me to think that you must be now very nearly through your six months' work. If I do not mistake it was about this time that you and I fussed off to the North German Lloyd and were given our ticket and change by that honest shorthand writer who had a few weeks before taken down a lecture on R.L.S. delivered at the Lexington. Old days—days gone—days lost in oblivion—how many throats cry Yankee Doodle to the cosmos now out of that crowd which paraded the Philadelphia streets in 1909 with dusty boots, dusty boots they were then, and now they are dust themselves and no little niggers to furbish them back to the respectable world. That little black boy who perused indecent literature (his only joy in the Rittenhouse lavatory) where is he now? Where is Mr. Winkle and his pretty wife—does he? do they still continue to eat ices after the guests have been served in some other Rittenhouse? Where is Kitchener the chemist and the little librarian who could not tolerate English staff lectures? Where is Sophy? and Atkins and Margaret Leipziger? It still remains to me an amazing fact that I am alive and able to remember these things and recall these people who served me with soft drinks, and mean jumps out of their oblivion. How the perpetual flux has submerged all of their purposes and occupations! It does not matter whether I was possessed of the three R's or whether Mother Wallis had grip or no.

Well, General Smuts has fairly begun his campaign here and

I await events and think of our Will surrounded by a million dangers. They have taken Morhi and are working away down the Tanga railway. Perhaps by the time this reaches you B.E.A. will have fallen, but will W.E.P. have fallen, that is the point. If he comes out safe I would gladly let them keep their colony. I shall not stay in the country forever. I keep repeating that to you and to myself. Now Marion has abandoned me I am free and the world is my terrace walk and I shall move about in it at my ease—smell Turk's Head lilies and even perhaps wander away out into Badgouljay wood. You have no conception how much I concentrate my mind and energies upon the business of farming. Very often 'The old refrain' comes back again 'how long how long how long!'[1] From sunrise to sunset I am occupied with this occupation, and all the time activity present. I think my next move will be to the highlands of America, but I daren't go while the war is on, or until I can discuss things with Willie. I hope you will be able to get those short stories published, some of them are 'good stuff' as Bertie would say, as good stuff as ever I shall write. I trust you are well. I long to hear from you again.

(No signature).

To Theodore Francis Powys

Gilgil, B.E.A.
April 23rd, 1916.

Well my dear Theodore,
   I like very much receiving your letters, and as for your book[2] I cannot tell you how highly I think of it. It may be that our Confessions will be more popular at first, but I agree with the marquise[3] when he says yours will be still read in far off future days. This book at one stroke puts you beyond half the great ones of the earth. Cole reads it continually and says he senses in its pages a most sensitive and super-refined soul like that of his cousin Lord Barrymore!!! I think your style is amazing, and your irony and your quips, there is not a single page that has not something in it that separates it from everything. I do not like the text at the beginning though. What a triumph to the true

[1] Reference to a phrase of Mr. Atkins.   [2] *The Soliloquy of a Hermit.*
[3] 'The Marquise', a character in Louis Marlowe's pamphlet *Blasphemy and Religion* (1916).

cause if we three gain a reputation as being men of parts and imagination—a victory for Court House,[1] for Studland,[2] for the left steps . . . and as for you, your company will be sought out by the mob, and the mob will get a poxy belabouring for their pains. HO! Ho! I see it plain, we are great men-of-letters, and can now loll at our ease and give a turd for the world!!!!

Yesterday I rode out in the afternoon to a far-away sheep camp and did not get back till after dark. I do not like being out after dark and I keep looking over my horse's tail. Two lions have been seen out there and I thought for certain they would give me a pat.

Your loving
Lulu.

To John Cowper Powys

Gilgil, B.E.A.
Sept. 23rd, 1917.

Dear Jack,

A letter from you—I am sorry your friends have betrayed you and I am dreadfully afraid that ennui and a return of dyspepsia will intervene now that there is no flaming background to your life. I wonder what kind of writing will all this turmoil and strain and sickness evoke. Will I read insane master words or will these months have produced nothing? There is absolutely no chance of my being relieved until Cole gets back from England. Whatever happens you must not expect it. *I am caught.* The burden of this vast farm lies on me alone, there is no other man within five miles of me. I cannot let the thing go until there is someone to take my place. I have an idea peace is not far off, but even then I see no prospect of seeing you for another year. Lions are here again, stampeding cattle and generally giving trouble. I have managed to kill two in a trap I set over a dead zebra. God! I know well how to set a gun, and how to give a great lion an unexpected biff at the back of the neck. What wit! what ape-like cunning for me, a scurvy philosophic coward who fears a personal encounter! . . . Two stations up the line there has been a settler *murdered at midnight* by natives— sometimes when I sit alone at night amid all these innumerable

[1] Then J. C. Powys's Sussex home. [2] Then T. F. Powy's Dorset home.

black men I think this may be my end, but no I shan't escape consumption for nothing. I have other work to do.

Your loving brother,
Lulu.

To John Cowper Powys

The White Nose, Owermoigne,[1]
August 19th, 1925.

My darling John,

I ought to write to you much more often. I do so adore your letters. Old Bertie has been staying here for the last fortnight and I think he enjoyed himself. We had some lovely days, one excursion to Wimborne Minster where we walked into the fields and came upon an old mediaeval bridge over the Stour. I made Alyse take off her stockings and wade across the Stour, and the tall flags and rushes on the banks were wonderful, also the look of a swan under the arches, also the crying of moorhens or coots or dab-chicks from hidden places. I was interested by seeing the ancient library of chained books at Wimborne Minster—Raleigh's *History of the World* and a first edition of Burton's *Anatomy*, and Matthew Prior's first subscription edition of the poems out of which he made £2,000, and among the names of his patrons Sir Littleton and Sir Thomas Powys and Elizabeth and Richard Powys. There was a clock going still in the Minster invented by a monk of Glastonbury in 1320 and its machinery still in use. . . .

Today we sat on Bats Head with Katie and saw two cormorants half way down the cliff on a steep chalk ledge and also some thirty others fishing in the green transparent depths below. When they fly over the sea past the White Nose, they fly always very low almost touching the sea. I have bathed twice with Florida's little daughter aged 11 who is very entrancing and makes me feel like some aged Abdel Krim as I follow her over the rocks. Abdel Krim—good luck to him. What a sly look he has and his sandalled feet stick out like the feet of a cormorant. I received since a sweet letter from our darling Phyllis and I

[1] Llewelyn Powys's first Dorset home after his marriage.

will write to her very soon. Give her my love. Will she come and stay with us next year do you think? Perhaps we will spend a summer abroad next year. I love you my dearest brother and miss you always.

Lulu.

To H. Rivers Pollock

The White Nose, Owermoigne,
Dec. 1925.

My dear Rivers,

. . . The frost continues. The little green pond actually bore last night and I stood in the very centre of it to my great satisfaction. Alyse and I came down to it from the down above Rat Barn where we had met the Diment's shepherd hurdling a flock of hoggets on a flint-strewn hill. We asked him whether he ever saw ghosts on the downs at night, and he said that once near Corfe Castle as he passed another green downland pond he had seen the ghost of a cow with a white face that plunged into the water and was gone! He said it did not matter seeing such sights, but if you threw stones at the object or hit at it there was danger! His discourse I found pleasing. It delighted me to discover, to talk with a man whose occupation was so simple that the very apparitions he encountered had to do with the horned creations.

Last night when I took the lid off the milk pail a whiff so foul hit my nose that I was immediately violently sick—the milk was apparently fresh as soon as the evil gas melted away into the air. What could this be? Dicken suggested that it was because they had begun feeding the cattle on hay but does this consumption of hay cause the milk when covered up to give off gas that smells like a devil's fart? Solve me this riddle my master. My stomach is still uneasy. Give Eveline my love and also darling Mary. Tell her never to lose the fox's tail. Beware Archer![1] I find my heart with regard to Archer virgin of tenderness. Let him caper to his death and be damned to him!

Yours,
Llewelyn.

[1] A very mettlesome bull which on one occasion chased Ll. P. and A.G. from the other side of a hedge.

To John Cowper Powys

The White Nose, Owermoigne,
1927.

My dear Jack,

. . . Violet's grandmother died and I went to the funeral in Dorchester and stood by her coffin with Theodore and looked upon her dead head. I never saw a dead head with so complacent an expression as was worn by this female cadaver who had lived upon earth for 86 years. There were two carriages but there was no room for me so I walked behind the coffin bareheaded through the streets of Dorchester along with the undertakers who were clever at picking their way amongst the puddles. The grave was dug out of chalk and did not look unpleasant. I observed a dead mouse at one end of it.

I returned to the White Nose in deep fog, walking up Upton Lane. Alyse found two primroses in the horse show wood at Ringstead, but the rooks haven't begun to build yet. We walked to Lulworth one night to take supper with our Catholic priest, when we passed under the three elms at the bottom of the road below Diffy's Farm they made a wonderful music and it was pleasant to meet boys and girls coming back from church in a wet and muddy lane in mild winter weather,

Yours,
Lulu.

To Roy Jansen

Austerlitz N.G. (?), 1931.

Dear Mr. Jansen,

[1]Of all experiences I think my spirit has been more stirred by the various dawns I have watched breaking in different countries. I remember an occasion in Africa when I was riding across the open country in the very early morning and watched the sun rise unconquerable over that alien and dazzling landscape. In an ecstasy of life birds cried and screamed from the damp jungle, the monkeys in the treetops chattered, the buck danced out of my way leaping from mound to mound, warthogs with backs shining with dew rushed through the scrub, tail on end—and

---

[1] Answer to a request asking what experience in the life of Ll.P. had made the deepest impression on him.

then all at once I disturbed a lion! I cannot tell what a revelation came to me as the splendid beast raised its golden head. The slanting sun rays touched the grass about it and transformed the animal into a creature of unsurpassed magnificence. Never had I felt so much the mystery of existence. I, a man, with the rare burden of consciousness on me, was looking at this beast of ancient lineage, while the sun, the only god visible to mortals, illumined with his divine light the wide flanks of the revolving earth, grass-grown, primitive, unregenerate, and mysteriously stirred with eager life as though still in the first hour of creation with the shouts of the sons of God only lately silent.

Yours,
Llewelyn Powys.

To A. R. Powys

White Nose, July, 1931.

My dearest Bertie,

This is to wish you many happy returns of your birthday. We shall think of you on Sunday and hope for your good fortune and for the fulfilment of your anticipations of a long life.

Yesterday we went into Weymouth to see the Prince of Wales. I liked the look of him. I thought he looked delicate and refined. Bernie was with us and rolled after us like a sun-warmed keg of Malmsey wine with a thousand spiggot holes having the gift of enjoyment and vision. He saw a gypsy baby 'Violet' born under Culleford's Tree and looking like a Buddha. He saw the curve of the breast of a young girl standing by an old Etonian outside the yacht club where we once lunched with Uncle Jack! and observed in Thurman's a new kind of cultivator. I often think that you go about after truth like a watchman with an enormous lanthorn and all the time the imp is chirping under the lappet of your hat. This is a slight reference to your letter which I was very happy to receive and I loved you for being able to write!

Eleanor Cole wants to come next Friday for the night and we will so arrange it. . . .

We enjoyed seeing old Littleton the other day. I very much liked to hear his voice sounding over the gorse bushes.

I long to know the date of your visit here so that I can look forward to it.

Yours,
Lulu.

To Edna St. Vincent Millay

Chydyok,
Chaldon Herring,
Dorchester,
Dorset.
November 26th, 1932.

My dear Edna,

I would so like to persuade you to stay for a little time in a cottage at East Lulworth four miles away from here. The cottage has no modern conveniences in the way of a bath, etc., but it is very snug and well furnished and has a very good library and exciting books and you could have it for ten shillings a week. At present Oliver Lodge (Junior) has it with his young wife Diana, but they will soon be going back to their house in Surrey. It is within a mile of the sea and East Lulworth is one of the loveliest villages of Dorset. It is a thatched cottage next to a tavern and within walking distance of us. Do try it for a fortnight, for a month, for two months. It is a lovely place. You could walk in the Park which has walks around it five miles long and here all the fairies of the county have been driven to take refuge, as well as others that have come from the North. I myself have seen the bluebells sway as they pass through them. It has a ruined castle in the centre where peacocks gather and the property is owned by Herbert Weld, an old man of eighty of very ancient lineage.

Now I beg you, darling Edna, to consider the proposal. A stay here will bring peace to your mind. You will write the best poetry you have ever written. The village is overlooked by Flowers-Barrow, an ancient Neolithic camp which in the winter breaks the sky line with the grave nobility of a chapter of Scripture. Never was there any place more fitted to succour the wounded spirit of a great poet. It is the kind of retreat that would have healed John Keats. Oliver Lodge is so happy there that I think he may well try to come back to it after Christmas, but if you write to me at once I think we could arrange for you and Gene to have it.

O! I should so love to be near you again if it was only for a little time. Do, do try to come. The days pass swiftly for us—

we plant bulbs and carry our goods over the downs and on these November evenings when we wait upon the Green we stand in breathless delight to see the tall elms spread out their noble forms against the fading light in the sky. The children come drifting by old cottage walls with their boots all muddy from the puddles, and from the village shop a small warm interior light shines out upon the cold damp grass. An old man, Mr. Wallis, sweeps the dead leaves from the steps going up to the churchyard where Walter Franzen is buried, and this autumn, because it has been mild, the bats flutter about over the leafless hedges. If you wish for company you shall have it. Mrs. Hardy is at Dorchester, my brother Theodore at Chaldon Herring, Sylvia Warner in the village, and Romilly John—the son of Augustus—at White Nose. Come, my sweet gallant Edna. I beg you to come. We have always brought luck to each other. Do let the thread of my life be once again entangled with yours here in my own land.

O! the cliffs are so deserted, so desolate is their beauty and from the lone headlands the gulls rise in proud defiance and I will take you to the cliff Foxes and this will teach you cunning and to the owls of the castle for wisdom.—Don't you go to Paris. Come, come here—I should love to be with brave Gene again. I have a bottle of champagne I have been keeping for him for a year.

With our love and with my love,

Yours,
Lulu.

To A. R. Powys

Chydyok, Chaldon Herring,
July, 1933.

My dear Bertie,

Here is a fine thing. I write to tell you I am ill with my old deadly complaint, ill and in bed and you write me no letter though I have to remain in bed *five weeks!* All you think of is stalking about with your own fine beard, hale and hearty, with tufts of black hair about your throat lusty as a bull. I never heard of such a thing, and yet I am glad you are so recovered. I hear good news of you and this is excellent, for if you are well and strong I have little doubt you will prosper and we will have time to be merry and happy in each other's company for many a day yet.

I am recovering. My temperature down, and am beginning to walk about as usual . . .

This weather is wonderful. Yesterday we walked to the sea for the first time since I became sick. It was lovely. I look forward to seeing you again so much. "It is necessary that we respect spiritual beings but at the same time keep as far as possible out of their way", that is a good saying.

Yours,
L.P.
I love you.

To Lynd Ward

Chydyok, Chaldon Herring,
1933.

My dear Lynd Ward,

You certainly do write me the most sensitive letters. I feel very moved by your concern over my sickness. I am getting better, still in bed, but getting better. I am tired of dying this particular death and hope that in the end I shall experience quite a new one. An old woman called Anne Pratt, tells me that when *you are dying* it is best to close your eyes, 'It makes it easier.' This seems rather terrifying to me—to experience that terrible *drop* in the dark!

. . . Both Miss Gregory and I so look forward to the day when we shall have the pleasure of meeting you, my most courteous and magnanimous friend,

Yours,
Llewelyn Powys.

To W. E. Powys

20 Brunswick Terrace, Weymouth.
April 1935.

My dear Willie,

I have now had all the top teeth out and the two wisdom teeth were Turks. How he tugged at them! He broke off a bit of the jaw and in the end broke the roots so that three tips still remain in my head. But he says I shall not feel them. By God I did not like it much. They would not budge! They would not move! They stood firm, as firm as the old stone in Wash Lane. We hope to go back in a week's time. I have to have some teeth stopped first. I have walked as far as Invicta House where old Bowles used to live. I remembered it very well. I walk usually in the early morning when the air is crisp. I am getting stronger, but I ought to eat fat—butter, milk! If I do I hurt my kidney so it is nothing but vegetables. . . . Also I hear from Tilly Cole—the pale one whom Mother used to like. She said 'Think of Miss Clare dying on Christmas Eve! What a HAPPY CHRISTMAS she must have had!' *Not my kind*, I thought. Ho! Ho! But she quite won my heart again by saying in the same letter 'This is the time of the year when your father used to tell the boys at children's service never to take more than one egg from the nest—and again I once saw him stoop and pick up and put in his pocket pages from a Bible that a lad had carelessly thrown in the street.'

I hear old Cobb is going to have a Hell of a bonfire on the top of High Chaldon for Jubilee. Do you know, from my bed I can see the top of High Chaldon above the White Nose down? Gertrude would not believe me, but I could see the top hedge clear with my little glasses (with the same glasses with which we watched Jasper and the black cat) and yesterday I asked Valentine Ackland to light a flare at 8.30 p.m. It was a dark rainy night, but at the exact time I saw the light and had time to call Alyse *clear as a star in the middle of the darkness*. It must be possible from the top of High Chaldon to see the tops of the Weymouth houses.

Your loving,
Lulu.

To W. E. Powys

Chydyok, Chaldon Herring,
Autumn 1935.

My dear Willie,

What a delight to get your letter with that glimpse of the early summer morning under Montacute Hill. It was as if I had been there with you waiting for pigeons. It was a description full of *Living Poetry*, like a tailpiece from Bewick—the wreathed mist, the lost slowly moving cows, and the hurried dairy man, himself close to the animal world—as unconscious as they and as innocent of culture. You certainly have been writing me some wonderful letters, some of the best *I have ever received from anyone* with these thumb mark sketches out of the past such as would make me to prick up my ears even if I was lying in a cupboard coffin. . . . How I used to walk about in Mombasa by myself—this way and that, just as you did. I remember crossing by that ferry and sitting in a little white missionary church on the other side. I remember the strange fish and the stone steps roughly cut leading up from the shore to the fish market, and the old dark fort and the smells of spicery and native turds and incense-bearing trees and the crying of the priests on the roof tops as the sun went down and the terrible swaggering English clubmen led by M——, blind and deaf to the whispers of creation, but by God! not dumb with their chatter, about 'blowing in' and 'blowing out'—always using those standardized words and expressions that destroy all poetry and are the hall marks of a common mind and an ill-descended spirit. They used to make me want to 'blow off' to hear them as they sat in their club over the whisky—their 'sundowners'! Well old—— has got his sundowner now. I wonder where he is buried. I remember his having a hell of a row with a ticket collector who swore 'Codfish' was above the age of an 'infant' when we were on our way to play cricket at Bournemouth and he had slipped me in as the 'scorer,' and I sat in the Pavilion before a huge field blazing in the sun—putting down the bloody 'runs' in the wrong places, scared out of my life, and helped by the other scorer *out of pity.*

I love to think of you three together again. It was sweet of Elizabeth to write me so long a letter from the boat.

With love
Lulu.

To Littleton C. Powys

Chydyok, Chaldon Herring,
Feb. 1936.

My darling Littleton.

I very much hope that you will not take it amiss my sending you a telegram, but I am very anxious that as few family letters are destroyed as possible. When Mabel in our conversation asked me what my opinion was about destroying letters I had no idea that she referred to letters that seem to me to have such very great family interest . . . I myself would be reluctant to destroy *any* letter that had survived fifty years and I cannot conceive anything that I would find more distressing that the destruction of these three charming letters 70 years old, these little envelopes alone would plead for them, let alone their references to Sherborne, to Uncle Littleton and Shirley etc. and addressed to *Miss* Mary Johnson. I implore you, dear Littleton, to remember that some of us have an intense and passionate interest in the past and letters of this kind are *a trust to posterity* and though all members of a family may not think the same, letters of this kind should be saved by those who are responsible *on principle*, for one member of a large family cannot even know for certain what would be valued by another and although under the stress of the moment the preservation of old family letters must be a nuisance to you they would be treasured by Marian, by myself , by Gertrude, and very likely by Bertie, and anyhow the children of L.A.P. or Francis, or Oliver, or Peter, or Rose might be interested or even one of these children only and it would still have been of importance that they should have been in safe custody. Tastes are different. I for instance have taken an eager interest in every scrap of writing about Stalbridge and looked over as many letters as I could with concentrated attention and I do not think you could say that I have abused the glimpse I have been so fortunately permitted into the past. I wish I could be more eloquent or could plead better. I see life as a river flowing, flowing away and would preserve what I could of the shadows as they pass, and there are many who share with me this passion . . . I pray you, before you decide on destroying such links with our past, remember that you have always been, *like a wise man*, one who is deeply absorbed in the passing moment and the *passing scene* and one who has also been inclined to take the attitude of your neighbours a little too seriously, allowing in many cases your judgment to be influenced by immediate reactions, and content if all is in order to the satisfaction of the passing view of people. I resemble you in this to a degree, and it is easy for us to be caught making very grave mistakes 'under the shadow of Eternity.' I am afraid I said what I have tried to say very badly. I would write it over again if I could to try to explain better. It has been a very great agitation to me and I wish I did not feel so strongly.

I wish I could make it clear to you so you could see it *in a flash* as I see it. These letters have value from so many points of view and it is terribly easy to be blinded by the insistent pressure of the immediate. People like—— always look on such things with *an unillumined eye*. Your letter proved that you saw them imaginatively, but did not altogether appreciate their particular value, or you would never have thoughtlessly contemplated their destruction, which once done would be an action *irrevocable*. I could plead the cause of these three letters on many counts (1) They are perfect reflections of the mood of their period. (2) They have great psychological interest for a reflective mind. (3) If you destroy these letters you destroy a possible vindication of the simplicity and natural goodness of Father's character. You know, and regret, that there is considerable interest in our family and that it is commonly said that Father was the subject of suppressed sexual impulses that are very unhappy—and these three letters *as long as they exist* provide splendid and almost irrefutable evidence that I am correct. If you destroy them there is little chance of the rumour (and these rumours are very tenacious) ever being corrected. I could write more but I am too tired, but dear Tom I do beg you to be careful about destroying these letters *of family and general interest*. I think we all have a perfect right to destroy anything that has to do with *our own* lives but when it comes to other letters the greatest circumspection is required before such immediate action is taken.

Your loving brother,
Lulu.

I so very much enjoyed seeing Mabel and we spent such a happy time with her. I do hope you are now better again. My great love to you.

To Mrs. Cobb

Chydyok, Chaldon Herring,
May 12th 1936.

Dear Mrs. Cobb,

How can we possibly contrive some plan by which Joseph will remember my eggs? Every week his mind is pondering over some theological conundrum put to him by his father at breakfast, or perhaps it is his girl that is in his mind all day this fine May weather? Or his ox in the stall with golden horns? but *never my breakfast eggs*. Continually we have had to get them elsewhere and sometimes (as last Sunday because of the confusion) I have had to send Miss Gregory to the cliffs for gull's eggs or to the furzen for thrush's eggs. What can be done? When the Greeks burnt a Persian city Xerxes had a slave stand by his bed every morning and say *Remember Athens*—and I shall send a goblin down the chimney of Joseph's room to say Remember Chydyok EGGS. I hope you are all well.

Yours sincerely,
Llewelyn Powys.

To W. E. Powys

Clavadel, Davos Platz,
March 1st, 1937.

My darling Willie,

 . . . Last week for the first time I drove in a sleigh to see an avalanche and then had lunch in a mountain village. I was free, I was merry. I saw a squirrel jump from a tiny twig on a larch tree —a far jump to another. I saw an old man digging a grave under five feet of snow for a fellow 42 who died of *measles!* (that made me shake my ears). I saw a lusty fellow through a crack in a door tarting one of the tavern wenches with a fine glint in his eye and I saw the ragged mountains beyond which is Italy all black like the teeth of a wolf under a blue sky, and coming back we met a tandem and the first horse rushed round, and an old chap like Montacute got out and told our driver what to do and his sleigh was full of foreigners and he told Lisaly his sleigh was 'full of swine,' and I was scared of the bloody horse and 'twas a job to get it by, we were so cramped in the snow. There were no bears in the valley and have not been for many years. Old Fraülein Gadmer remembers seeing one carried down by the woodsmen when she was a little girl, but one was shot last year in the next valley. My chest still gets steadily better. My digestion is my trouble. I have to be careful and eat frugal, but I begin to feel well and lusty. Ho! Ho! I went to the dentist in the Sanatorium last week! I like so much to hear about Rose. Why, what sport next year! If I have to be here in March then I hope you will get out at Naples and be here for a fortnight and all come home together in April. Lisaly will find you snug rooms by yourselves in a peasant's house up the valley, and then what a summer we will have. God every moment we will be together will be a frolic. . . .

With my love always,
Lulu.

To John Cowper Powys

Clavadel, Davos Platz,
May 3, 1937.

My dear John,

Louis is coming to stay at the Kurhaus on the 5th of May and Gertrude on the 20th. I must have a care with the first not to laugh myself back to the ferry banks of Charon. . . .

Yesterday I walked down to Davos Platz but it was a little too far and although I enjoyed it I flagged and when I came back felt a very old man, and yet as you can guess I was happy to see the greenness of the firs on both sides of the familiar *going down*, and the sunlight shining so bright on the main street of the cursed city and a cockatoo in the flower shop, thirty years old, which must have been on its perch when you told me that even if I were dying and wanted to see you, *I must not say so* for fear you would have to go against your dame's will! The cockatoo was white with faintly yellow underwing and a yellow comb which it could stretch out, but alas its breast bone was bare of feathers *from age* so the Flower shop man explained.

Have you read *Piers Plowman*? How many thousand times have I wished to call Mother from the grave to read this old man's words into her ears of clay! It would be one of her favourite books *I know it*. Lisaly has gone to see her mother for 6 days. Nobody ever looked after us better. This evening we go out to supper with my Baumgartner cousin! Oh! what a relish I have still for *all* experience. I walked one day to Frauenkirch and put a cowslip on the grave of Dr. Frey who told Alyse at Christmas that he feared the year 1937 and that to him Life was so sweet and that he had always believed in the wisdom of the Twelve Months. My love to Phyllis

Yours,
Lulu.

Anonymous

Clavadel, Davos Platz,
1938.

My dear ——,

I read your letter with sadness for your plight but also with a certain irritation. You must not be so simple and so foolish and so lacking in spirit—what's the word they used to use at Montacute—' so meek-hearted.' I feel impatient with you, *fond of you*, but impatient with you. You must learn to see things with a clear eye objectively. Of course there exist many people—many men both young and old—who would eagerly cherish someone so rare as you are and there is a chance that one day you will meet them. You have to rely upon chance but at the same time *build up your life as it is* with clear-eyed resolution. *Face the facts.* You ought to be grateful to this man for giving you a little pleasure, love-making is not to be despised however it is come by, especially as we get older, and it is a mistake at once to associate it with passionate Tennysonian ideal love. I think I would have advised you to hold back nothing from this man and probably it would have been a mistake for he seems to have been an ordinary, greedy, vulgar philanderer and nothing more, but you should have had enough insight to have seen this, taken what pleasure you could get, but not cling to things he says that are like feathers and straws, and call him false. He was not false because he was never faithful. Your position was a difficult one, but you were silly to create an imaginary situation and then when it did not fall in with *your* vision to drown yourself with self-pity and feel betrayed instead of grateful for the compliment the man paid you. As you see I would have taken all risks; if you had become pregnant there would have been jars and jolts but after a year your problem of the emptiness of life would have been solved by having a baby on your knee and your neighbours would have been used to your 'fall' and you would have had something to love of your own, for it is the frustration of your deep capacity for loving that is at the root of all your depressions. On the other hand, the man might have become emotionally involved and you might have had to live with him and discovered his limitations and grossness of nature when it was too late and been miserable. No, I think you are well rid of him, and well quit of the situation.

The class to which you belong is responsible for much of your trouble. Its codes of respectability adamant, its lechery immeasurable and covert, and its intellect and honesty non-existent except in rare cases, as in your case, and then it is subjective, introspective, and cannot really be trusted. Your culture has been proved not deep enough to help you. Even when you are emotionally hurt you do not go to the great masters to strengthen you, but instead stay in misery complaining and blaming and reproaching. Of course you have had handicaps, but you have had great advantages also. Learn to love your Fate and make what you can out of it. Very likely if you had married like —— you would have felt unfulfilled. Your husband might have been stupid and heavy and your life would have passed with even less understanding and experience of life than at present. You cannot now expect to compete with younger women on the sexual plane, but you can compete with everybody in the realm of sensitive responsiveness and understanding and sympathy. You have a charming vulnerable nature and don't allow it to become ineffectual and tiresome and always murmuring like the Israelites in the wilderness. I would take a course of secretarial work. This is often very good I think, but always realize that a deep consciousness of existence is of more importance than any temporal necessity of life. Be happy that you are alive to enjoy nature and to observe the foolishness and *egoism* of *other* people at work automatically; and whenever you see unhappiness of any kind fly to help so that you can escape from your dungeon by the only proved way, through the release that comes *from love*. If you go forward with a brave heart and reconcile youself to living your life by understanding life, which is the most any of us can do, happiness may come unexpectedly and you may even *at the end* meet the one you *can* love. But you must get out of morbid states of introspection—many of the people you think are so happy are because happy their minds and emotions are superficial, yours are not so, so you must not expect ease on such simple terms. Let them go, and you yourself take a truer deeper path than your nature makes it possible for you to tread. And do try not to make the world after your own vision and then blame it and others for what is largely the fault of your own imaginary pleasure-longing, or your own silliness. In any case you are half through your life now and you will soon be dead and all your agitations forgotten. This is the fate of all, even the most lusty and happy—so turn back to life and through books and your love of nature and *Love* try to build a little *personal bower* that swings upon reeds that are independent of the malicious accidents of a Fate that cannot be remedied.

With my love always,
Llewelyn Powys.

Anonymous

Clavadel, Davos Platz,
Autumn 1939.

My dear ——

. . . Your case has been in my mind ever since I got your letter, I am confident that you will be able to navigate your little craft through these dangerous waters and I hope and believe that a suitable appointment will be found for ——. My advice to you however is to shake your mind clean out of the ordinary vision and to face the situation at its worst and then build up from the bottom with a full realization of present hazard and a resolution to be as happy as you can be in this Ragnarok which causes even the elves to shiver. . . . Nobody can alter the great tidal river of Fate, they can only, like water fleas, sit merry on their straw ship and even possibly give it a kind of direction now and again. (Each for himself and God for us all!) Now imagine that in the end you go on the dole. You know about diet, are very sensible and intelligent, and even under such circumstances would, better than any, be able to get —— and the boy across these stormy waters. It is lucky that there is a dole! Now take a worse view still. Suppose —— gets ill and you get ill. You both die—your boy who is so strong and gay will recover from his sorrow and maybe live in a better-arranged world. But all these things have not happened and *will not happen*. There are many things to be grateful for .—— does not have to go to war. You are in little danger really of being starved to death or of becoming refugees in a country which is falling to pieces. . . . Live light and travel light while the sandstorm lasts but remember *it also is* life. You have done wonders already. You have given —— the happiest years of his life. As long as you are together things need not be so bad. It is worry that killed the cat. Why, if you live in a goose stable it is still possible to have hours of happiness. 'Who so merry or make such sport as they that belong to the poorer sort.' Keep cool and calm. Expect the worst and 'face it down' and still be gay while life lasts! Deep in my heart I know a pair like you two will not be left with the unemployed, but, even if this should happen, as long as you keep your minds 'unintimidated' all is not lost, no, not till the last crust has been eaten and the last glass of water drunk. Remind —— of that passage in *The Dynasts* when the soldier in Spain—the Somerset soldier—under Wellington, cries out suddenly 'Would I were back in England a-leaning over Bristol Bridge with the afternoon sun a-slanting down and nothing said!' As long as the sun shines there is a chance of happiness, and an hour's happiness can redeem a week, and a week's happiness a month, and a month's happiness a year, and a year's happiness a life time. You must not worry, you must not stay awake at night. Be as far-sighted as you can be and leave the rest to chance, knowing that you will do your best as each occasion and opportunity arises. . . . We are all in for hard times and likely to be shaken out of our shells like peas from a dry pod. My brother John, for example, is finishing his huge book on Owen Glendower with the money that he manages to earn by the week, and there will be worse to follow. You must keep me in close touch with your affairs and prospects and disappointments and I will try to plan with you.

I do not believe that you will founder. Don't keep trying to go up the ladder unless it is easy—plan to be happy and at ease on the lower rungs. Don't get the crowd hypnosis and think 'this is poverty, penury and misery,' keep a philosophic mind and cry 'Hullo! a famine in England begins at the manger and we must keep awake and know where the mushrooms grow.' Don't allow yourself to be intimidated—keep your intellect above water like a periscope. —— is a good one at this but the poor old bugger always sees nothing but God Almighty's backside as Moses did from *his* cleft in the rock of the Waste Land. . . . In any case *you must not worry*. You must take a large and deep view of the case. Plan to be happy from hour to hour, be short-sighted and *long-sighted*. As long as we live all is not lost. 'We live, and Lords do no more.' Remember the words of Confucius, 'The way of the superior man is three-fold, but I am not equal to it. Virtuous, he is free from anxieties; wise he is free from perplexities; bold, he is free from fear.' Keep me in touch with all that happens of importance. *Good hope lies at the bottom*. . . . 'Oh blackbird what a boy you are. How you do go at it!' You may see more of each other and be able to walk together *in the mornings* when the daffodils first show.

With my love to you all three,
Llewelyn Powys.

The foregoing letters are here first published.

Three Chapters from

LOVE AND DEATH

Three Chapters from

LOVE AND DEATH

I

Too weak the wit, too slender is the brain,
That means to mark the power and worth of love;
Not one that lives, except he hap to prove,
Can tell the sweet, or tell the secret pain.

Robert Greene

AFTER that first morning I met Dittany every day in the wood. Once we walked to Ham Hill and I showed her the chasm between the two unused ivy-covered quarries that as boys we used to leap, but I did not jump it as she became frightened climbing along the slippery bank. She was not happy when on Ham Hill: it was, with its short turf, its thyme and eyebright, too open for her, too much under the the dominion of the sun. When whins are out of bloom, kissing is out of fashion. She favoured the gorse-bush alleys in the sloping field which my mother had named the Cathedral, having noted the elevated habit of the trees that grew there, with branches lifted high above the spreading primrose-beds by trunks smooth, powerful, and perpendicular as pillars. Under these trees, in hidden fastnesses of furzen, we would find inaccessible rabbit lawns entirely to our pleasure. In such places I could wait for hours looking into her soft eyes where I was 'mirror'd small in paradise'; while the linnets, rosy-feathered, sang fragmentary madrigals, now from this thick-set thorny spray, and now from that.

> *The chuckling linnet, its five young unborn,*
> *To sing for thee.*

To Ham Hill she much preferred the fragmentary earthworks, mossy and cool, or the shady glens, or the sunny warren-dips sequestered behind the high forest trees—silent places in the deeper recesses of Stoke Wood, where it used locally to be said fugitives from the Battle of Sedgemoor had hid themselves, for months together, to escape the bloody wrath of Judge Jeffreys. From Ham Stone to Dogtrap Lea a squirrel may leap from tree to tree. How ravishing she looked in such retreats, where lights came fitfully down upon her bare arms through an awning of green confederate leaves, as if she were in very truth the milk-white hind.

> *But be sure ye touch not the milk-white Hynde,*
> *For she is o' the woman kind.*

I would return for lunch, and, after, would sit in the Terrace-Walk and my mother would presently come and read to me with a brown Shetland shawl about her head and shoulders. I remember that she read to me that summer the poems of Walt Whitman, the poems of Thomas Hardy, *The Confessions* of Rousseau, *Tom Jones,* and the *Autobiography of Benvenuto Cellini.* She would sit by my side on a stiff garden chair, and I would give but half my attention to the cadence of her gentle voice, and for the rest my mind would be going over and over what had happened in the morning, recalling the frock Dittany had worn, recalling her sweet ways, her varying expressions, the words she had spoken.

> *He might not in the house, field, or garden stir,*
> *But her full shape would all his seeing fill.*

Dittany! The very syllables of the name had for me a peculiar peculiar charm. I had learned all I could about the old medicinal herb. The leaves of the herb dittany (*dictamnus*) are pinnate in form and of a habit feathery soft, its flowers being white. In summer weather this exceptional plant is often enveloped in a mist, a mist of the blue colour of the smoke of a wood fire and of so igneous an endowment as to be set alight should a flame be carried to it. Botanists explain this mysterious property from the fact that the leaves and stems of the plant are decorated with innumerable hairy glands which in Dog-day sunshine exhale, moment by moment, an aethereal vapour, a vapour which, like a sort of veil of Isis, affords an airy covering for this most sensitive and most singular hedgerow wort. I discovered too that the ancients were by no means ignorant of some of the strange qualities possessed by this weed, for in the *Encyclopaedia* of Bartholomew Anglicus, which used to stand next to Young's *Night Thoughts* in the spare-room, I came upon the following remarks: 'It is said that a hind taught first the virtue of dictamnus, for she eateth this herb that she may calve easlier and sooner; and if she be hurt with an arrow she seeketh this herb and eateth it, which putteth the iron out of the wound.'

Presently my reveries would be disturbed by the voices of the turkeys from the orchard field belonging to Sam Hodder on the other side of the lane—gobble, gobble, gobble they would go, and once more gobble, gobble, gobble—and listening to their farmyard clutter I would come to be aware of how stationary those summer afternoons could be in the process of time moving no faster than the standstill shadow that the flowering elder-hedge made upon the orchard grass. Then at last I would see 'The Stunner' come sauntering up from behind the summer-house holly tree, pipe in mouth, and bowler hat, turned green with age, tilted sideways on his head, and the cows, red of hide and in good case, would move slowly away beneath the apple trees for their milking, their hairy ambling legs struck again and again by the tiny clubs of the taller buttercups. Then Mary Hockey would appear from the kitchen-garden path carrying my afternoon glass of milk on the very same silver salver that in the division of my father's property I later inherited. The glass of milk, milk from the udders of these orchard cows, had been standing all the morning in the larder, securely protected from flies, and was often so rich and thick that the first few mouthfuls I took would be of pure cream.

Dittany and I planned one day to meet by the great beech tree and walk from there through Dogtrap and across the Battlefield to Norton Covert. I wanted to show her a spring that I knew, a spring to which it was rumoured the fairies brought their cradle changelings from Bagnel, from Park Plane, from Norton, and from Cheselborough. It was a pool, deep-matted with moss and banded about with roots like snakes.

The morning we selected for the expedition was cloudless. I arrived at our trysting tree and waited. As always I began to dread that she might not be coming, that her heart might misgive her.

For if I gang to the Broomfield Hill,
My maidenhood is gone;
And if I chance to stay at hame,
My love will ca' me mansworn.

I never failed to feel on such occasions that for those few scattered hours with her I would make any sacrifice. If only I could see her appear between the familiar guardian trunks! The value of the current time, which alone was sure of her in the sunshine, seemed infinitely greater than any problematic future good. An antic ancestral prophet, wise in counsel, kept crying to me from somewhere in earth, air, or water:

Yesterday returneth not;
Perchance to-morrow cometh not;
There is to-day; misuse it not.

I ran to meet her. How my whole breathless being danced at seeing her again. When I reached her I threw my arms about her and kissed her many times. She flushed at my ardour. I never had seen her looking more lovely. We began walking up the slight incline that separated us from the great forest beech;— 'Oh! I was so afraid you weren't coming,' I exclaimed. 'I thought something had prevented you, your mother perhaps.' She caught a certain nervousness in my voice conveying my apprehension lest sooner or later her mother might really interfere, for scarcely had we taken a few steps together than she began mockingly to repeat:

'*My father is the nightingale*
Who sings within the bosky dale
On the tallest tree.

The mermaiden my mother is,
She who sings her melodies
In the deep salt sea.'

And then just as suddenly grew grave. 'You need not fear,' she said, 'my mother would never prevent me, she always lets me do what I want to do, and anyhow she knows we meet and doesn't mind.'

We arrived at last at the tall white wooden gate opening into the woodland cart-track that runs round the foot of Hedgecock. It was still early in the morning and the track was so shadowed, with laurels on the left and with the trees of the wood on the right, that the dew had not dried. Dittany got her shoes and stockings drenched with the long grass and purple water-mint over which we trod. 'How lovely it is,' she said, looking up the green lonely thoroughfare. 'It's as though it was all under a spell and we were walking in the land of Shea!—How still the lane is! The butterflies are the only creatures that *can* move.' We stood side by side, gazing before us along that green roadway, rank, luxuriant, and magical. I can still in my mind's eye evoke it— the bracken, already ladle tall, the pink campions above and the blue-bells below, and the sunshine slanting down upon wavering marbled-whites, whose soft bodies were invisible under fluttering wings. I threw myself on my knees before her, and as I looked up at her I remember feeling as if this homely drong, familiar to me since my infancy, had been transformed to a royal path in some greenwood, vert and eldritch, of the Sely Court.

As I walked a little ahead of her, beating down the brambles that trailed over the cart-track, and pushing back the overhanging bracken lest their wet fronds should spoil the freshness of her summer frock, made out of white linen, I told her how I re-membered coming here with my brother John and my Aunt Dora and how I ran before them, a little boy, on just such a summer morning, and how I kept beating off the heads of the pink campions with the stick of the wooden hoop that I carried, and how John had called to me, and, because I had taken no notice, had hastened after me, and held me in his arms, and said, 'Llewelyn, you must never, never do that again, never in your whole life—for you must not forget that every tree, every leaf, every flower is alive *as we are alive* and it is only very stupid or very wicked people who can be indifferent to the destruction of their earth companions.' I had never forgotten his words because he had looked at me so very earnestly with his small green-grey tabby-cat eyes. 'It is best,' he said, 'never even to pick flowers; but you must at any rate never injure them wan-tonly as you were doing just then.'

Dittany listened eagerly. 'I have always felt like that,' she said, 'especially when I sleep in the garden, and each one of them seems like a different, separate person.' She begged me to tell her more about my brother. We had reached the place where the road turned to encircle the southern side of Hedgecock and led up to the woodland avenue known as the Beeches. In a few words I tried to give her some conception of my eldest brother, named after John the Baptist, tried to describe his appearance, his low-browed, primordial, soothsayer's skull and his long-fingered hands, thin as autumn leaves, the hands of a very old man, and yet with the gripping power of a demon, and I told her how tall and lean and stooping was the body that housed so mighty a spirit.

At the turn of the avenue we stopped at the foot of the corner beech. No tree in the whole wood was so old or so large as this tree. Dittany had made her shoes so muddy coming up the lane that I gathered a tuft of grass and tried to clean them. She didn't want me to do this for her. She tried to snatch the grass away from me and doing so she got her hands covered with black leaf-mould mud. 'Come,' I cried, 'I will show you a basin where you can wash them,' and I led her round the great trunk of the beech to where two protruding roots had formed a stoup of woodland water. Often as a child I had left the side of Miss Beales to run to examine the cider-coloured liquid in this wooden bowl. 'I will wash your body, Dittany, in the water of the wild rain,' I took her meek hands in mine and dipped them deep into the tree trunk's hollow. 'How lovely!' she exclaimed, and I was delighted by the delight she experienced as she felt the lukewarm water upon her thumbs and upon each of her four fingers. She was entranced by the little catch-basin, made all of wood and surrounded by its tod of softest moss. ' Do the birds come here to drink?' she asked, 'whitethroats, and chaffinches, and long-tailed tits?' I dried her hands with my handkerchief. Her little finger was so small that I am sure it could have reached to the end of any of the round holes made by the mason-bees in the sun-hot wall of the East Garden of Montacute House, holes that used to astonish me when we took our nursery walks through the Park, on sunny autumn mornings, to pick up the sycamore leaves which our nurse Emily had taught us to value for the variation of their colour.

Oh! how wonderful it all seemed to me that day. What rapture, to be alive with Dittany, a thousand leaves spreading open to the air about her, and the small birds darting over the meadows below us, and the blackbirds and thrushes singing, and the grey battlements of the Abbey visible as we walked forward under the great trees!

We crossed the waste land called Dogtrap, but before we went through the gate into the Battlefield I took her to the Wishing-Stone that is under the beeches above Forster's Gully. I let her stand first upon the stone. With a secret joy I saw her so seriously silent upon this wizard stone of the walks of my childhood. 'All ignorant that soul that sees thee without wonder.' Her eyes were fast shut. 'I think this is really and truly a place of mystery,' she said at last, when she stepped away to make room for me. 'What a sombre lane!' I did not answer. In my turn I was occupied with projecting my very individual and pertinent wish into the air about us.

> *For your grace, lady,*
> *Lovely and white,*
> *My heart leaps up*
> *By day, by night.*

When I had made my simple invocation I explained to her that the road going up to Ham Hill was the old coach-road to Exeter, and that Forster's Gully was so called because a highwayman of that name had been caught here and hung up in an iron cage to starve to death, and that there were old people in Montacute whose grandparents remembered hearing of the man's cries, 'Forster's starvin'! Forster's starvin'!' 'It is said,' I told her, 'that a woman got leave from the guard to speak to the prisoner and pushed a couple of tallow candles through the bars of his hanging prison for him to eat'. I wished I had not repeated to her the old hearsay. Dittany had an extraordinary capacity for imaginative sympathy and could never bear to be told of cruelty, even though it might have happened centuries ago. She shrank from pain in all its forms. Once I noticed a spider eating a struggling house-fly at the top of a dim dusty window. I stood upon the window-seat to observe more narrowly what was taking place, calling to Dittany to do the same. When I looked round, she was pale as a ghost. I used to fancy sometimes that her body was covered by only one skin instead of the seven that the rest of us carry, a skin as white as a lily and of a texture as tender.

We now went through the five-barred gate on the other side of the road. We skirted the Battlefield, keeping to the sheep-tracks that ran under the top hedge. The mouths of each of the sandy rabbit-holes shone yellow bright in the morning sunshine. The field's real name was Witcombe. It was my brother John who had named it the Battlefield because it was formed with two steep slopes rising opposite to each other, suggesting to his imagination the topography of the old-fashioned pictures of battles that our uncle Littleton had painted on large sheets of drawing-paper, and which had remained in my father's album since the Stalbridge days, the French charging down on one side and the English charging down on the other side, with the ugly iron cannons of the Napoleonic period shooting balls over the heads of the two combatants, and over their flags bright-coloured as popinjays. At the bottom of the opposing slopes was a level valley in which Dr. Hensleigh Walter, the local antiquarian, used to tell me there had once stood the village of Witcombe, abandoned at the time of the Black Death and never reinhabited. I told Dittany about this forgotten village, and from where we had sat down, elbows on knees, we could distinguish the shadowy outlines of the foundations of its cabins under the grass. The morning was unequalled. I could hear the yaffle, laughing and calling in Horse's Covert—'What fools, what fools you mortals be!' From the mild pastoral slope on which we were resting I could see growing in the grass, where the cottages had used to stand, clusters of yellow flowers. I knew what they were, wild daffodils! They had always grown here, possibly descended from the fourteenth century garden flowers, very short in the stalk now and yet carrying bravely enough their cold single trumpets. Dittany noticed another vegetable growth of a darker foliage and I explained to her that this was hellebore, also probably brought here by those old peasants who had sat by wood fires in mud-and-wattle huts discussing battles in France and the prowess of their Black Prince, as they whittled away at their long bows of churchyard yew. England were but a fling save for the crooked stick and the grey-goose wing.

II

Surely she was the most beautiful woman that ever water washed.

Ballad

WE WENT through the little gate into the wild bracken-grown ground above Norton Covert. It is a rough acreage, bordered by an earthwork that leads away to Ham Hill. Everywhere the hawthorn trees were in blossom. I had never seen them more beautiful nor the turreted bracken so tall or of so tender a green. She was now a little in front of me and I observed her distinctive walk as she adventured through the ferns. She did not dance or trip along lightly as other girls. Her advance possessed no hint of resolution in it. On all occasions, whether she was going through field or forest, along sheep-walk, or over cow-pasture, it seemed that her course might be diverted by a bramble, by a breath! We climbed through a shard in the hedge into the wood. I wanted to discover a secret place and soon was successful. In the heart of the wood a great tree had fallen and by balancing along its prostrate trunk we were able to reach a secluded patch of green ground surrounded by blackberry-bushes and hazel-nut trees. It was here that I made her a bed. As if she guessed what was in my mind she took her hat off and hung it with shy deliberation upon a branch of the fallen tree. It happeth in one hour what happeth not in seven years. I was trembling.

> *These blue vein'd violets whereon we lean*
> *Never can blab, nor know not what we mean.*

In silence, without speaking a word, we drew together. Her cheeks were flushed.

My love for her, my desire for her, could never be appeased. My passion for her was so inordinate that I saw her beauty as it were with the vision of a God, with the eyeballs of Siva. Although she was unwilling to concede the last union, to be fast joined, that is to say, as fell to flesh and as hardly to be separated, our loving was passionately intemperate. Every inch of her body shone for me like the radiant skin of Aphrodite when she lay entangled—a shining silver-white dace of a lady—in her good-man's meshed net of gaudy brass.

> *Take care, take care;*
> *If anyone look,*
> *If anyone stare,*
>   *Tell it me!*
> *In the leafy thickets over there;*
> *Beware, beware*
> *If anyone stare!—*

'Look at that dragon-fly sitting guard over me so faithfully,' she cried once. The great horse-stinger, with its net-veined glittering wings, had settled on a leaf above us and there sat with globular compound eyes regarding Dittany's disordered frock and scattered looks. ' For all his rude staring he is a dragon that hasn't guarded me so very well,' she complained. The place where we were lying smelt of the summer wood, of newly burgeoning leaves, of inconspicuous flowers, moschatel, wood-sage, wood-sorrel, wood-saxifrage, and also of countless un-recognizable sap-filled vegetable stalks. The air was alive with the muffled murmur, now loud, now soft, of the race of flies, each separate insect of the petty multitude steering this way and that, on untraceable quests of love or hunger. Dittany lay now indolently reclining under the restling branches with her laces still loosened, her sweet body, after such impassioned usage, languid, fragrant, and relaxed. My senses ached to see her there so idly defenceless, rumpled, sense-drugged, looking dreamily up at the leaf-fretted summer sky, her head resting on one of her hands.

We had had one hour to spend and it was over, swift-passing as an April shower, as always when Dittany and I were together alone.

> *Say, is there aught that can convey*
> *An image of its transient stay?*
>
> .   .   .   .   .   .
>
> *'Tis a shuttle in its speed;*
> *'Tis an eagle in its way,*
> *Darting down upon its prey.*

Whenever we were alone, hours became minutes, and minutes seconds. I had to teach myself to remember this on those occasions when a preliminary silence, charged with significance, would suddenly fall between us. It would then be no longer wise for me to rely upon clocks or watches for measuring time. From the moment that I kissed her first, from the moment that the scent of her body came to me as it were like rose-flushed white-clover found in a hayfield when the men and jangling horses have all left, I would be lost to the common world. After the very first touch had passed between us I would have no further power of calculation. My moments with Dittany seemed to share in eternity, and yet more richly still did they belong to the fugitive now of the life of this corn-planted planet. I kissed her that morning till she was tired out. I kissed her 'by the pot' as the old expression has it, that is, holding her head between my hands by her two ears, by those two ears that she always kept so closely hidden under her hair and which were, for all that I ever knew, 'loave' or 'prick' in shape; and then sometimes I would kiss her anywhere, everywhere, as best I might, so full I was of joy.

The sunlight fell upon her face, and the shadow of a tall pink-campion waved and flickered across her Orion-sealed forehead fairer than that 'full star that ushers in the even'. One hand was shading her eyes. As I looked at her I could see that her softly curving chin was covered with almost invisible hair like the down on one of the odorous peaches that my father would bring in to my mother fresh-gathered from the kitchen-garden wall. And below the beautiful curve of her small chin was a sheltered area that continually held my vision, so inviolable did this part of her neck appear, less blemished than the lip argent of a Madonna lily across which an enamel-sharded garden-beetle might tread with pricking feet. My very bones were idolatrous of this morsel of mortal matter more admirable than the under side of a snow-finch's wing. Suddenly her whole attention was awakened as though she had seen an angel in the sky. 'It's a bird', she cried excitedly, 'a white bird.' I looked up between the tree-tops expecting to see a dove from Norton Mill, but, instead, a large gull passed across the open space flying towards the sea. It was a rare thing in those days for one of these birds to traverse the Montacute district. Only once had I known such a thing to happen, and then we had all come running to the house calling our father from his study and our mother from her sewing to watch the hungry ocean fowl breast its way southward and seaward far up over the inland flowerbeds, where humming-bird hawk moths flickered and poised over sultry geraniums. 'I think that must be a bad omen,' she said gravely, when the bird had finally disappeared in the direction of the Chinnocks. I reminded her that the unlucky bird John Oxenham had seen had been a white dove. 'The sight of a white sea-gull,' I said, 'ought to be read as a sign of good fortune.' 'How can you tell ? I don't know,' she replied, rising impetuously from the ground. A moment later, however, she had thrown her arms about my neck—'Anyhow, I don't care,' she said.

> *O lovely and immaculate lady,*
> *I have no answer to give to you,*
> *Save the trampled grass and the boughs shady;*
> *And nothing I used to know is true.*

The ambiguous lines of poetry recklessly spoken, the free spontaneous gesture and the fragrance of her neck, like lilac in the sun, revived my body's memory of its recent meeds. She became aware of its renewed eagerness. 'No, no, we mustn't, we mustn't,' she whispered nervously, 'we must go now or we shall be late. Besides, I want to visit the changeling pool we came to see,' she said, with a smile that was tender and yet at the same time not without regret. 'We will have to come another day for that,' I answered. 'It is difficult to find, and very overgrown on all sides.'—'I know I shall now never see it,' she responded ruefully. Her voice still had a hint of reproach in it. I tried to reassure her. 'We will come especially to see the pool and nothing else,' I explained. 'I know we shall never reach it,' she continued. 'We never could, not on Monday, Tuesday, Wednesday, Thursday, Friday, Saturday, or Sunday, take more than a few steps in such a lovely dragonfly wood without making love, and so we will never get there.' She stood before me with eyes so full of an authentic sadness that I was more than ever bewildered. Seeing this she became at once gentle, kissing my frowning forehead. With her head shadowed by the constellated leaves, and with her feet upon the woodland mould, she seemed to embody all the undefined delights that my spirit had ever craved, and I became overwhelmed by a sensation of ineffable happiness. It was no celestial happiness that surrounded us. It was an earth happiness, golden, all-embracing—a benison from gods older and wiser than Jesus. Her level eyes seemed lightly to carry the burden of everything lovely and free— snowdrops in the rain, seaweed, ground-ivy in a February ditch, blackberries in a basket, river-rushes! Surely all the sweets of June were encompassed within the fresh-laundered whiteness of her dress.

As we clambered together down the steep side of the wood, what did we care for omens ? Our youth was so sanguine that it could not be intimidated by rumours of disaster. Such misgivings served but to add to our passion. The intensity of the love that we felt for each other cancelled all apprehensions except the apprehension of wasting a single opportunity of indulging it to the last quivering fulfilment. We reached the lane and had only a few yards to walk before we arrived at Tinker's Bubble. It was here that the overflow from the fairy pool burst out of the wood, its stream being carried over the wall of the sandy lane in the hollowed-out trunk of a young larch tree. Emily used to take us here on our nursery walks, pushing us when we were tired in a three-wheeled open perambulator large enough to carry three of us side by side. I remember once we came at Easter-time and picked ' pussy willows,' or 'palms,' as she taught us to call them, and brought them back with a bunch of daffodils from the Battlefield, to be placed in a large china bowl on the nursery table.

It was past twelve o'clock and yet the water that fell from the rude wooden spout in one continuous flow was ice-cold. The dust of the lane was darkened with its splashings. I made a cup of my hand as I had often seen my father do for my mother on his summer holiday walks, and she drank, this creature of an hour, more rare than ever was the nymph Eurydice before her fateful race,—fly, little maiden! fly away across the snake-grass fells of ancient Greece. When Dittany's thirst was satisfied, when, with a last swift rippling sip she had raised her head, laughing to feel the water run down her chin, I let the gushing fountain splash over my own scalp. The water was chill. It wetted my flannel shirt. This fountain-stream seemed to celebrate our happy solacings in the wood, its bright sparkling waters giving, so it appeared to my romantic fancy, a sort of wild consecration to the love that we felt for each other.

III

Though but a shadow, but a sliding,
Let me know some little joy!
We that suffer long annoy
Are contented with a thought
Through an idle fancy wrought:
O let my joys have some abiding!

John Fletcher

One of the happiest days that Dittany and I spent together was on the river Yeo. We had arranged to be with each other from dawn till evening. I told Ellen that I was going out for the whole day and asked her to make egg, honey, and lettuce sand-wiches overnight and to put out supplies of sponge-cake, buns and raisins, ready for me on the kitchen dresser. With the idea of sleeping out of doors I had ordered a garden tent. It had come that morning, but I had not had time as yet to put it up so was forced to go to bed as usual in the nursery. I might, however, have been sleeping in a hammock woven of flowering clematis cords, so strongly did the room carry the odour of those little white blossoms thick clustering about the window.

For a long time I could not get to sleep. A lover's soul lives in the body of his mistress. I felt as I used to at school on the last day of the term. I could not wait for the hours to pass. I would put my head on the pillow, first lying on my left cheek and then on my right, closing my eyes ; but try as I might I could not sleep. Then I would say to myself, 'Well, I don't care if I don't sleep . . . I will stay awake all night,' and I would turn over, and, lying on my back, listen to the dulcet silence of the summer garden. The sash-window was up, and over the muffling folds of the clematis I could see the spreading branches of the acacia, against the dimness of the night. There was a moon almost full, but many stars also were illuminating the cold midnight lawns, the bark of the trees alive with insects under dark rustling branches, and the crinkled sapless moss on the old garden walls. How actual it all was to me outside. I could almost feel the air, the soft summer garden air, pass through the shining leaves of the Portugal-laurel, could feel it turn up the tiny hairs on the plump, hirsute bodies of moths scavenging with gleaming, goblin eyes through the crowded spears of the lavender bush that porcupine-like bristled at the centre of the Crescent-bed. How lovely, how consecrated on a summer's night, are the inter-spaces between dreaming garden trees! As a child I had played in this room. It was here I had looked at my first picture-book, it was here that I had seen my nurse, as it were an angel in a vision, entering from the night-nursery in her Sunday apron. I knew every inch of it, the particular shapes of the marks and spots on the window-sill, where in the shivering precipitations of atomic matter the old Goodden varnish had been withdrawn! I knew each irregularity of the darker tracings that showed in the marble of the fire-place tiles. I knew the picture of the farmyard cock and hen, the table of plain deal which we used to revolve upside down like a gigantic turtle, balancing it on a hard hassock and running round and round, clutching the one of its four legs which was thinner than the others. At any moment I could rise and sit upon the sofa of fairy-story-reading memories, a sofa covered over with webbed hair from the manes and tails of horses—shiny, slippery, and jet black. Those hairs had been pulled from mares and geldings who had plunged and snorted and stood about by the hedges of green paddocks long before I had been born. In this room I had carried my brother Willie on my shoulders and let him fall, and had witnessed my mother's alarm as, at the sound of his cries, she came running to the room to see a green bump rise upon his forehead as large as a heron's egg. In this room I had, with cradle straw scarce out of my breech, outwitted my brother Bertie over a matter of three biscuits. We—Bertie, May, and myself—had been playing with building bricks when Emily came with three sugar biscuits which were to be given to us when we had tidied up the room. She placed the biscuits on the chest-of-drawers, and presently I noticed that the largest had been slipped under a book out of sight by my brother. Waiting my chance, baby though I was, I stretched up and put into my brother's chosen hiding-place the smallest of the biscuits, being myself alert silently to consume the largest before the last of the bricks had been put away. It was an incident my brother never forgot all through his life, so deeply impressed was he that so newly-born an infant could contrive to be master of such a knavery.

> *Many a merry meeting*
> *My love and I have had;*
> *She was my only sweeting,*
> *She made my heart full glad.*

I was wide awake at five o'clock. To my surprise I found that I had slept soundly for several hours. I got up at once. Dittany had promised to try to meet me by Bob Chaffey's white gates in Marsh Lane at half-past six. I walked to Marsh Lane through the meadows by the station-stream. It was a perfect midsummer morning. The sun was already 'kissing with golden face the meadows green.' When I looked back over the station-field I could see the track of my footsteps in the dew. The turned-up ends of my flannel trousers were soaked and covered with grass-seeds. Over the pollarded willows, over the hedges, over the dairy meadows, and over the hay-fields that had been already mown came the singing of birds. My ears might have been licked by grass-snakes and slow-worms, so sensitive had they become. The joy of the birds was without stint. They sang like creatures enchanted, like creatures thrilling with ecstasy from claw to feather-tip. It seemed as though the early sunshine had utterly redeemed those Somersetshire meadows. They were light as paddocks of Arcady. They quivered, danced, and laughed, and at the same time they retained their solid actuality, thick bespattered with cow-pats loose and emerald green. I have never forgotten the lesson I learned that morning. Of course men and women are created to be happy, their capacity for happiness is without bounds. The greatest villainies can be laid at the door of old men moralities, exaggerated beyond all reason by the clergy, and by mind-cramped masquerading judges with their ears hung about with white ewes' wool, all of them looking out at the world, as Rabelais says, through one hole. He breaches well who lives well, that is all the Divinity I know.

I passed the place where a tributary stream from the Tintinhull side of the railway-line comes through a culvert. As a little boy I had crawled with Bertie along the diminutive tunnel, holding in my hand a bucket full of sticklebacks for our aquarium. I knew well the intimate life of the little stream, its deep holes and shallow holes. I knew where the loaches were to be caught under the islands of rushes. I knew how the sticklebacks looked when you held them flickering in your hand, these marvellous little fish in miniature, with eyes, scales, fins in perfect proportion, such trout as a buttercup-high fairy might fish for, with a creel of woven quaking-grass hung about his shoulder.

I reached the lane. I had as yet seen no sign of human life, but now as I climbed the stile I could make out wisps of blue smoke curling up from Wulham's Mill. They are preparing their fires for heating their coppers, I thought, either for washing, or that they may have water ready for making sweet their dairy-pans and pails.

I soon reached our meeting-place, but nobody was there. I waited and waited, straining my eyes in trying to catch the first glimpse of her between the distant green hedges. She is not coming, I thought. She will never come. I waited as I had often waited in dreams with a half-conscious recognition at the back of my mind that the reality I was experiencing was of no very steadfast essence. I thought of the feathers of a dead hen-blackbird I had just seen by the side of the lane, caught on its nest, perhaps by a marauding stoat. These feathers would linger for a time, gnawed at by little hungry mice, examined and scattered by predatory crawling insects with minute retractile claws, and then as the winter advanced would be drenched, degraded, and disgraced still further.

> *All things making for Death's taking!*
> *—So the green-gowned faeries say*
> *Living over Blackmoor way.*

It was in this unreliable world of floating appearances, of shadowy apparitions, a world foredoomed to extinction, that I was now living.

> *She is walking in the meadow,*
> *And the woodland echo rings;*
> *In a moment we shall meet.*

There she was! No, it was someone from the farm, a dairy-maid in her milking-apron, but there she really and truly was a little way behind. I could see her unmistakably between the grass-green twigs of the hedge. It was teasing that this other should have appeared just at the same time. I had intended to run to meet Dittany and now I had first to pass this unknown young woman, had to pass her as though my business on that fine morning were in no way exceptional. Dittany must have felt much the same, for it was a very demure hand she put forward with an amused bow, stately and reserved, such as she used when we met at parties. I experienced the same shock of surprise that I always did at seeing her again. She was wearing her wide summer hat decorated with a blue ribbon, and a blue sash was about her thin cotton frock, a frock marked with little roses so small that they would have been suitable for that same stickleback fisherman to have sent as a garden gift to his true love.

It was not long before the farm girl got over a field gate and we were alone. We then took each other's hand and went slowly down the lane. 'Think,' she said, 'what long hours we have before us. Do you know, when I saw you coming up the lane to meet me, a verse out of a love poem came into my head?' And as we walked with springing footsteps between the hedges she repeated the words:

> *I have loved the beauty of your talking,*
> *All the words you said*
> *Nested in my mind like blackbirds singing*
> *Treasured in the head,*
> *I remember all, I have remembered*
> *Every word you said.*
> *All your grace of mind and grace of body,*
> *Patterns that your feet*
> *Made on paths of fern on hills of bracken,*
> *Counsels wise and sweet,*
> *How your face looked brighter than the morning*
> *I had come to meet.*

As I listened to her voice it was as if I were holding happiness in my hands as a child holds up a sun-warmed apricot. Near the bridge where the railway crosses Marsh Lane, there is a gate hidden from view beneath a willow-tree. It was here that we kissed for the first time that day. The fields were golden with buttercups, and through the air, yellow and green under the sunshine, the birds went flying, now up, now down, with see-saw flights. I do not think the cuckoo was ever silent for more than five minutes.

Against the gate I held her, this lovely creature of my own kind. I was wildly, madly alive to the proximity of her body, of her body so close to mine, naked under her frock, her breasts as firm and explicitly rounded as wall fruit. Near is my kirtle but nearer is my smock. I knelt down. I threw my arms about her. She seemed to me transfigured. She was encompassed by my love. It was an aureole about her beautiful head, a girdle about her belly, and golden rings about her ankles. Her cheeks grew flushed, her eyes shone, she laughed to feel my love run over her as lightly and as gaily as moorland water in the sun.

From *Love and Death, an imaginary autobiograpy* (1939).

A CHECK LIST OF BOOKS

A CHECK LIST OF BOOKS BY
LLEWELYN POWYS

1. CONFESSIONS OF TWO BROTHERS.
   By John Cowper Powys and Llewelyn Powys. The Manas
   Press, Rochester, N.Y. 1916.
   *Not published in England. The second and shorter part of this
   book consists of extracts from Llewelyn Powys's diaries, connected
   by a commentary.*

2. EBONY AND IVORY.
   With a Preface by Theodore Dreiser. American Library
   Service, New York, 1923.

2a. EBONY AND IVORY.
   With a Preface by Edward Shanks. Grant Richards,
   London, 1925.
   Sketches and Essays of life in East Africa.

3. THIRTEEN WORTHIES.
   With a Preface by Van Wyck Brooks. American Library
   Service, New York, 1923.

3a. THIRTEEN WORTHIES.
   Grant Richards, London, 1924.
   Essays appreciative of great writers and eccentrics.

4. BLACK LAUGHTER.
   Harcourt, Brace & Co., New York, 1924.

4a. BLACK LAUGHTER.
   Grant Richards, London, 1925.
   Sketches of life in East Africa.

5. HONEY AND GALL.
   Haldeman-Julius Co., Girard, Kansas, 1924. Wrappers.
   Not published in England.
   Essays on diverse subjects.

6. CUP-BEARERS OF WINE AND HELLEBORE.
   Haldeman-Julius Co., Girard, Kansas, 1924. Wrappers.
   Not published in England.
   Essays on famous writers.

7. SKIN FOR SKIN.
   Harcourt, Brace & Co., New York, 1925.

7a. SKIN FOR SKIN.
   Jonathan Cape, London, 1927. Limited to 900 copies.
   Autobiographical.

8. THE VERDICT OF BRIDLEGOOSE.
   Harcourt, Brace & Co., New York, 1926.

8a. THE VERDICT OF BRIDLEGOOSE.
   Jonathan Cape, London, 1927. Limited to 900 copies,
   uniform with *Skin for Skin.*
   Autobiographical, mainly of his life in U.S.A.

9. HENRY HUDSON.
   John Lane The Bodley Head, London, 1927.

9a. HENRY HUDSON.
   Harper & Bros., New York, 1928.
   A biography of the explorer and navigator.

10. OUT OF THE PAST.
   Grey Bow Press, Pasadena, California. Edition limited
   to 25 copies. Not published in England separately, but
   included in *Earth Memories.*
   An Essay.

11. THE CRADLE OF GOD.
   Harcourt, Brace & Co., New York, 1929.

11a. THE CRADLE OF GOD.
Jonathan Cape, London, 1929.

11b. THE CRADLE OF GOD.
New edition, with an introduction by Ernest Carr. Watts & Co., London, 1949.
An account of the Old Testament background.

12. THE PATHETIC FALLACY.
Longmans, Green & Co., London, 1930. Published in America as *An Hour on Christianity*. Reprinted in the Thinker's Library, Watts & Co., London, 1931.
An interpretation of the Christian teaching.

13. AN HOUR ON CHRISTIANITY.
Lippincott, Philadelphia, 1930. Published in England as *The Pathetic Fallacy.*

14. APPLES BE RIPE.
Harcourt, Brace & Co., New York, 1930.

14a. APPLES BE RIPE.
Longmans, Green & Co., London, 1930.
A novel.

15. A PAGAN'S PILGRIMAGE.
Harcourt, Brace & Co., New York, 1931.

15a. A PAGAN'S PILGRIMAGE.
Longmans, Green & Co., London, 1931.
An account of his journey to Palestine.

16. IMPASSIONED CLAY.
Longmans, Green & Co., New York, 1931. With a woodcut by Lynd Ward.

16a. IMPASSIONED CLAY.
Longmans, Green & Co., London, 1931. The English edition lacks the woodcut by Lynd Ward.
A philosophical essay.

17. THE LIFE AND TIMES OF ANTHONY À WOOD.
Edited, with an introduction by Llewelyn Powys. Wishart
& Co., London, 1932. Not published in America.
An abridgment of Andrew Clark's edition of Wood.

18. NOW THAT THE GODS ARE DEAD.
Illustrated by Lynd Ward. Equinox Press, New York,
1932. Limited to 400 copies signed by the Author and
Illustrator. Not published in England.
A philosophical essay.

19. GLORY OF LIFE.
With wood engravings by Robert Gibbings. Golden
Cockerel Press, London, 1934. Limited to 277 numbered
copies.

19a. GLORY OF LIFE.
New edition by John Lane The Bodley Head, London,
1938.
A philosophical essay.

20. EARTH MEMORIES.
With woodcuts by Gertrude Mary Powys. John Lane The
Bodley Head, London, 1935.
Essays, mainly of country life.

21. DAMNABLE OPINIONS.
Watts & Co., London, 1935. Not published in America.
Essays, mainly controversial.

22. DORSET ESSAYS.
With photographs by Wyndham Goodden. John Lane
The Bodley Head, London, 1935. 18 of the essays were
included in the American edition of *Earth Memories.*
Essays, autobiographical and of country life.

23. THE TWELVE MONTHS.
With wood engravings by Robert Gibbings. John Lane The
Bodley Head, London, 1936. Limited edition of 100 copies

signed by Author and Illustrator; and a trade edition. Not published in America.
Essays on the progress of the year.

24. SOMERSET ESSAYS.
With photographs by Wyndham Goodden. John Lane The Bodley Head, London, 1937. Not published in America.
Essays, autobiographical and of country life.

25. RATS IN THE SACRISTY.
With Preface by John Cowper Powys and wood engravings by Gertrude Mary Powys. Watts & Co., London, 1937. Not published in America.
Biographical essays of great writers.

26. THE BOOK OF DAYS.
Thoughts compiled from the philosophy of Llewelyn Powys by John Wallis. Illustrated by Elizabeth Corsellis. Golden Cockerel Press, London, 1937. Limited edition. Not published in America.
A quotation from Llewelyn Powys for every day of the year.

27. EARTH MEMORIES.
W. W. Norton & Co., New York, 1938. With an introduction by Van Wyck Brooks. Contains the 23 essays published in the English edition of *Earth Memories,* together with 18 essays selected from *Dorset Essays.*
A representative selection of essays.

28. LOVE AND DEATH.
With an introduction by Alyse Gregory. John Lane the Bodley Head, London, 1939.

28a. LOVE AND DEATH.
Simon & Schuster, New York, 1941.
An 'imaginary autobiography.'

29. A BAKER'S DOZEN.
With an introduction by Lloyd Emerson Siberell and

illustrations by Mathias Noheimer. Trovillion Private Press, Herrin, Illinois, 1940.

29a. A BAKER'S DOZEN.
With an introduction by John Cowper Powys and decorations by Gertrude Mary Powys. John Lane The Bodley Head, London, 1941.
Essays, autobiographical and of country life.

30. OLD ENGLISH YULETIDE.
With an introduction by Violet and Hal. W. Trovillion. Trovillion Private Press, Herrin, Illinois, 1940. Contains two essays, 'A Somerset Christmas' and 'The New Year' from *A Baker's Dozen.* 202 copies privately printed for the friends of Violet and Hal. W. Trovillion, Christmas, 1940.

31. THE LETTERS OF LLEWELYN POWYS.
Selected and edited by Louis Wilkinson with an introduction by Alyse Gregory. John Lane The Bodley Head, London, 1943. Excludes all those letters published in *Welsh Ambassadors* by Louis Marlow.

32. SWISS ESSAYS.
John Lane The Bodley Head, London, 1947.
Essays, mainly of life in Switzerland.

33. ADVICE TO A YOUNG POET.
John Lane The Bodley Head, London, 1949.
A collection of letters addressed to Kenneth Hopkins.

*

A VOYAGE TO THE WEST INDIES
This long essay was first published in *The Pleasure Ground,* an anthology edited by Malcolm Elwin and published by Macdonald in 1946.

THE COLLECTED EDITION

Messrs. John Lane The Bodley Head, have issued the following volumes in a Collected Edition of Llewelyn Powys's Works:

Skin for Skin and *The Verdict of Bridlegoose*	(together)	(1948)
Glory of Life and *Now That The Gods Are Dead*	(together)	(1949)
Advice to a Young Poet (here first published)		(1949)
Love and Death		(1950)

BOOKS RELATING TO LLEWELYN POWYS, OR WITH IMPORTANT REFERENCES TO HIM

SWAN'S MILK.
    By Louis Marlow. Faber & Faber, London, 1934.
    Louis Wilkinson's 'autobiography' in the form of a novel, with many important reminiscences of Llewelyn Powys.

AUTOBIOGRAPHY.
    By John Cowper Powys. John Lane The Bodley Head, London, 1934.
    Contains much important material relating to Llewelyn Powys.

WELSH AMBASSADORS: POWYS LIVES AND LETTERS
    By Louis Marlow. Chapman & Hall, London, 1936.
    Contains a selection of letters by Llewelyn Powys and much reminiscence about him.

THE POWYS BROTHERS.
    By Richard Heron Ward. John Lane The Bodley Head, London, 1936.
    Contains a long essay on Llewelyn Powys.

THE JOY OF IT.
    By Littleton Powys. Chapman & Hall, London, 1936.
    Contains much material relating to Llewelyn Powys.

THE LIFE OF LLEWELYN POWYS.

By Malcolm Elwin. John Lane The Bodley Head, London, 1946.

FORTH, BEAST!

By Louis Marlow. Faber & Faber, London, 1946.
The continuation of Louis Wilkinson's 'autobiography'.

THE BROTHERS POWYS.

A Paper read to the Royal Society of Literature by Louis Umfreville Wilkinson, F.R.S.L. ('Louis Marlow'). In *Essays by Divers Hands*, Vol. XXIV. Geoffrey Cumberlege, London, 1948.

Several introductions in Llewelyn Powys's books are specially valuable in studying his life and work particularly those by Alyse Gregory in *The Letters of Llewelyn Powys,* and by John Cowper Powys in *A Baker's Dozen* (English Edition).